3000 BC

Europe's farmers had begun settling the mountain regions, grazing their cattle on elevated pastures in summer. The discovery of Ötzi, a New Stone Age man frozen in Alpine ice, is one of the pieces of evidence for this.

2500 BC

The megalithic practice of monument-building reached the British Isles. Stonehenge is the most famous of the many monuments raised all over the islands at this time.

3000 BC

Native Americans in the Great Lakes region were working with copper, a metal that is beaten into the desired shape by cold hammering.

2500 BC

Simple ceramic vessels are in use in some coastal regions of southeastern north America.

00 BC

2400 BC

3100 BC

Narmer of Upper Egypt conquered Lower Egypt, uniting the two in one nation. This marked the beginning of the ancient Egyptian civilisation.

2500 BC

King Khufu had his pyramid built at Giza, near modern-day Cairo, the first and tallest of the Great Pyramids.

3000 BC

Sumerian settlements in Mesopotamia – the land between the Euphrates and Tigris rivers – had developed into the first city-state civilisations. By this time, the Sumerians already had writing; around 2700 BC they introduced a new writing tool – the stylus.

2500 BC

The cities of Mohenjo-Daro and Harappa become the centre of the Indus Valley civilisation. They are the first cities built to a strict grid plan and have advanced drainage systems.

2350 BC

Sargon of Akkad conquers the Sumerian city-states to create the first large state in the Middle East, with its capital at Akkad.

EUROPE

1800 BC

During the Bronze Age in Central Europe, the solid disc wheel was replaced by the spoked wheel, making carts lighter.

AMERICA

2000 BC

Native Americans in the Arctic region were getting about in specially designed boats – kayaks – and using harpoons to catch fish.

1800 BC

AFRICA

2052 BC

After a century of chaos following the end of Egypt's Old Kingdom, Pharaoh Mentuhotep reunited Upper and Lower Egypt, founding the 11th Dynasty.

1792 BC

King Hammurabi acceded to the throne of Babylon. During his 40-year rule he conquered almost all of Mesopotamia and compiled the first codified laws.

ASIA

2100 BC

The Sumerian city of Ur experienced a revival of power when King Ur-Nammu reunited the Mesopotamian city-states under his rule.

OCEANIA

1600 BC

The Bronze Age reached northern Europe, where the lur (left) was a popular musical. At the same time, the Mycenaean culture was on the rise in ancient Greece.

1400 BC

The Minoan culture of Crete – the major trading power in the Aegean for more than a millennium – came to an end.

1500 BC

The Olmec culture emerged in Mexico, the first advanced civilisation of Central America. They created huge head sculptures and devised a ceremonial ball game.

1600 BC

c.1500 BC

Hatshepsut – widow of Thutmose II and regent for the future Thutmose III – was crowned as the first female pharaoh.

c.1370 BC

Pharaoh Akhenaten instituted a monotheistic sun cult and banned the worship of ancient Egypt's many other gods. After his death – in about 1360 – he was declared a heretic.

1260

Rameses II had temple carved in cliffs, just one of list of building ach in his 67-year reign

1650 BC

The Hittites established their power in what is now Turkey. King Hattusilis I built his capital at Hattusas.

c.1550 BC

The Shang dynasty came to power in northern China, establishing its dominance over neighbouring warlords and ending the period known to history as the '10,000 kingdoms'.

5400 BC

The people of Central Europe had begun to build large permanent houses, with walls of wood or stone and thatched roofs.

5000 BC

The sun observatory at Goseck in Germany was constructed. The earliest known structure of its kind, it enabled people to mark the solstices precisely.

9500 BC

Early American toolmakers were crafting deadly stone spear points. Examples like these have been found all over North America.

5000–3500 BC

Early farming settlements on the Nile gradually developed into towns of several thousand people, such as Hierakonpolis and Naqada.

5000 BC

Craftsmen from the Yangshao culture on the Huang He river in China were producing sophisticated ceramics, like this pottery mask. Artisans of the Liangzhu culture in the south had mastered working with jade.

oldest
5m
stone
ower.

3500 BC

Early seafarers from eastern Asia colonised Polynesia. They are known as the Lapita culture after the first find site of their pottery.

30 000 BC

Modern humans had supplanted the Neanderthals across Europe. Still living as hunter-gatherers, they had begun to express themselves through art, creating images on cave walls as well animal sculptures.

25000 BC

Images of humans were rare in Stone Age art. The Venus figurines are an exception – examples have been found all over Europe. They are believed to be symbols of fertility and motherhood representing the Mother Goddess.

40000–15000 years ago

recent estimates put the arrival of the first s in America as early as 40,000 years ago. A nservative figure is around 15,000 years ago, re the end of the last Ice Age.

25 000 BC

10000–5000 BC

In the post-Ice Age world, the Sahara was a fertile landscape. Deep in what is now desert are thousands of rock paintings by Stone Age artists that reveal the rich life of this lost world.

9000 BC

People were starting to settle to a farming way of life in the Fertile Crescent region of the Middle East.

7500 BC

Jericho, the world's known town, had a (20ft) high defensive wall with a look-out

20000 BC

Australia's Aborigines invented the boomerang, used for ceremonial purposes as well hunting. They also used spears.

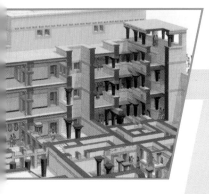

900 BC

Europe's Bronze Age ended with the emergence of a new metal – iron.

1200 BC

The Chavín culture came to prominence in the Andean highlands of Peru. They demonstrated technological mastery of irrigation, metallurgy and architecture.

1000 BC

Large settlements developed in the Eastern Woodlands culture of North America.

1200 BC

BC

he Abu Simbel
o sandstone
an impressive
ievements
.

1050 BC

The Shang enjoyed a peak of power during the 11th-century rule of Wu Ding. After his death decline was swift, and the dynasty was defeated by the Zhou c.1050 BC.

1006 BC

David became King of Judah, one year after King Saul's death. Shortly afterwards, he also became King of Israel.

1200 BC

The Phoenician city-states of Byblos, Sidon and Tyre established control over the sea trading routes around the Mediterranean.

1000 BC

Some aboriginal artists began to paint in the X-ray style, one of the later styles of rock art to emerge in Australia.

900 BC

Polynesian seafarers had colonised some 800 Pacific islands, including the Fiji Islands, Tonga and Samoa.

THE DAWN OF
CIVILISATION

PREHISTORY – 900 BC

PUBLISHED BY THE READER'S DIGEST ASSOCIATION LIMITED
LONDON • NEW YORK • SYDNEY • MONTREAL

Inspirational landscape The Tassili n'Ajjer plateau in Algeria was the artistic centre for prehistoric artists, who used the rocks themselves as their canvas. The name 'Tassili' means 'many rivers', harking back to the time when the land was rich in all manner of wildlife.

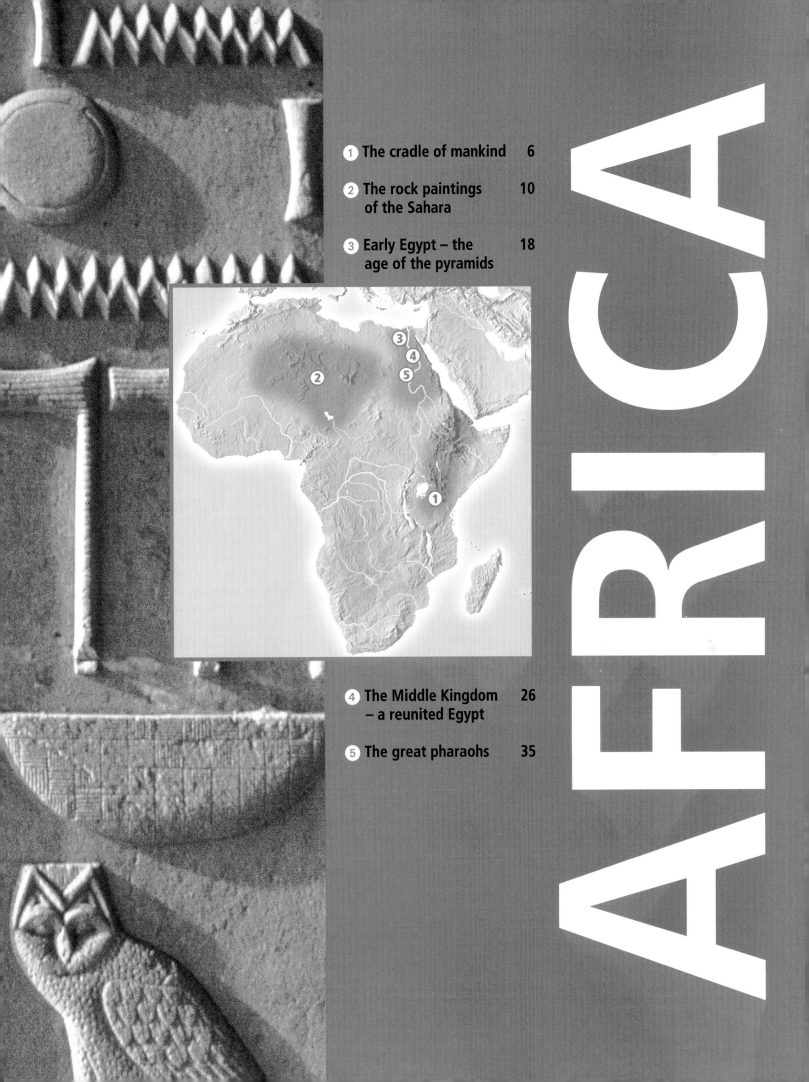

AFRICA

The cradle of mankind

Human prehistory got under way on the African savannah where, millions of years ago, the first primates raised themselves up onto two legs and opened up a new world.

In November 2000, a stir of excitement swept through the worldwide palaeontological community as news spread of a remarkable discovery. The remains of five prehistoric chimp-sized creatures had been recovered in the Tugen Hills of central Kenya. What fired the scientists' interest and imagination was the age of the finds: the bone fragments, including teeth and jaws, dated back six million years, meaning that they belonged to the oldest human-like beings yet found.

Evidence from a femur suggested that its owner was developing the ability to walk upright – a crucial advance that helped to separate mankind's ancestors from the apes. Even the timing of the find seemed significant: in the very first year of the new millennium, palaeo-anthropologists Martin Pickford and Brigitte Senut had made a breakthrough that opened fresh horizons on human evolution. Their discovery was officially tagged *Orrorin tugensis*, from a word meaning 'first human' in the language of the local population, but the media quickly christened it Millennium Man.

Is this how our early ancestor looked?
A reconstruction of Lucy, the most famous australopithecine hominid, who for a long time was considered to be the ancestral mother of all humans.

The Tugen find provided fresh backing for a view that had been gathering increasing support in scientific circles – that the human 'family tree' is more like a broadly spreading bush with various different branches, large and small. Excavations over the past 30 years have produced a multiplicity of different hominid or human-like types, making it ever more difficult for scientists to explain the relationships between the different lines of descent

The hominid family line includes not just the genus *Homo*, which produced our own modern human species *Homo sapiens sapiens*, but also embraces *Australopithecus* (literally, 'southern ape'), an entirely separate genus that, like *Homo*, divides into species and subspecies. Further complicating the picture are other finds that have yet to be definitely classified. Besides Millennium Man, this group includes 4.4 million-year-old *Ardipithecus*, first found in Ethiopia in late 1993, and *Kenyanthropus*, reckoned in spring 2001 to be approximately 3.5 million years old.

How climate change helped to shape prehistory

All hominids share a common feature: they stood upright. Many theories have been advanced to explain exactly why and how individual groups of apes should gradually have adapted to walking on their hind legs. The development took place in the late Miocene era, about 8–10 million years ago, against a background of global climate change that was linked in turn to massive tectonic movements when the Earth's continental plates were shifting extensively. In East Africa the pressure was so great that an enormous rent was torn open along a fault line some 4000km (2500 miles) long. The eventual result was eastern Africa's Great Rift Valley, which presented an almost insurmountable barrier for early primate populations, physically separating the ancestors of humans from those of the anthropoid apes.

At the same time that these immense tectonic changes were underway, the world

was also cooling down. Ice caps spread across the polar regions, locking up huge quantities of water. Africa developed a seasonal climate, featuring distinct wet and dry periods. The vast rain forests that had covered most of the continent began to shrink, making way for savannah grasslands dotted with clumps of trees and small patches of woodland. The Great Rift Valley also served as a watershed: clouds drifting over from the Atlantic tended to drop their rain to the west of the divide, while the land to the east found itself in a monsoon zone, washed by heavy seasonal rains interspersed with long periods of drought.

These dramatic natural changes had far-reaching consequences for the region's fauna. The apes that lived on the forest edges in areas east of the Great Rift Valley had to adapt to the savannah conditions. In the view of some scientists, the apes' enforced isolation may have encouraged them to adjust particularly rapidly to the new circumstances in which they now found themselves living.

Lucy and life on the savannah

When the first hominids came down from the trees, their upright stance gave them several advantages. To begin with, standing

The Olduvai Gorge
Situated in the north of Tanzania, this eroded valley is one of our richest sources of hominid fossils and stone tools. The abundance of hand axes and knapped stone fragments found here inspired the name 'Oldowan Culture' for the early people who created them.

up on two legs made it possible to peer over the top of the tall grass and to keep an eye out for trouble. This made it easier to cross the dangerous open terrain between clumps of trees that provided cover. Another distinct advantage was that it left the hands free while walking – to gather food, perhaps, or to carry tools.

The earliest of the australopithecines discovered so far date back about 4.2 million years. The fossil remains of these creatures suggest an evolutionary compromise: they were already quite good

manner of a quadruped. She and others like her would have continued to retreat to the treetops for protection against carnivores and to sleep.

The dangers of the new savannah environment brought about changes in the social life of early hominids. They began to group together in small bands of about 20 individuals. Larger groupings would have given them even more protection, but at a cost: they would have to forage over wider areas to feed the extra mouths.

Lucy was apparently unfussy in her eating habits. Although her diet, like that of her predecessors, was mostly vegetarian, she also obtained animal protein in the form of eggs, termites, small reptiles and birds. She may have already been using sticks and simple stone tools to dig up and break open food. Most implements were probably fashioned from wood or other perishable materials.

The first humans

About 2.5 million years ago, when the Ice Age was getting under way, renewed drought made living conditions difficult in Africa, triggering two very different evolutionary responses. The 'robust' branch of australopithecines developed formidable chewing apparatus, marked by large molars and premolars for grinding up roots, nuts and fruit skins. Another branch relied instead on versatility and inventiveness: this was the line that produced the first representative of the genus *Homo*.

One current theory claims that the earliest *Homo* species was *Homo rudolfensis*, named after Lake Rudolf in Kenya (known since 1979 as Lake Turkana) on whose banks the first remains were found. Dating back about 2.5 million years, *Homo rudolfensis* was contemporary with the last australopithecines. The *Homo* species, however, had a larger brain and showed increasing use of stone tools to extend the range of food in the diet. While the brains of Lucy and her relatives were still only about the size of chimp brains, around 320–480cm³ (20–30cu in), *Homo rudolfensis*

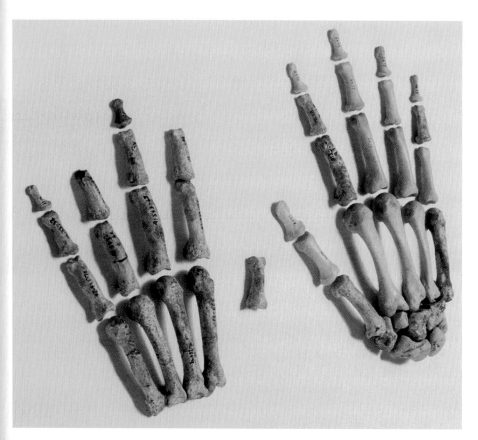

Purposeful and dextrous
Lucy's finger bones (left) were more strongly curved than the more delicate bones of a modern human hand (right). Her curved fingers still enabled her to climb well, but they were also flexible enough to be able to manipulate small sticks and stones to use as tools.

at walking upright, but were also still adapted to treetop life. The most famous of all *Australopithecus* finds indicates this duality well. Found in 1974 in Hadar, north-east Ethiopia, the 3.6-million-year-old skeleton of an *Australopithecus afarensis* female was affectionately named Lucy by her finders. Her bones show a slender, gracile build, well suited to an upright stance, but to walk Lucy still had to swing her hips quite considerably, in the had double that capacity – some 750cm³ (45cu in). A modern human brain is 1200–1700cm³ (70–100 cu in). *Homo rudolfensis* used this increased brainpower to develop new survival strategies. One of these was to exploit carrion as a source of protein-rich food which, as it turned out, fuelled further brain development.

The upright stance was a huge advantage to *Homo rudolfensis* when they had to cross open ground quickly to reach prey – if the sight of circling vultures, for instance, indicated where a dead animal lay. Speed and stamina were of the essence if they were to get there before other carnivores could fight them off. Their jaws, evolved for an omnivorous diet, were not equipped to tear meat, so they needed the help of tools. Sharp-edged stone scrapers were used to cut a carcass into smaller pieces that could then be carried off to be eaten somewhere safe. Larger stones were used to crack bones open to get at the nutritious bone marrow within.

Mastering tools and fire

Step by step, early humans learned how to put tools to use to secure their survival. By about 1.5 million years ago, *Homo erectus* ('upright man') was shaping efficient hand axes. Advances in technology made humans less dependent on nature, enabling them to survive even in wintry conditions. By this time *Homo erectus* is thought to have mastered fire. Fire provided warmth, kept wild animals at bay, and it also brought in a whole new dimension in cooking food.

Early humans learned to plan hunting forays and kills were brought back to fixed camps, where they were cut up and shared out. Group cohesion and solidarity were

TIME WITNESS

The stones speak

Stones have a history, too, even if they do not look as if they have. The oldest-known worked stones date back to a time more than 2.5 million years ago. Simple, sharp-edged flakes were split off from a raw nodule of stone with the help of a hand-held hammer stone. The chipped surface was then worked further, until the core stone took on the desired shape. Hacking stones, scrapers and blades, all worked on two sides, were often made of quartz or basalt.

About a million years later, *Homo erectus* took another great technological step forward with the development of the hand axe, the manufacture of which required considerably greater skill and knowledge.

becoming all the more important because the evolutionary changes were affecting human development. As brain capacity increased, children took longer to mature. Women had to devote more time to child-rearing, while the children themselves went through a prolonged phase of learning and practice before reaching adulthood. The men's role as hunters became pivotal to ensure the survival of the group.

As social interaction within each small band became more complex, the need for language grew. Full speech capability is thought to have evolved in the later stages of human evolution, some 500,000 years ago, but no-one knows exactly when people first began to express themselves in words. It seems likely that *Homo erectus* must have had some form of rudimentary speech.

The preconditions for cultural evolution were already in place by the time *Homo erectus* first left his African home, perhaps 2 million years ago. A great divide had been crossed: mankind was already on the path that, about 1.9 million years later, led *Homo sapiens* to fan out across the globe.

Technological beginnings
Among the earliest stone tools fashioned by *Homo erectus* were hand axes like this one (bottom left). Splitting off hard-wearing, sharp-edged stone tools like these from the raw stone required great dexterity and skill.

The rock paintings of the Sahara

Thousands of years ago, the Sahara teemed with life. Early artists captured the rich fauna of this fertile world before the climate changed and the desert closed in.

The lost world of the Sahara was created by a radical change in North Africa's climate as the last Ice Age came to an end about 12,000 years ago. Increased rainfall turned much of what is now desert into a green and fertile landscape that provided favourable living conditions for several thousand years. An extraordinary record of the rich and flourishing animal life has survived in thousands of rock paintings, created with great skill and sophistication by the people of the time. Because of these anonymous artists we know that herds of elephants, antelopes and buffalo grazed on the grassy steppe, lions and other carnivores preyed on the migrating herds, and crocodiles and hippos cruised the rivers and lakes.

No-one knows for sure when people first moved here, but archaeological remains include stone circles, barrow graves and ancient settlement sites, all bearing witness to the presence of early humans. What is known is that when these people began to create their legacy of rock engravings and paintings depicting the world about them, the human race was on the brink of a great revolution. Throughout the long millennia of the Stone Age, small groups had supported themselves by hunting and gathering wild foods. From about 9000 BC, however, communities, first in the Middle East and then across the world, learned to herd and domesticate animals and grow crops. The Saharan rock art era coincided with this shift to farming, and the paintings recorded the change.

Other evolutionary developments had taken place in the aeons before the rock artists set to work. Since the time of the early hominids, human mental faculties had advanced hugely through tool and weapon-making. People had begun to employ logic and abstract thought, and at some point after the emergence of *Homo sapiens sapiens* they had begun to feel the urge to express themselves in art.

The earliest forms of artistic expression were probably songs and dances, which could be handed down through the generations; these depended on memory and so were essentially transitory. Rock art was a means of passing on knowledge, skills or ideas in permanent form, which also recorded for posterity the special achievements of the culture.

Art in remote places

From about 8000 BC, the climate of much of the Sahara region once more began to dry out, but upland districts

Desert dancers
This rock painting is thought to show a masked figure in a ritual dance, with smaller figures moving rhythmically around him. Human images date from the later periods of Saharan rock art.

A ledge under an overhanging rockface provided a convenient worksite for the early Saharan artists.
Overhangs have helped to protect thousands of images from weather erosion through the years.

continued to enjoy ample rainfall and remained fertile. One such was the plateau of Tassili n'Ajjer in what is now southeastern Algeria. With an average altitude of 1000m (3250ft), Tassili is a bizarre landscape dotted with small lakes and combed by ancient riverbeds that run in canyons up to 700m (2275ft) deep. Even today torrents of water gush through these canyons following the heavy rains that occasionally drench the region.

It can never have been easy to gain access to Tassili's ancient river valleys, choked as they were with acacia trees and grasses, but nonetheless the plateau became a centre for rock art and remained so for around 8500 years. Today, some 500,000 images still survive in over 400 locations on the plateau, giving a vivid impression of life in the Sahara in the late Stone Age.

Animals observed

Meticulously ground out of the rock with a scraper, this animal head clearly represents an oryx, a type of antelope still widely distributed across Africa today.

Living spaces

Thousands of stone tools and pot shards indicate that this fantastic landscape was occupied from an early date. Natural rock formations as tall as towers create an illusion of futuristic cities, that seem in the valleys to be crossed by networks of tiny paths and winding alleys, opening out into plazas or leading to extensive cave systems where the prehistoric peoples made their homes. People also took refuge under rock overhangs, a natural feature of the region formed by erosion at the base of rock masses. These shelters offered ready-made protection from the wind and weather.

For their canvases, the artists chose suitable rock surfaces either inside caves or beneath overhangs – the sandstone walls provided plenty of smooth surfaces to work on. The paintings probably lent the sites the same sacred aura that temples and cathedrals held for people in later millennia. They may have been places for contemplation, where individuals sought communication with the divine.

For the most part, individual pictures are difficult to date, but occasionally a fairly accurate figure can be obtained – for example, if a broken-off fragment of a painting is found lying in an archaeological stratum that also contains dateable items such as food remains, pollen or animal bones. At some sites archaeologists have been able to infer a chronological sequence when pictures in markedly different styles have been found painted one on top of another.

The art of the buffalo-hunters

By comparing pictures across all the various North African sites, five main stylistic groups have been identified. The first dates back at least 10,000 years, and consists exclusively of incised images. It is known as the 'Bubalus' style, after a genus of wild cattle that today includes the wild water buffalo and the anoas. The representative of the genus at the time was *Bubalus antiquus*, a long-extinct giant buffalo that provided the early artists with their favourite motif. In this period, the hunter-gatherer lifestyle was still in full swing. Small bands of humans armed with stone weapons followed migrating herds of their favourite prey animals; bows and arrows had yet to be invented.

At some point, it appears that individuals in the groups began to use their stone tools to start drawing pictures. Hunter-gatherer groups have left evidence of their passage all across North Africa in the form of rock engravings. Some have survived even in open-air locations thanks to a layer of so-called 'desert varnish'. This natural varnish is in fact a protective black pigment exuded by iron and manganese deposits through chemical reactions that then seal the rock's surface. Pictures that have been conserved in this way depict giraffes, rhinos, elephants, and many other animals still found in Africa today.

These very early artists used small stone hammers to chip the silhouette of the image into the rock; alternatively, they scraped out the outline with other stone tools. Several people must have worked together to produce large groups of pictures, but it was still a time-consuming process that would sometimes have taken years. The sheer effort involved gives some indication of the significance that the sites must have held. The whole community would have had to contribute as the artists, busy with their work, would not have been free to help hunt for food yet still needed to be fed.

Helping the hunt

One of the rock engravings from this early period is an image of a cow about 5m (16ft) long. The beast's eyes are close together, and its body is covered in mysterious spirals and horizontal figures of eight. No-one knows exactly what the significance of these patterns might have been, but it has been suggested that they were fertility symbols. Close by, the artists created elegant images of antelopes.

Given that the people who produced these images relied on hunting for their survival, it seems unlikely that the pictures were made simply as decoration. More likely they had some ritual or magical significance. By creating a realistic image, the

Duelling lions
Like heraldic beasts, two lions face up to one another, seemingly poised for combat. Four small ostriches can be made out between their upright bodies.

hunter – or perhaps a shaman on the hunter's behalf – sought in some way to gain control over animals: in effect, to help conjure them up in flesh and blood.

Human images emerge

No images of people have survived from this early period, so we simply do not know what these first artists looked like. The earliest representations of humans date from the so-called 'Roundhead' period, beginning around 8000 BC. This was followed, about 3000 years later, by the 'Bovidian' or 'Cattle-herding' period. However, the transitions between the different styles were not clear-cut. People continued to hunt throughout all of these periods, so it is impossible to say whether pictures of wild animals and the hunters pursuing them predate images of herd

Capturing movement
This picture of three hares (top) clearly tried to capture the creature in motion – the artist's intention seems particularly evident in the ears. Movement is certainly conveyed in the elaborately costumed figures above, which seem to be dancing in a flowing rhythm.

animals. However, over the thousands of years in which the Roundhead and Cattle-herding styles prevailed, the paintings evolved from naturalistic, partly schematic line drawings into complex, colourful and amazingly vivid pictures showing scenes of everyday life.

The artists of the Roundhead era depicted people with circular heads set directly on their shoulders with no facial features. These neckless beings are sometimes referred to as 'Martians' – indeed, the best-selling author Erich von Danniken once claimed them in support of his controversial theory that Earth was visited by spacecraft in the distant past. A more likely explanation for the lack of features is that portraying the human face was probably taboo.

From their physical appearance the Roundhead peoples are generally thought to have belonged ethnically to the Negroid branch of the human race. For the most part they lived as hunter-gatherers. Later on in the period, however, images of domestic cattle – recognisable by their spotted hides – make a first appearance, indicating that herding was being adopted as a way of life, and that the hunter-gatherer bands were gradually becoming more settled.

Depicting the spirit world

While the hunter-gatherers of the Bubalus era had only drawn single animals, the Roundhead artists created more complex scenes. They drew detailed pictures of everyday life in which people had a central role. They also passed down images of rituals and the spirit world. There are paintings of musicians and dancers; others show the making and wearing of masks. There are also some highly surrealistic images that appear to have been created under the influence of hallucinogenic mushrooms – indeed, some actually show the mushroom that inspired artists to paint fantastic beings, monsters and spirits.

One of the most enigmatic images in the entire Tassili region shows a huge dancing figure, approximately 3m (10ft) tall, which probably represents a god. The figure wears a mask, its outline is delineated in brownish colours although the body itself is white, and the arms are outstretched, seemingly in an attitude of blessing. The loins are covered with a cloud-like shape from which rain appears to be falling. An antelope is shown leaping from the cloud and may also be symbolic of rainfall – the creature is linked to rain in African myths. Another interpretation, however, is that the cloud symbolises the opening of the god's belly, from which the antelope is emerging newborn. Some smaller, apparently female figures can be seen approaching in reverent attitudes. Another woman lies nearby in the act of giving birth. The painting completely dominates the great shell-shaped grotto in which it sits.

The image has a naive and childlike quality, and has no parallel elsewhere in the region – there simply are no other paintings that might help to clarify its meaning. Consequently it remains a mystery and subject of debate. Some scholars think it was meant to have magical significance in summoning rain; others see it as the icon of a fertility cult.

Colourful dance rituals

Art styles changed in the latter part of the Roundhead period, as figures came to be drawn almost naturalistically and in finer detail than before. The artists made clever use of irregularities in the rock surface to create three-dimensional effects that must have increased the impact the works had on viewers. They also expanded their palette of colours: in addition to the reddish, brown and white shades previously employed, yellow, blue-violet and greenish shades now came into use.

The colours were made by grinding up stones of suitable hues then mixing the powder with acacia gum and a milk protein called casein. It is assumed that the colours were then applied directly to the rock with a finger or a stick. The porous sandstone provided an ideal surface as it absorbed the excess moisture from the paste, enabling the colours to survive, in sheltered spots, for thousands of years.

The largest work from this period is more than 5m (16ft) long and 1.6m (5ft) high. It depicts many aspects of everyday life, but the significance of some of the detail remains unclear. Two graceful female figures, with cloths tied around their hips, can be seen moving in a dance. Their heads are still faceless in the Roundhead

manner, but they now display elaborate hairstyles or head-dresses that are shown in careful detail. Their arms and upper bodies seem to be painted or tattooed, and they have cloth strips or bracelets around their wrists. A ram with larger-than-lifesize horns is depicted beneath the women. Slightly smaller Roundhead figures surround the female dancers, along with rain clouds and animals. The overall scene is thought to illustrate a ritual intended to placate the spirits of animals killed in the hunt.

It is hard now to imagine the effect that these paintings would have had on people at the time. The rock formations are like works of art in themselves, as natural light and shadow constantly

VIEWPOINT

The Saharan charioteers

Among the many thousands of rock drawings in the Sahara are some of horse-drawn chariots. Scholars still argue over who might have built and driven the vehicles. Some think they were probably used by local traders. Others have suggested that the owners might have been the pharaohs of distant Egypt – the Egyptian rulers were certainly well versed in the use of horses and chariots, and some are known to have penetrated deep into the desert on military campaigns.

Another theory holds that the charioteers were a people called the Garamantes, who were described by the Greek historian Herodotus in about 500 BC. Herodotus reported that the Garamantes inhabited an oasis in southern Libya and rode in four-wheeled chariots; he also claimed, however, that they ate snakes and reptiles and squeaked like bats. Scenes painted on the walls of pharaonic tombs in Egypt depict the Garamantes as fair-haired and blue-eyed. Early Egyptian inscriptions also refer to clashes with inhabitants of the Sahara region.

The chariot pictures seem to support environmental findings that the Sahara experienced a final wet period around 1500 BC. The increased rainfall improved living conditions in the region and the more widespread availability of water would have made it possible, at least along certain routes, for horse-drawn vehicles to cross the Sahara.

Flying chariots
This horse seems to be flying through the air at full gallop, with a two-wheeled chariot in tow.

An unexpected find
These barbed fish hooks and harpoon points shaped out of ivory were found in the Sahara, compelling evidence that humans once caught fish here.

Tools of wood
In addition to stone, bone and ivory, the Saharan peoples also fashioned wooden tools like this versatile and elegant sickle.

change, echoing the mystery of spirits and a world where nothing is as it seems. For outsiders coming to the plateau from the flat monotony of the savannah, the monumental rockforms alone must have been extraordinary. The sight of the paintings under the overhanging rocks probably filled them with holy terror. Some no doubt preferred to stay at a safe distance, using these magical places simply as familiar landmarks marking the way to the camps of local settlers.

A melting pot of peoples

A new era began around 3500 BC, when the Saharan peoples finally adopted a more settled way of life. They no longer followed herds of wild animals along traditional migration routes, as their hunter-gatherer forebears had done. Instead, they kept their own cattle and cultivated crops. Cattle became their most precious possessions, so it is not surprising that they turn up frequently in rock art. The Cattle-herding period was underway and most of the artworks in the Tassili region date from this era.

Scholars still argue over who exactly the cattle-herders were and where they might have come from. The rock pictures seem to depict peoples of Negroid and Mediterranean ethnic stock side by side, giving the impression of a colourful mix of peoples. The two populations are clearly differentiated in their dress, with Negroid individuals usually shown naked or wearing a loincloth, while the lighter-skinned people sport decorative clothing and wide capes. One theory holds that the

Negroid people were the region's original inhabitants and that the lighter-skinned groups arrived later from the north and east. It is conceivable that light-skinned cattle-herders could have migrated to the Sahara region from the Nile Valley when the spread of arable farming in Egypt robbed them of the grazing space their animals needed. Other experts think that the cattle-herders practised a form of nomadic pastoralism, grazing their animals in the fertile valleys in the summer months and then retreating to the Sahara grasslands, which were still extensive at the time, for the winter.

Life and leisure among the herds

The prehistoric Saharan artists used the ready-made surfaces that the rocks provided to depict most aspects of everyday life. Some of the pictures show round huts equipped with hearths and quernstones. These shelters housed extended families, providing a focal point for the group where meals were prepared.

There are scenes of cattle-herders at work, and of women chatting together or playing with their children. Both men and women are shown participating in rituals and festivities involving dancing. Most wear masks or other special apparel for these occasions. There are even cartoon-like drawings caricaturing people with pot bellies and bald heads.

Some of the rock paintings depict the tools that helped the Saharan people cope with their environment – stone axes for chopping and shaping wood, stone sickle blades, and some early pottery. Thread was also being manufactured now, as the discovery of devices for turning spindles has shown.

Successful cattle-breeders

No subject crops up more often in the rock paintings, however, than cattle. Literally thousands of images have survived and they show at least two domesticated species, distinguished by their differently-shaped horns. The artists

evidently took great delight in portraying the animals that were so essential for the wealth and well-being of their people, and they depicted them with a loving eye for detail. Spotted cattle – possibly the result of interbreeding – were reproduced with particular attention to specific characteristics, such as the shape of the horns and hooves. Paintings also record the way in which the cattle-herders tied up their calves more than 5000 years ago, using a technique that can still be seen today among the Fulbe, a nomadic people who tend cattle to the south of the Sahara.

The Saharan artists had also mastered the arts of perspective and correct proportion in their work. Their skills enabled them to produce action-packed pictures of herdsmen on the move with their beasts. Some scenes show cattlemen under attack from raiders – bows and arrows had evidently come into use by this time. Another noticeable feature of the artistic style in this later period is the use of deliberate exaggeration in some paintings, perhaps for dramatic effect, or perhaps to discourage enemies. For example, artists sometimes drew running figures with longer, stronger legs than could really have been the case.

The end of an early culture

Around 1500 BC, the conditions for life changed fundamentally in North Africa, permanently altering the Saharan ecosystem. Rivers and lakes dried up for want of rainfall, and the greenery that was left was increasingly swallowed up by desert. Living conditions for the people there became increasingly tough.

The first indications of the climatic changes are already evident in paintings from the final phase of the Cattle-herding period. Alongside cattle, the images now depict goats and sheep, which were better able to cope with the deteriorating conditions than larger animals. Horses, too, make their first appearance in the rock art at about this time, usually shown in pairs hitched to two or four-wheeled wagons. The use of horse-drawn vehicles may well be an indication that trade with peoples outside the region was beginning to grow. The pictures are found primarily along the main access routes in the region, so it is hard to be sure whether they were created by indigenous artists or by peoples on the move.

At some point, the cattle-herding people were forced to abandon the Tassili region, but it is not known when or where they went. The trail of the Sahara cattle-herders is lost in the desert sands, but the legacy of their artists lives on.

Herds on the move
The rock art in the Sahara evolved from simple line drawings of single animals to complex scenes like this one showing a herding community rounding up cattle. The curved shapes at the left edge of the picture may represent the huts in which the herders lived.

Early Egypt – the age of the pyramids

In the words of the Greek historian Herodotus, Egypt was 'the gift of the Nile'. The great river supplied its people with all the necessities of life, providing the foundations for one of the world's most enduring cultures.

Birth of a nation
The palette of Narmer is one of Egypt's most ancient relics. Narmer was the ruler who united Egypt in about 3100 BC, and he is shown striking down an enemy. The palette is made of dark green slate and was used for grinding up minerals such as malachite for use in ritual cosmetics.

The first farmers settled the banks of the Nile in the centuries before 5000 BC. Over the course of the next two millennia these early settlements developed first into fortified villages and then into towns, such as Hierakonpolis and Naqada, each inhabited by several thousand people. Local kings reigned over populations still divided into tribal groups, and these rulers already claimed greater-than-human powers. Each town had its own presiding deity: in Hierakonpolis, for example, the falcon god Horus protected the citizens.

Around 3500 BC, rival rulers began to raid neighbouring territories with the aim of forming larger realms. Gradually, the fiefdoms coalesced until finally only two kingdoms were left: Upper Egypt in the south and Lower Egypt in the north.

According to ancient tradition Egypt was finally united by Narmer, a semi-legendary ruler sometimes also known as Menes, who extended his power from the upper Nile to the delta through a combination of diplomacy and military might. Narmer built a new capital to celebrate his victory over Lower Egypt and the ensuing unification of the kingdom. The city was constructed on a strategically important site at the head of the Nile delta, and was called Memphis, 'city of the white walls'. The Memphis region would be the principal home of the pharaohs for almost 1500 years, until it was replaced by Thebes, on the Nile's upper course, at the start of the New Kingdom period.

Narmer's new state was able to establish itself with little outside interference; in the early years, attacks from beyond Egypt's borders were extremely rare. The peculiar geography helped in preventing incursions as the land to east and west was enveloped by deserts, the Nile cataracts hindered access from the south, and the northern frontier was the Mediterranean Sea.

The rulers wore a double crown, combining the white crown of Upper Egypt and the red of Lower, in recognition of the two kingdoms that made up the realm. Other royal insignia included a crook, flail and artificial beard worn on the chin as a sign of masculine power.

In time, the kings of the united land took the title of pharaoh, a word derived from the Egyptian term for 'great house' or palace. The pharaoh was an absolute ruler whose word was law, although in practice he delegated some responsibilities to government officials. In theory, the whole of Egypt was the pharaoh's property: he could control trade and distribute land among his subjects as he chose. He was a symbol of national unity and also served as high priest to the

The weathered Sphinx stands guard over the pyramids of Giza.

VIEWPOINT

Were the pyramids aligned by the stars?

In ancient Egypt the study of the night sky was deemed so important that a special class of priests was trained to observe the movements of the heavenly bodies. In more recent years, some scholars have found possible links between the positions of the pyramids and certain astronomical features, and argue that the architects must have used astronomical calculations to orient the buildings. Some believe that the pyramids and other structures were aligned with sunset at the time of the winter or summer solstices. Others think that the siting of the pyramids reflects the constellation of Orion or the circumpolar stars, both of which are often depicted in the artwork of pharaonic tombs. Enough evidence can be interpreted on both sides to ensure the argument keeps running.

The Step Pyramid
Pharaoh Djoser's pyramid at Sakkara marked a turning point in Egyptian architecture: it was not only the first pyramid to be built, but also the first large structure built entirely of worked limestone blocks. A wall 1.6km (1 mile) long enclosed the king's tomb complex, which covered an area of 15 hectares (37 acres).

nation's many deities. The pharaoh took on semi-divine status, becoming a god after his death.

The civil service and writing

The pharaoh's most important aide was his vizir, whose duties included supervising the royal palace and all public buildings, including the irrigation channels along the Nile. His main task, however, was collection of taxes and customs duties, in which he was helped by a hierarchy of treasurers, provincial governors and lesser civil servants. This led to the development of one of the ancient world's most extensive bureaucracies, all under the tight control of the pharaoh.

Egypt's efficient system of government could never have functioned without the invention of writing. During the 3rd millennium BC, a pictorial script with characters known as hieroglyphs came into use, mainly for inscribing religious texts and for carving inscriptions on monuments. A simplified script known as hieratic was preferred for daily use – notably for drawing up tax accounts and detailing the amount of tribute individual landholders owed to the state. Even though the hieratic script was easier to use than hieroglyphics, it still posed a tough challenge for students, who had to master around 800 different picture signs. Those who stayed the course, typically through 12 years of strict schooling, could expect to win social respectability and a well-paid position as a scribe.

Egyptians wrote with sharpened reeds and a long-lasting ink made by grinding pigment (usually ochre) and mixing it with water. In the early days they used writing tablets of clay or limestone, but these were unwieldy and short on space. As ever in Egypt, the Nile provided a solution – in the papyrus reeds that grew in abundance, then as now, along its banks.

To produce a cheap, efficient writing surface, Egyptians chopped the reeds into lengths, stripped away the green outer skin and cut the white pith inside into thin slices. Dampened strips of pith were laid on a block, in two crossed layers, and pounded together with a wooden mallet, then left to dry. The end product was a membrane with a slightly wavy surface, not unlike modern writing paper. Lightweight and relatively tear-resistant, papyrus was easy to handle and could be rolled into scrolls or cut into sheets that could be bound in book form. The oldest surviving papyrus roll dates from the 12th century BC and is almost 45m (145ft) long.

The Rosetta Stone

For many centuries after ancient Egypt's final collapse the meaning of the ancient scripts was lost, and the fact that scholars can read hieroglyphs today is due to a fortunate find. At the end of the 18th century, Napoleon invaded Egypt. Archaeologists accompanying the French army discovered a stone slab inscribed in three languages. One was hieroglyphics, another was a simpler form of Egyptian writing known as demotic script, but the third was Ancient Greek. By 1822 Frenchman Jean-Francois Champollion had used his knowledge of Ancient Greek to decode the Egyptian. The stone slab became known as the Rosetta Stone.

By the start of Egypt's 3rd Dynasty, in about 2700 BC, the power of the pharaohs was complete. Their political supremacy was unchallenged, and they had an efficient, well-organised bureaucracy in place to underpin their rule. This era is associated above all with the names of Djoser and Imhotep. Djoser was the second of the dynasty's five rulers, and several pioneering innovations were introduced in his reign, among them a radical change in the design of royal tombs.

The first pyramid

The Egyptians built their tombs as homes for eternity. They believed that the souls of the dead could only be resurrected in the afterlife if the body remained intact. In early times the dead were buried in the desert, where the warm, dry sand naturally preserved the remains. Later, Egyptians perfected the art of mummification.

The pharaohs of the 1st and 2nd Dynasties were interred in stone-lined pits in mastabas – rectangular, mudbrick buildings topped with a flat roof. Even the earliest mastabas incorporated several separate chambers to house the royal sarcophagus, along with grave goods including food, tools and weapons.

Djoser commissioned a very different kind of tomb: a structure built out

of stone that was to reach to the heavens. The builder was Imhotep, the earliest architect whose name has come down to modern times. Imhotep was far more than just an architect: he was ancient Egypt's Leonardo da Vinci, a genius of many talents who served as Djoser's vizir while also pursuing careers as a physician, sculptor, philosopher and astronomer. He was one of very few non-royal Egyptians whose fame entered popular legend. Long after his death he was

considered the personification of knowledge, and in the late period of ancient Egyptian history he even came to be worshipped as a god.

Under Imhotep's supervision Djoser's tomb was built at Sakkara, about 20km (12 miles) south of present-day Cairo. Completed in about 2650 BC, it was to become the prototype for all later pyramids. Imhotep still used the traditional mastaba design, but he placed six of these

Hieroglyph inscriptions
Tomb chambers like this one (above) in the mastaba of the vizir Mereruka were typically covered with hieroglyphic texts describing the career and accomplishments of the dead man. In early times each hieroglyphic character (inset) was a pictogram respresenting the object it depicted, but as the script evolved the signs also came to stand for sounds, as letters do in the modern alphabet.

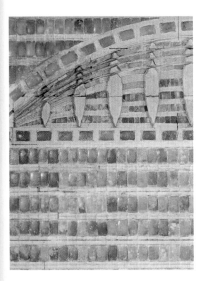

The blue room
Djoser's tomb chamber was clad in cobalt-blue ceramic tiles. The pigment was manufactured by mixing quartz sand, chalk and soda, then heating the mixture to more than 800°C (1470°F). Copper compounds were added to create the blue tones.

structures one on top of another, with each layer slightly smaller than the one below. The result is known as the Step Pyramid – even though, strictly speaking, it does not have the square form of a true pyramid: at 125 x 105m (405 x 340ft), its base was rectangular, in the mastaba style. Even so, the effect was totally different from earlier structures. Djoser's monument was an impressive 60m (195ft) tall and, in the words of one temple text, was a 'stairway to heaven' for the king to mount up to the skies.

The cult of Re

This inscription begs a question: did the Step Pyramid merely seek to glorify Djoser's power, or did it also have symbolic religious significance? To answer that question, it is necessary to remember that the rank and status of the various Egyptian deities changed over time. For example, while Narmer and his successors gave pride of place to falcon-headed Horus, under Djoser the sun god Re (or Ra) moved to the head of the pantheon. A temple was built in Re's honour in Heliopolis, northeast of today's Cairo, at about this time. This temple, and the city in which it lay, became the centre of the new sun cult, which was to predominate until the end of the 6th Dynasty around 2190 BC.

According to the Re cult, after death the pharaoh could expect to accompany Re on his daily journey through the heavens; in a sense the ruler became an incarnation of the sun god. In one inscription Djoser is addressed as Re, and from the 4th Dynasty pharaohs held the title 'Son of Re'. In this context, the pyramid was probably conceived as a stairway in the literal sense – the means by which the pharaoh ascended to join the sun. When the sun's first rays hit the apex of the pyramid each morning, the soul of the dead ruler stepped into the sun barque to journey with Re across the sky.

Everyday life in country and city

The bulk of ancient Egypt's population were farmers or farm labourers, whose lives revolved entirely around the flood cycle of the Nile. Sowing began as soon as the high water receded in October; harvesting took place between February and the beginning of June, at the time of the lowest water levels. In July the regular inundation arrived, and a cleverly designed system of reservoirs, dykes and canals ensured that the waters could be retained to irrigate the fields in the dry months.

The main crops were emmer wheat and barley, used to make Egypt's staples, bread and beer. In good years surplus harvest was

---

EVERYDAY LIFE

Of bread, cakes and ale

Bread was baked fresh daily in ancient Egypt, even though the process required a great deal of effort. First the grain had to be pounded in mortars, then finely ground between grinding stones or querns. The flour was mixed with water to form dough, then shaped into large loaves or other shapes such as stars, dumb-bells or cones. The baking ovens were made of mudbrick and sited outdoors, usually next to an open fireplace in a backyard kitchen. The ovens were used not just to make bread but also cakes flavoured with honey. Beer was a staple drink and brewing it was a task that fell to housewives. The Egyptians brewed their beer out of fermented barley bread, which they sweetened and flavoured with honey, dates and other ingredients.

Baking bread
The favourite loaf of the ancient Egyptians was cone-shaped.

stored in silos against times of shortage when the Nile flood faltered or failed. Pulses, leeks and onions were cultivated, as were melons, dates, figs and pomegranates. The river provided plentiful supplies of fish, and poultry was also a regular part of the diet. Geese were ubiquitous in the meadows along the Nile, and roast goose was a favourite main course for feasts.

With the Nile supplying most of life's essentials, many of Egypt's citizens had time left over for creative pursuits. The cities housed a large population of craftsmen and artisans, including potters, stonemasons and weavers, who soon began creating works of art as well as standard everyday wares. Pottery was manufactured in many different shapes and sizes for home use and for export – archaeologists have found plentiful evidence of trade links with Mesopotamia and the Near East.

The Egyptians loved jewellery, which they made from a variety of materials, and they also spent much time and attention on make-up. Kohl was habitually used in a thick line to highlight the eyes. In contrast, clothing tended to be simple. Workers wore nothing but a loincloth. For the rest, the usual item of male attire in early Egypt was the apron, while women as a rule wore a simple tunic held up by shoulder straps.

Building the great pyramids

The great pyramid-building epoch began in the reign of Snefru, founder of the 4th Dynasty in about 2613 BC. Snefru had a long and prosperous reign, but his first attempt to build his own tomb was not a success. Due to calculation errors, his edifice at Dashur, south of Sakkara, ended up off-centre and has been known ever since as the Bent Pyramid. His second attempt, however, resulted in a near-perfect pyramid almost 100m (325ft) high.

Snefru's son Khufu (Cheops), who reigned from 2551 to 2528 BC, set himself the ambitious goal of outdoing his father's efforts and commissioned the Great Pyramid – first and largest of the pyramids of Giza, the only one of the Seven Wonders of the ancient world to survive into the

modern age. Today, the Great Pyramid stands on the outskirts of Cairo; like all royal tombs, it is on the Nile's west bank, the side of the setting sun. Constructing this extraordinary monument used an estimated 2.3 million blocks of limestone, each weighing about 2.5 tonnes, and it reached a height of 147m (478ft).

Raising such a structure without the aid of modern lifting equipment or even pulleys seems at first sight to be an almost superhuman task, but lengthy research has given a clear insight into the building techniques employed. Clearly a huge

Hunting for game
Meat was scarce in the Egyptian diet and birds of all kinds were considered delicacies. Traps or nets were used to catch ducks and geese in the papyrus thickets along the banks of the Nile. The wealthy hunted birds for sport in the riverside marshes using wooden throwing sticks.

workforce was needed, but the people who built the pyramids were not slaves. Rather, tens of thousands of farmers and farm labourers answered the Pharaoh's summons, and worked on the pyramids when the fields were submerged by the Nile. Building the pyramids was no picnic, and many of the workers no doubt resented the demands made on them; presumably some did not survive. Others, however, may have taken a more positive view, regarding this work for their god-king not as drudgery but as an honour.

Stone by stone

The stone for the pyramids came from quarries fairly near the building site. To cut the huge blocks, workers first drove a wooden wedge into a natural split in the rock. Water was then poured over the wedge until it swelled and split off the stone. Each dislodged block was rolled on tree trunks to load-bearing sledges and then dragged to barges waiting on the bank of the Nile. The boats transported the mighty blocks to a disembark-ation spot as close to the pyramid as possible. The techniques used by the pyramid-builders to lift the blocks into place were surprisingly simple. Workers carried small stones on their shoulders. Larger blocks were pulled by ropes along ramps made of air-dried mud bricks coated with a layer of Nile mud. The blocks glided so smoothly over the slippery surface that, according to French researchers, one man alone could move a one-tonne limestone block. Evidence of the techniques can be seen in stone reliefs and tomb paintings which illustrate the methods. After use, the ramps were disassembled and the bricks were thrown into the Nile, where they dissolved back into mud.

Modern estimates suggest that it would have taken around 36,000 workers some 20 years to build the Great Pyramid. A further 10,000 would have been needed to quarry and transport the stone blocks, boatloads of which probably arrived every few minutes. The infrastructure required must have been immense: entire road systems would have had to be built and giant ramps and canals constructed. A town to house skilled workers was even constructed from scratch.

The architects and engineers had few tools to guide them: the plumb bob, the protractor, a measurement system based on the ell (equivalent to about 1.15m/45in) and the vizir's rod as a ruler. With the aid of these simple tools and a sure grasp of the basic principles of geometry, they were able to calculate the surface areas and volumes involved. The end product of all their efforts was truly awesome: a vast pyramid pointing skyward like a giant arrowhead. The outer surface was clad in flat white casing stones, making it completely smooth, and the apex was crowned with a gilded capstone that must have shone like a second sun.

The interior of the pyramid was equally splendid, with corridors and chambers of multicoloured granite pillars and polished alabaster floors. Other rooms were adorned with statues and wall reliefs, as well as furniture and other funerary goods. Narrower passageways led below ground. The tomb chamber itself lay in the centre of the pyramid: this was where the Pharaoh's body was laid to rest in a huge stone sarcophagus.

Priest and public dignitary
This lifesize statue of the priest Kapher was carved in about 2490 BC from the wood of a sycamore, a tree considered sacred by the Egyptians. It was found in a tomb near Sakkara.

The Great Sphinx

Sometime around 2500 BC, sculptors employed by Khufu's son and successor Khafre (Chephren) shaped an outcrop of rock alongside the Great Pyramid into a colossal, lion-like figure with the head of a man. From its front paws to its tail, the Sphinx – the name was given to it by travellers from ancient Greece – measures an impressive 73 metres (237 ft). The head is thought to represent Khafre himself, or so the royal headdress with snake-like uraeus and false beard, both symbols of sovereignty, would suggest.

Sphinxes probably owe their form to the Egyptian view that lions made apt guardians for holy places. The Giza Sphinx, the largest and oldest of its kind, no doubt had such a function, protecting not just the Great Pyramid but also the pyramids built nearby for Khafre and his successor Menkaure. In later times entire alleys of sphinxes lined the entrances to temples, fortifying the power of the pharaoh to preserve the sanctuary.

The fall of the Old Kingdom

In the long run, mammoth projects like the building of the Great Pyramid turned out to be more than the economy could bear. While Khafre was able to raise his pyramid to a height of nearly 140m (455ft), only 7m less than Khufu's, later pharaohs had to scale their monuments back considerably. The later pyramids were also built with far less care and attention to detail. This change was already apparent in the reign of Menkaure, and is reflected in the size of his pyramid – the third and last in the Giza complex and by far the smallest. But there were other factors involved, besides the huge financial burden, in bringing the great age of the pyramids to an end. Evidence points to a long-lasting drought that affected the entire Near East region towards the end of the 3rd millennium BC. Egypt was hit by famine.

To cope with the crisis, the pharaohs had to delegate considerable powers to provincial governors, known as nomarchs. These officials took the opportunity to build up their own local power bases, weakening the central authority. The outcome was a time of troubles and civil war that plunged Egypt into chaos and brought the first era of ancient Egyptian history – the Old Kingdom – to an end. More than a century would pass before Mentuhotep, a strong pharaoh of the 11th Dynasty, finally succeeded in reuniting the country in about 2052 BC.

The pyramids of Giza
The Great Pyramid of Khufu – the largest pyramid ever built – stands in the centre, with the tomb of Menkaure behind and the pyramid of Khafre on the left. In the fore-ground are smaller pyramids thought to have been built for the pharaohs' wives.

Furniture for a royal bedroom
Unlike neighbouring peoples of the time, the Egyptians slept in beds. Beautifully crafted pieces of furniture, like these that belonged to Heteferes, Khufu's mother, were inlaid with gold and silver or decorated with ivory.

The Middle Kingdom – a reunited Egypt

A hundred years of civil war finally ended during the 11th Dynasty, with the start of the Middle Kingdom period in ancient Egypt's history. The next four centuries saw Egypt reach a zenith of power and wealth.

Model warriors
Figures like these Nubian archers were popular grave goods in Middle Kingdom times. The bowmen fought in the pharaoh's army.

Following the collapse of the Old Kingdom, Egypt descended into anarchy as rival warlords engaged in a bloody struggle for supremacy. Eventually, in about 2060 BC, a resourceful 11th Dynasty pharaoh called Mentuhotep came to the throne at Thebes in Upper Egypt. Within a decade of coming to power – by about 2052 BC – he had reunited the country under his rule, bringing Upper and Lower Egypt back together under a single crown and giving peace to a war-weary people. Even so, the nomarchs who had brought down the previous regime were not entirely tamed; these provincial nobles managed to retain some of the additional powers they had won following the Old Kingdom's decline.

Securing Middle Kingdom power

To restore the authority of the pharaoh, Mentuhotep reorganised the machinery of government, establishing an efficient bureaucracy to match that of Old Kingdom days. Egypt began to recover economically as farmers and artisans once more started paying the taxes that had been withheld during the intervening troubles, a time known to modern historians as the First Intermediate Period.

The first pharaohs of the Middle Kingdom also had to secure the nation's borders. In the north they pushed back the Libyans of the western desert, and put an end to incursions by Asiatic nomads raiding from the northeast. In the south the rulers of the succeeding 12th Dynasty established sway over Nubia as far downstream as the Second Nile Cataract. This was an important success as Nubia supplied soldiers for the Egyptian army and was also rich in mineral resources, particularly gold and precious stones.

Egyptian traders were in contact with another country even farther south: the mysterious Land of Punt, that is now thought to have been somewhere in the Horn of Africa. The pharaohs enjoyed peaceful relations with Punt, which had long been a source of luxury goods such

as ivory, ebony and especially incense, which was in constant demand for religious ceremonies. During the Middle Kingdom, this grew into a thriving trade along the Red Sea coast.

Building new homes for the dead

In the meantime, a new city of the dead was being created to the west of Thebes, which briefly served as the capital under Mentuhotep and his immediate successors. (It would later regain this position as the home of the New Kingdom pharaohs.) Mentuhotep had a magnificent tomb complex built for himself in the bowl-shaped valley of Deir-el-Bahri, on the west bank of the Nile just downriver from Thebes. The complex was stepped, rising up against a dramatic cliff backdrop. The mortuary temple itself was in the form of a gigantic hall supported by 140 columns, with a small pyramid rising from its roof. The design – a synthesis of the pyramid tombs of the earlier pharaohs and the

Symbols of power
This fragment of a relief comes from the mortuary temple of Pharaoh Mentuhotep at Deir-el-Bahri. It shows him wearing the distinctive royal insignia of the artificial beard and the uraeus, or serpent headdress.

A warrior pharaoh
This painted sandstone statue shows Pharaoh Mentuhotep wearing the red crown of Lower Egypt. Variously designated Mentuhotep I or II by different sources, this is the pharaoh who reunited the nation by conquering Lower Egypt from his capital of Thebes in Upper Egypt, thus establishing the Middle Kingdom era of Egyptian history.

rock-cut tombs of Theban provincial nobles – symbolised the nation's restored unity, but also served as an expression of changing ideas about the afterlife.

By Mentuhotep's day Egyptians no longer believed that the pharaoh rose up to join the sun god Re on his daily journey through the heavens. Instead, they thought that when the pharaoh died he became one with Osiris, god of the dead and the focus of an increasingly important cult. Osiris had been restored to life in the branches of a sycamore, and significantly the great inner courtyard of Mentuhotep's temple contained a grove of these sacred trees.

The cult of Osiris

Today, Osiris is probably the best-known god of the Egyptian pantheon. According to legend, he was once king of all Egypt, ruling alongside his sister Isis, who was also his wife and queen. The couple were so well-loved that they aroused the jealousy of Osiris's evil brother Seth, who hatched a wicked plan. He tricked Osiris into lying down in a particularly splendid sarcophagus, then locked the lid and threw the coffin into the Nile.

When the faithful Isis learned that her husband was missing, she set out to search for him, if needs be to the farthest ends of the Earth. Eventually she traced the sarcophagus to the port of Byblos on the eastern Mediterranean coast, and brought her dead husband back to Egypt. Seth, however, had not exhausted his malice. Getting hold of his brother's corpse, he cut it in pieces and threw them into

the river. Once more Isis set out and when she had gathered almost all her husband's scattered body, she reassembled Osiris and breathed life back into him. Thereafter Osiris became Lord of the Otherworld. Horus, the son of Isis and Osiris, set out to avenge his father. After a long struggle and many battles with Seth, the gods awarded Horus victory.

Egyptians recorded their beliefs about the afterlife in inscriptions on tomb walls and on papyrus scrolls. These texts have since been brought together as the Egyptian Book of the Dead. They believed that when people died they were carried across the Nile into the kingdom of Osiris, somewhere on the river's west bank where the sun set. There, they were received by the jackal-headed god Anubis in a great hall of judgment. With Isis, Osiris and the falcon-headed god Horus in attendance, each dead person's heart was weighed in the balance against the

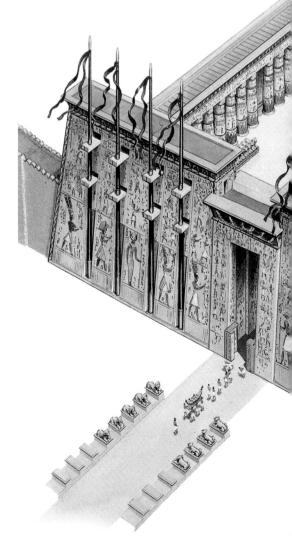

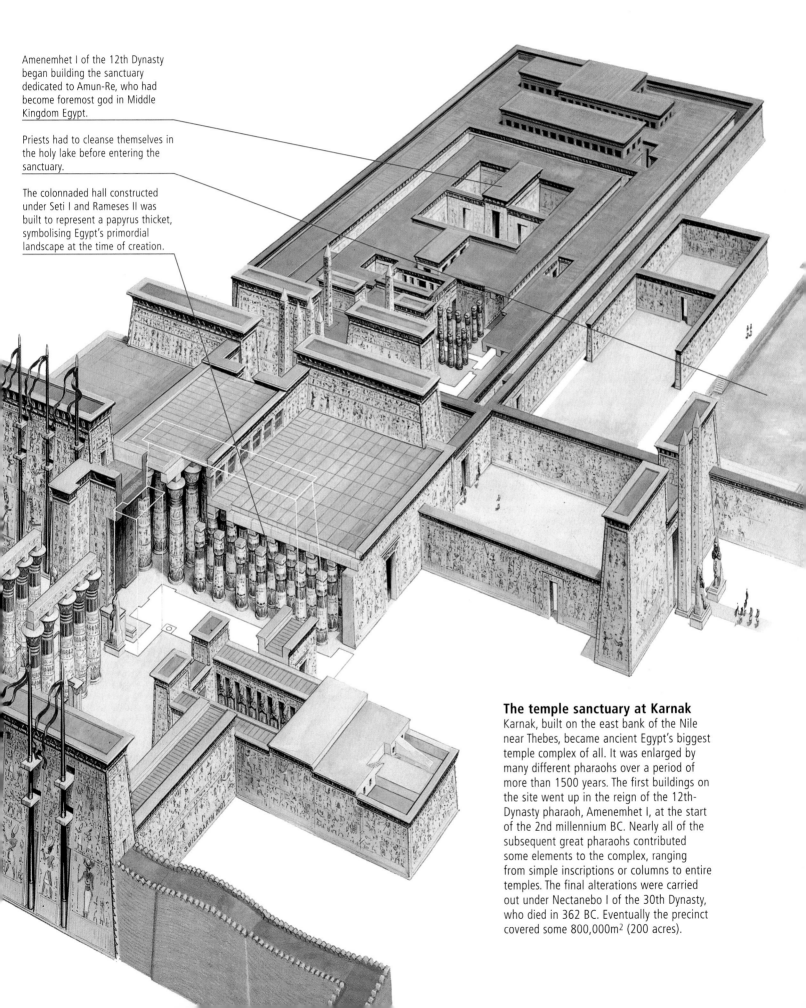

Amenemhet I of the 12th Dynasty began building the sanctuary dedicated to Amun-Re, who had become foremost god in Middle Kingdom Egypt.

Priests had to cleanse themselves in the holy lake before entering the sanctuary.

The colonnaded hall constructed under Seti I and Rameses II was built to represent a papyrus thicket, symbolising Egypt's primordial landscape at the time of creation.

The temple sanctuary at Karnak
Karnak, built on the east bank of the Nile near Thebes, became ancient Egypt's biggest temple complex of all. It was enlarged by many different pharaohs over a period of more than 1500 years. The first buildings on the site went up in the reign of the 12th-Dynasty pharaoh, Amenemhet I, at the start of the 2nd millennium BC. Nearly all of the subsequent great pharaohs contributed some elements to the complex, ranging from simple inscriptions or columns to entire temples. The final alterations were carried out under Nectanebo I of the 30th Dynasty, who died in 362 BC. Eventually the precinct covered some 800,000m^2 (200 acres).

Stories in stone
The pharaohs had inscriptions carved onto the monumental columns of the temple sanctuary at Karnak commemorating their military victories and other important events of their reigns.

feather of truth. The dead had to give an account their life. If they failed to tell the truth, their heart, weighed down by falsehood, would upset the scales, and the guilty faced the terrible fate of being swallowed up by a monster – Ammut the Devourer. The virtuous, however, being light of heart, were released into blissful eternal life in the otherworld.

The cult of Osiris offered the possibility of salvation for all virtuous people, effectively democratising the afterlife; in future, not just the pharaoh but any individual who lived an upright and honest existence could hope to gain eternal life. The new beliefs not only offered solace to ordinary Egyptian citizens but also went some way to undermining their belief in the divine status of their rulers.

The great age of temple-building

The pharaohs of the 11th Dynasty laid the groundwork for Egypt's recovery, but it was under the 12th Dynasty that the Middle Kingdom reached its peak. The dynasty was founded in about 1995 BC by a former vizir, Amenemhet I.

One of Amenemhet's first steps was to move the capital from Thebes, which lay far to the south, near to the centre of the country. A new city was created at Lisht, about 30km (20 miles) south of the Old Kingdom capital of Memphis. Thebes lost its political importance, but acquired a fresh religious status as the centre for the worship of a newly important deity – Amun. Hitherto, Amun had been a relatively little-known local god of Upper Egypt, but in time he would merge

with the old sun god Re to become, as Amun-Re, the foremost god of the whole kingdom.

The first temple to Amun-Re was built at Amenemhet I's behest on the east bank of the Nile at Karnak, near Thebes. In time a gigantic complex developed on the site – over the next 1500 years it would grow into a labyrinth of monumental gateways, courtyards and colonnaded halls. The immense wealth of the Karnak complex was testimony to Amun-Re's pre-eminence over the other Egyptian gods, as was the extent of the political influence that the priests of Amun came to exercise. Yet Karnak was also a monument to the glory of the pharaohs. No other Egyptian site bore so many inscriptions commemorating royal victories, and none was so often built and rebuilt to accommodate additional expressions of royal piety.

In 1971 BC Amenemhet I decided to appoint his son, Sesostris I, as co-regent. This decision proved vital to the future of the dynasty, for after a successful 30-year reign the ageing pharaoh fell victim to a palace coup. Sesostris, who was away at the time campaigning against the Libyans, came rushing back to court on receiving news of his father's death and assumed power as the nation's sole ruler.

An outpost in Nubia

Sesostris's reign marked the start of a long period of wealth and internal peace. There was an upsurge in building activity, although relatively few of the temples and palaces have survived to bear witness to the Middle Kingdom's splendours.

Sesostris energetically continued his predecessors' policies in Nubia. Egypt's position as the Middle East's principal trading nation, and the political influence that accompanied this standing, was largely dependent on Nubian gold and Sesostris was particularly eager to control the rich gold resources in the south of the country. To secure his gains, in 1950 BC he ordered the construction of a mighty fortress at Buhen, on the west bank of the Nile near the Second Cataract. The stronghold was designed to serve as a command centre for Egyptian forces in Nubia. Its massive walls stood 9m (29ft) high and 5m (16ft) thick and were pierced with arrow slits so that the Nubian bowmen, who now formed a significant part of the Egyptian army, could rain down arrows on besiegers. Any attackers who survived the fire would also be subjected to a volley of stones from the ramparts. Buhen was the largest of a number of outposts built around this time at strategically important points along Egypt's borders. Some commanded the principal trade routes to the north, where Sesostris founded other new cities.

Life-giving waters

Economic considerations also provided the impetus for an ambitious irrigation project southwest of Memphis, undertaken in 1890 BC by Sesostris I's grandson, Sesostris II. The wealth of Egypt depended on the Nile: prolonged failure of the annual flood could have devastating consequences, as painful past experiences had shown. To prevent such disaster in future, Sesostris built a canal that tapped one of the Nile's western branches, diverting its waters into a vast natural depression. The water flow was controlled by means of a dam and a system of lock gates. In the flood season these gates could be opened to create a gigantic reservoir, and the waters were used in the dry months to irrigate fields for many miles around. The Fayum oasis remains one of the country's most productive regions to this day.

Such ambitious schemes required precise knowledge of the timing and extent of the Nile's annual flood. A device

known as the Nilometer was installed at Aswan, near the river's First Cataract, to record the river's rise and fall. Every July, at the start of the flood season, the water's height was carefully noted: the mean measurement was about 8.5m (28ft). If the figure diverged from the norm, or the flood arrived early or late, messengers were sent to inform the pharaoh so that measures could be taken in advance to lessen the negative impact on the nation's farmers.

The Nile not only watered crops, it also fed the cattle that grazed the green meadows fringing the river. Cows were Egypt's most important domestic animal; they provided meat and milk, and were also harnessed to plough the fields. Asses were also important as beasts of burden (camels were not domesticated until later).

The divine uraeus
The uraeus-serpent was part of the royal insignia worn on the pharaoh's brow. It was an expression of the fiery eye of the primordial creator god Atum.

A burgeoning trade network

As the principal highway for traffic, the river was as vital for trade as it was for agriculture. Countless boats and barges plied its waters every day, carrying grain, cattle, building materials, luxury goods and much besides. Simple boats made by lashing together clumps of papyrus reed had been in use since pre-pharaonic times, and these remained popular as they were well adapted to the Nile's calm waters. By Middle Kingdom days, however, shipwrights were also constructing seaworthy vessels made of wood and powered by sails

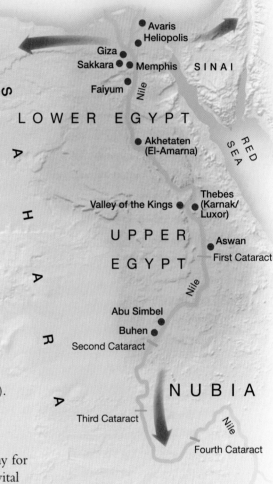

MEDITERRANEAN SEA

Avaris
Heliopolis
Giza
Sakkara • Memphis SINAI
Faiyum Nile

LOWER EGYPT

Akhetaten
(El-Amarna)

RED SEA

Valley of the Kings Thebes
(Karnak/
Luxor)

UPPER
EGYPT Aswan
First Cataract

Nile

Abu Simbel
Buhen
Second Cataract

NUBIA

Third Cataract Nile

Fourth Cataract

■ Middle Kingdom
● Key sites
➤ Egyptian expeditions

Counting cattle
These colourfully painted clay figures were fashioned to serve as grave goods. They depict a landowner named Meketre counting his cattle with the help of his scribes. From such lists, we know that some Egyptians owned huge herds.

as well as by oars. The wood to build the ships was not grown in Egypt, however; the palms and acacias that flourished along the Nile were unsuitable because they only supplied short planks of inferior quality. Instead, cedar wood was imported from the city-state of Byblos in what is now Lebanon, the most important trading port of its day.

Besides timber, Byblos exported resins, oils and silver to Egypt, as well as copper from Syrian mines. Egypt also imported copper from the Sinai peninsula, while wine, olives and delicately worked gold jewellery came from Crete. In return, the Egyptians shipped out surplus grain as well as paper and rope, both made from the versatile papyrus reed.

Trade remained a state monopoly in Egypt. In theory at least, the pharaoh owned the whole of the nation's output just as he owned the land, which was merely worked by his subjects. Even arts and crafts were concentrated almost entirely in state-owned workshops.

Artistic transition

When Sesostris III came to the throne in 1878 BC, Egypt was experiencing something of a cultural blossoming. In Old Kingdom days the arts had been strictly ruled by tradition; styles were fixed by past custom, and there was little in the way of experimentation. In the peace and prosperity of the Middle Kingdom era, however, the fine arts became lighter and livelier. Painters were not just more generous in their use of colour; they showed a new interest in everyday subject matter, creating vivid vignettes that have bequeathed to posterity a detailed picture of Middle Kingdom life. Sculptors explored new artistic conventions and poses, while jewellers made broad collars and necklaces of semi-precious stones and wrought amulets in gold. In literature the Middle Kingdom produced a wealth of stories, satires and love songs, of which only fragments have survived.

The administrative machine

The general affluence that Egypt was enjoying provided a stable background against which the pharaoh was able to push through political reforms. Royal authority had not been seriously called into question since Mentuhotep I reunited the country, but the different provinces had retained a degree of autonomy, maintaining their own separate traditions of government under powerful local governors. Sesostris III put an end to this state of affairs, imposing a single system of centralised rule for the whole of Egypt, directed uncompromisingly from the royal palace. No contemporary records have survived to document the change, so historians can only speculate about the degree of resistance that the ruler had to overcome in imposing these new measures, but it was probably considerable.

No matter how great the pharaoh's power, in practice he relied on the efficiency and competence of an army of civil servants. The leading administrators owed their position entirely to the ruler – he could replace or even execute them if he saw fit. However, they exerted considerable influence, not least because all information passed through their hands before reaching the pharaoh himself, who must often have found himself simply rubber-stamping decisions that had already been made further down the chain of command.

Life of luxury

It was the pharaoh's custom to reward his most important aides and advisers with elaborate gifts intended to encourage their lasting commitment and loyalty. Some of them amassed considerable wealth in this way and owned expensive boats, jewellery and costly clothing. High officials lived in comfortable villas with walled gardens and Nubian servants at their constant beck and call.

The luxurious lives of these senior civil servants were mirrored in their splendidly equipped tombs, for Egyptians, always conscious of the afterlife, were eager to preserve their creature comforts beyond the grave. The paintings on tomb chamber walls are full of the joys of life, offering a detailed picture of the celebrations and banquets that were part of the lives of the wealthy classes. Guests garlanded with flowers take their ease at well-stocked dinner tables. Young serving girls dispense drinks, particularly red and white wines.

Naturally, the master of the house also provided entertainment for his guests. Poets told stories or recited verses. Acrobats, dancers and singers performed to the accompaniment of musicians playing the lyre, flute or harp.

BACKGROUND

Religious practices of ancient Egypt

Egyptian temples were more than simply places of worship; in a very real sense they were thought to be the home of the gods. Egyptians believed that the nation's many deities needed shelter, food and clothing, just as humans do. The role of the priests was to look after the physical wellbeing of the god or gods to whom their own particular temple was dedicated.

First, they performed the ritual burning of incense to purify the air. Then the high priest took the statue of the god from its resting-place, undressed it and cleansed it. The statue was then dressed again in fresh clothes and replaced in the shrine. Offerings of food, water and flowers were left in the sanctuary to provide physical and spiritual refreshment for the deity.

Many Egyptians would have had small domestic shrines in their homes where they carried out similar daily rituals. To secure divine protection at all times most people wore amulets, which also accompanied them into the tomb when they died. The udjat eye was particularly popular as an amulet because it was thought to protect the wearer from harm and, above all, to guarantee fertility.

Watchful eye
The udjat symbolised the all-seeing eye of the falcon god Horus.

PAST VOICES

The life of Sinuhe

One of ancient Egypt's best-known literary works described how a young court official called Sinuhe had the misfortune to be present when Sesostris I received the dreadful news of his father's murder. Fearing that he might have overheard a state secret without permission, the young man fled to Palestine in fear of his life and remained there for several years, supported by Bedouin tribesmen who took him in and gave him shelter. He raised a family in his new home and in time became wealthy, even being made a sheikh. Yet Sinuhe could never forget his old home, and so was only too happy when Sesostris I eventually recalled him to take up a high position at the Egyptian court.

Fertility charm
This blue faience hippo represented Taweret, a goddess who protected women during childbirth.

Luxury on an altogether different scale prevailed in the pharaoh's palace. A host of servants took care of the ruler's person and dress. There were barbers to cut his hair and shave him each morning; hairdressers to maintain the royal wigs; manicurists to tend his hands and nails; and perfumers who bathed him in sweet-smelling oils. There was even a special attendant charged specifically with the task of supervising the royal sandals.

Each pharaoh had a number of wives and concubines, one of whom – the Great Wife – served as his official consort and first lady; her children had priority in the succession to the throne. Often the queen was a close relative of the pharaoh, not infrequently his sister. Although incest was not tolerated elsewhere in Egyptian society, for the semi-divine pharaohs sibling marriage was considered quite desirable as a way of avoiding dilution of the royal bloodline.

The beginning of the end

Sesostris III waged successful military campaigns to secure vital trade routes in southern Nubia and in Palestine. His victories raised Egypt's military might to new heights, and he was considered one of the greatest pharaohs both by his contemporaries and subsequently. His son Amenemhet III consolidated the gains his father had made, but soon after Amenemhet's death the Middle Kingdom started to fall apart. The reasons for this abrupt decline remain unclear, but it seems likely, given the centralisation of power in Egypt, that leadership failings on the part of the pharaohs who succeeded Amenemhet must have played a part.

Foreign rule

As the rulers' grip relaxed, there was renewed insecurity along the nation's borders. The conquered territories in Palestine stopped supplying tribute, and both the northeastern and southern frontiers came under attack. In the 17th century BC, the incursions in the north turned into a flood. A group called the Hyksos, made up of various Semitic tribes from the Mediterranean's east coast, took control of Lower Egypt.

They first entered the country peacefully, establishing a presence as traders and foreign workers. Later, however, they defeated the Egyptians in battle, not due to superior fighting skills, but thanks largely to new military technology. Their fighting men wore chain mail and wielded battle axes and improved bows, but their greatest weapons, previously unknown in Egypt, were horse-drawn battle chariots which gave their commanders a degree of mobility on the battlefield that the Egyptians could not hope to match.

The Hyksos celebrated their conquest of Lower Egypt by destroying the Middle Kingdom capital of Lisht. Then in about 1650 BC they established a ruling dynasty of their own, based at Avaris in the eastern Nile delta. They absorbed Egyptian culture but also brought contributions of their own, introducing such novelties as an improved loom for weaving as well as the lute and other musical instruments. Local rulers once more established some degree of independent authority under their rule, which lasted for almost 100 years until about 1570 BC – a time known to history as the Second Intermediate Period.

The great pharaohs

In the New Kingdom period, from 1570 BC on, a succession of exceptional rulers extended Egypt's frontiers and built a legacy of magnificent buildings to astonish later civilisations.

As the Second Intermediate Period dragged on, the oppressive tribute levied by Egypt's foreign Hyksos rulers caused growing resentment. The heart of the resistance movement was in Thebes, but it spread out from the city through all of Upper Egypt. By this time, Egyptians had learned the lessons of their defeat by the Hyksos and had started building war chariots of their own. The struggle came to a head under the leadership of Ahmose, founder of the 18th Dynasty. During his reign (1570–46 BC), he destroyed the Hyksos capital of Avaris and drove them back to Palestine and Syria. So began the New Kingdom, a glorious period in the history of ancient Egypt.

The first New Kingdom pharaohs concentrated on securing Egypt's borders in the northeast and in the south, where they re-established control over Nubia. Internally,

The mask of Tutankhamun
Inlaid with quartz, lapis lazuli and obsidian, the golden mask of Tutankhamun immortalises the most famous face of Egypt's New Kingdom – the boy pharaoh who died in 1352 BC, aged just 19.

Stone sentinels
An avenue of sphinxes leads between the temple complexes of Luxor and Karnak, built on the banks of the Nile some 500 miles south of Cairo. The modern town of Luxor is on the site of the New Kingdom capital of Thebes, the 'city of a hundred gates'.

Thebes became once again the nation's capital and royal authority was consolidated across Upper and Lower Egypt. These goals were largely accomplished during the reign of Thutmose I, a warrior pharaoh who waged successful campaigns in Syria and Nubia. After his death in 1518 BC, a period of peace and prosperity began during which, for the first time, a queen became the ruler of all Egypt.

The first female pharaoh

Hatshepsut was clever and ambitious. When her husband Thutmose II died, she came to power as regent for her stepson, the future Thutmose III, who was still a boy. Her position as *de facto* ruler of the country challenged convention: although Egyptian women were accorded relatively high status and legal standing by the standards of the ancient world, they were far from being treated as the equals of men. Hatshepsut clearly had a strong personality as well as great determination, for within a few years she had gone from ruling by proxy as regent to being made pharaoh herself.

As there were no traditions of female kingship, Hatshepsut adopted the practices of her male predecessors. At her coronation she wore the traditional male apron, leaving her breast bare but for the jewellery that glittered on her neck and shoulders. Later, she even took to wearing the pharaoh's artificial beard along with other insignia of royal power. Such behaviour no doubt shocked large sections of the population, but Hatshepsut had the backing of a strong court faction.

She also turned out to be an extremely able ruler. Avoiding military adventures, she concentrated on revitalizing cross-border trade. On her initiative, an important mission was dispatched to the Land of Punt on the Somali coast. Five great trading vessels made the journey down the Red Sea. Her emissaries were made welcome, and returned with their holds laden with what a contemporary record described as 'wonderful plants of many kinds, myrrh trees, ebony, real ivory, gold, incense, eye cosmetics, leopard skins' and much more. In return, the merchants presented their hosts with rings and pearl necklaces.

A monument fit for a queen

Hatshepsut commemorated this trading expedition in the imposing terraced funerary temple that she had built for herself at Deir-el-Bahri, near the mortuary complex of Mentuhotep I. Few architectural structures in the world blend so well with their surroundings as this extraordinary monument, large parts of which were hollowed out of the mountainside. Reliefs in one of the halls recorded details of the expedition to Punt, while live myrrh trees brought back from there were planted in a place of honour in the temple garden.

For all the splendour of the temple, however, Hatshepsut chose not to be buried there. Instead, she had her tomb dug 96m (310ft) deep into the rock of the hills nearby, taking care that it was completely inconspic-uous from the outside. In doing so she was reflecting a growing concern about the activities of grave robbers and how to ensure the security of burial places. The trend had been started by Thutmose I when he became the first pharaoh to site his tomb in the Valley of the Kings, an isolated spot located at the foot of 300m (1000ft) high cliffs across the Nile from Thebes. Almost all his New Kingdom successors followed his example, choosing to be buried in tombs that were dug in great secrecy deep into the rock. Women of the royal house were interred farther south in the Valley of the Queens.

Hatshepsut left her mark on the great temple complex at Karnak. She had two mighty obelisks erected there and also ordered the construction of a monumental gateway opening onto the sacred lake. The ancient Greeks gave the name 'pylon' to such gateways fronting Egyptian temples.

BACKGROUND

Ensuring comfort in the afterlife

Believing firmly in life after death, wealthy Egyptians took pains to equip their tombs with specially selected furniture, clothing, food and other items that would enable them to enjoy the afterlife in style and comfort. Small clay figures and models depicting scenes from everyday life – a bakery, a grain harvest, a hunt – have been found in many tombs, and it is thought that these grave goods were believed to provide the dead person for eternity with the products of the activities they depicted.

Hatshepsut reigned in peace and prosperity for about 20 years before her stepson rose up against her. Thutmose had long since reached maturity, and now sought the power he thought was his due. His rebellion cost Hatshepsut her throne and possibly also her life. The new pharaoh subsequently did his best to erase her from memory: at her temple at Deir-el-Bahri, even her name was chiselled from the stone inscriptions, and hardly a single statue of the female pharaoh survived Thutmose III's destructive revenge.

Building an empire

Thutmose soon abandoned Hatshepsut's pacific foreign policy. In about 1480 BC he set out with an army to conquer nearly all of northern Palestine and southern Syria, a region of city-states and small

Hatshepsut's temple
Built into the mountainside at Deir-el-Bahri, the building was originally constructed as a mortuary temple for Hatshepsut and her father. When Hatshepsut was deposed and fell from favour, it was rededicated to the god Amun-Re.

EVERYDAY LIFE

Beauty care in ancient Egypt

Egyptians set great store by their physical appearance. Men and women of all ages loved precious jewellery, cosmetics, perfume and wigs, which served to express their status and, above all, to keep them looking young.

People expected to experience the same needs in the afterlife as in this life, so utensils for applying cosmetics were standard equipment in high-status tombs. Archaeologists have discovered kohl eye make-up, powdered lead sulphite that was used to rouge the cheeks, ochre mixed with tree resin that served as lipstick, and various scented oils for perfuming the hair or massaging the body. Small curling tongs for dressing wigs have also been found. Mirrors – items indispensable for daily beauty care – took the form of flat, carefully polished discs of copper, bronze or silver, with wooden handles. Manicure sets, razors, hair pins, make-up boxes and a variety of mixing vessels completed the usual beauty kit.

One unusual feature of Egyptian adornment can be seen in a number of wall-paintings which show women, formally dressed for banquets or other celebrations, wearing cones on their heads. These cones were made of wax and balm, and would have slowly melted, pervading the hair with scent, and also perhaps serving as a skin freshener or even a sun lotion.

A must-have make-up box
This inlaid casket belonged to a woman called Merit, the wife of an architect from Thebes. The ceramic bottles are filled with scented oils, salves and perfumes.

kingdoms that he forced to accept Egyptian overlordship. The new pharaoh's warlike ambitions remained unsated, however, for he dreamed of an Egyptian empire extending to the mid course of the River Euphrates (in present-day Iraq) and to southern Turkey.

In pursuit of this goal, Thutmose marched his armies northward up the Mediterranean coast each summer, steadily pushing back the boundaries of Egyptian power. Eventually he did indeed reach the Euphrates, reducing the small kingdoms of Palestine and Syria that lay on his route to vassal states. Year after year their rulers sent a stream of tribute to Egypt: horses, cattle, sheep, goats, timber for building, copper, silver and precious stones, particularly turquoise and lapis lazuli.

A military career

The Egyptian army had never before had such a high profile as it gained under Thutmose III. Military service became a launch-pad for a successful civilian career. Men who had proved themselves on the battlefield found new possibilities for wealth and advancement opening up for them in public life. It was not unheard of, for example, for a trusted general to rise up to become 'governor of the estates', with responsibility for managing royal lands. In the later years of the New Kingdom, more than one successful general usurped supreme power to become pharaoh himself.

When Thutmose III died after three decades of rule in about 1448 BC, he left his successor a mighty empire, a powerful army and an overflowing treasury. Wealth continued to stream into Egypt from its new conquests, and the old trade routes to Asia Minor, Babylon, Assyria and Crete had been secured once more.

A flowering of architecture

The long reign of Amenhotep III, who succeeded to the throne about 40 years after Thutmose's death, marked a high point in the New Kingdom's fortunes. Amenhotep was a peace-loving ruler who enjoyed the pleasures of life at court, and in later times his reign would come to be seen as something of a golden age. It was Amenhotep above all other pharaohs who turned the capital into the 'hundred-gated Thebes' whose fame reached the ears of Homer on the Mediterranean's farther shores. The gates in question must in fact have been the monumental temple gateways known as pylons.

The city of Thebes stretched out along a 2.5km (1½mile) central avenue that linked the two great temple complexes of Luxor and Karnak (see page 29). The temple dedicated to Amun-Re at Luxor was built on Amenhotep's orders, and according to one contemporary source was 'comparable to the celestial horizon, a favourite dwelling place of the King of the Gods'. The pharaoh had endowed the temple with sculpted columns, gilded statues of the gods and pharaohs, and above all magnificent buildings whose walls glowed with brightly painted reliefs, all shining in the African sun.

Glittering banquets

Amenhotep wanted an equally glorious dwelling of his own, so he built a palace for himself at Malkata near Karnak. The inner walls of the palace were bright with blue, green and orange flower and bird motifs. The surroundings well suited the elaborate feasts that the pharaoh enjoyed, where wine flowed and the guests were treated to such delicacies as fillet of wild antelope and gazelle. Amenhotep also had a man-made lake, almost 20km (12 miles) long, built next to the palace for the pleasure of his Great Wife, Tiy. The king and his courtiers sailed across the lake whenever their presence was required at religious ceremonies or public festivals.

Grave goods from the tombs of Amenhotep's wealthier subjects give some indication of the enormous wealth of Egypt at this time. Luxury items from much of the civilised world found their way to the banks of the Nile, among them the world's oldest known glass bowls. Amenhotep's death in about 1377 BC marked the end of the most prosperous epoch the country had yet known.

The 'heretic' king

His son and successor, who came to the throne as Amenhotep IV, was a different character altogether. The new ruler would soon set in motion a religious revolution that shook Egypt to its very foundations.

Amenhotep had been brought up conventionally enough to accept the cult of Amun, which had been the dominant faith in Egypt for more than 600 years; indeed, the very name Amenhotep meant 'Amun is satisfied'. Yet the new pharaoh

himself found the traditional religious beliefs less than satisfactory. He preferred another, less familiar deity – the Aten. In contrast with Re, who was the sun god in human form, the Aten was the sun's disc as it appears in the sky. Theologians in Heliopolis, a longstanding centre of the solar cult, had suggested during Amenhotep III's reign that the heavenly body itself had a divine presence, and the Aten had duly become an object of veneration for many Egyptians.

There was nothing particularly unusual about adding another god to the crowded Egyptian pantheon. What was startling, however, was that soon after his accession the young pharaoh decided to recognise the Aten as the only god. Before long, he outlawed the worship of the many other deities popular in Egypt. In abandoning Amun, Amenhotep was obliged to change his own name. He chose instead to call himself Akhenaten, 'he in whom the Sun's Disc is well-pleased'.

A flourishing metropolis

The pious pharaoh also decided to quit Thebes, which was the focal point of the cult of Amun-Re and the seat of its powerful priesthood. Instead, he build a new capital on the east bank of the Nile

Selket, goddess of death
Selket was one of four goddesses who acted as divine mourners. They protected the coffins and the canopic jars, which contained the internal organs – liver, lungs, stomach and intestines – removed during mummification. This gilded wooden sculpture of Selket came from Tutankhamun's tomb.

Symbol of life
This wooden mirror case is in the form of the ankh, the Egyptian symbol for life. It is decorated with gold and silver foil and inlaid with semi-precious stones.

about 320km (200 miles) to the north, at a site known today as Tell el-Amarna. At the time the city was called Akhetaten, reflecting its position as the centre of the new mono-theistic creed. The city was built in just four years, and during its construction Akhenaten lived with his beautiful wife Nefertiti and their children in a giant tent nearby, so he could oversee the works. He remained in his new capital until his death, never leaving it again.

While Akhetaten grew into a flourishing city with a splendid royal palace and five temples dedicated to the Aten god, the old capital of Thebes fell into decay. The great temple of Amun at Karnak was closed, as were the temples of all the other gods: the Aten alone was now worshipped. To add insult to injury, Akhenaten confiscated the immense riches accumulated in Amun's honour by his priests, and he had the names of Amun and all other deities except the Aten erased from public inscriptions. Only one image was allowed: the sun's disc, shown radiating benefits down to the Earth on rays that ended in open hands.

New god, new art
The fine arts changed radically with the new religion as a fresh spirit of realism found expression, particularly in the natu-ralistic depiction of individual people. In Akhenaten's view, the true god had no human form, so personifications of the Aten were forbidden. Instead, artists created naturalistic images of the courtly world that gave an unprecedented insight into the private life of the pharaoh and his immediate family circle. Many scenes portrayed Akhenaten relaxing with Nefertiti and their six daughters; one even showed Nefertiti sitting on the king's

knee, giving him a kiss. Such a display of intimacy and mutual affection would have been unthinkable in earlier days, when the pharaoh was invariably portrayed as a distant authority figure.

Equally shocking for observers used to the greater formality of the past was the ruthlessly realistic treatment accorded to Akhenaten himself, who was portrayed with soft, strangely elongated features, a pot belly and plump thighs. There may have been some religious motivation behind the new style, perhaps based on the idea that nothing could be disguised or hidden from the all-seeing Aten. The new art style detracted nothing from the beauty of Queen Nefertiti, however, and her image became a universal icon of elegance. Yet beyond the name Nefertiti – which means, fittingly, 'the beautiful one has arrived' – virtually nothing else is known about her.

The downfall of the heretic
Akhenaten's religious revolution stirred deep misgivings among traditionally-minded Egyptians who had always worshipped a multiplicity of gods. The ordinary people had no way to express their disquiet except through passive resistance, but Akhenaten had created influential and persistent enemies in the priesthood of Amun-Re when he stripped them of their power and wealth. His position might have been stronger if he had paid more attention to state affairs, but his religious concerns absorbed so much of his time and energy that he disregarded the pharaoh's duties. Public works were neglected and trade declined, sapping Egypt's prosperity.

Worse still, the security of the nation's borders was threatened once more. There had been signs of renewed unrest even in his father's day, but now disturbing reports flooded in, from Syria in particular where vassal states there were coming under attack from the Hittites, a rising power in the Middle East, and from other neigh-bouring peoples. When Akhenaten failed

A royal pastime
This wall-painting from the tomb of Nefertari, wife of Rameses II, shows the queen playing a popular board game called senet. Players threw sticks to determine their moves.

to send reinforcement troops to bolster the Egyptian presence in the region, much of Syria and Palestine threw off the shackles of Egyptian hegemony and stopped paying tribute.

This rebellion was disastrous for Akhenaten. Apart from the damage done to Egyptian pride and prestige, the financial loss was enormous. For a century or more the royal treasury had derived much of its income from these tribute payments. Now, the coffers were empty. Meanwhile, the neglected internal administration of the kingdom had descended into chaos. For these reasons alone, most Egyptians probably breathed a sigh of relief when Akhenaten finally died, in about 1360 BC.

The Aten cult did not long survive its champion. After the shadowy two-year reign of a figure known as Smenkhkare (who some scholars think may have actually been Nerfititi), the throne passed to the child pharaoh Tutankhamun. At his behest – or more likely, that of advisers who served as his regents – the traditional religion was re-established and the nation's capital moved back to Thebes. Building recommenced, but Tutankhamun was not able to accomplish much else in his short reign, for he died at the age of 19.

Today, Tutankhamun is probably the best-known of all Egyptian pharaohs, but he owes his fame not to his own deeds but to an accident of archaeology. Although the pharaohs of the New Kingdom had attempted to secure their tombs against grave-robbers, by and large they failed. Despite the lengths they went to in the Valley of the Kings to conceal the rock-cut resting places, digging down as much as 100m (300ft) and carefully covering and sealing the entrances, tomb raiders managed to find a way through. Of more than 60 tombs in the valley, nearly all were eventually plundered. The only one known to escape that fate was the burial place of the otherwise little-remembered Tutankhamun.

A world-famous discovery
The archaeologist who made the breakthrough was an Englishman named Howard Carter. In 1922 he was digging in the Valley of the Kings when he came across a concealed doorway that bore the royal seal of Tutankhamun. Beyond this obstacle a passage filled with rubble led to a second door, also marked with the royal seal. But beyond this second barrier lay a hidden treasure chamber, piled high with all the valuables provided to accompany the boy pharaoh on his journey

Pharaoh with a curl
This relief shows Rameses II, the builder of Abu Simbel, as a child; he still sports the long lock of hair that was cut off when a boy reached adulthood. Rameses lived well into his nineties.

Pointing heavenward
Carved out of rose granite, this obelisk was erected on the orders of Pharaoh Rameses II on the east side of the gateway to the Luxor temple complex. It stands almost 30 metres (100 ft) tall and weighs 254 tonnes.

into the afterlife. Alongside beds, sofas and armchairs, objects of alabaster and faience, ostrich feather fans, and countless small chests and boxes, was Tutankhamun's gilded and splendidly decorated throne, with a picture of the king and his wife on the backrest.

It took Carter a whole year to catalogue and secure all the treasure from the antechamber alone. Only then did he and his team attempt the difficult task of opening the royal sarcophagus – an enormous stone structure that almost filled the burial chamber. When Carter, using a hoist, finally managed to open the lid, he found a gilded wooden mummy-case, within which a second fitted snugly in the manner of a Russian doll. The coffin itself, which lay inside the second mummy-case, weighed 112kg (247lb) and was made out of 22-carat gold. Inside lay the untouched mummy of Tutankhamun, the head and shoulders covered by the now-famous gold mask, decorated with quartz, lapis lazuli and other gems.

In contrast to the well-preserved grave goods, Tutankhamun's mummy was in poor shape. An initial examination suggested that he had died of tuberculosis, but when the body was re-examined in 1968 doctors noted some damage to the skull, sparking speculation that the boy pharaoh might have been murdered. If so, his immediate successor, an elderly courtier named Ay, gained relatively little from the deed. He reigned for just a short time, dying heirless in about 1350 BC.

Buildings for eternity

Ay's successor, Horemheb, was the first of a new breed of military commanders to hold the Egyptian throne. Horemheb had been commander-in-chief of the army under his predecessor. He ruthlessly set about expunging all memory of the heretic pharaoh Akhenaten, but he also proved a competent ruler and busied himself with a reorganisation of state government aimed at encouraging efficiency and stamping out corruption. He too died without an heir, appointing another general to take his place. This man was Rameses I, the founder of the 19th Dynasty in 1293 BC. Both he and

his son and successor, Seti I, were competent military leaders; between them they managed to re-establish Egyptian control over much of Palestine.

They were also enthusiastic builders. It was Rameses I who started the construction of a gigantic colonnaded hall at Karnak. By the time of its completion under his grandson Rameses II, it covered a total area of more than 5000 square metres (1.25 acres), making it one of the largest temples ever built. Rameses II decorated the hall with reliefs of the Battle of Kadesh, which he fought against the Hittites in about 1275 BC. Huge reliefs show him standing in his war chariot and aiming his bow at his enemies. Although Rameses chose to portray the battle as a victory, it actually ended inconclusively, with both sides withdrawing. Thereafter, a wary truce prevailed for 20 years until a peace treaty was agreed between Rameses II and the Hittite king, Hattusilis III – the oldest peacy treaty known to history.

Rameses II occupied the throne for 67 years, one of the longest reigns of any pharaoh. He went down to posterity as Rameses the Great, not so much for his military exploits as his building activities, for he drew on the nation's revived prosperity to create many great monuments. One that has survived almost intact is the temple that he had cut into the sandstone rock of Abu Simbel, 500km (300 miles) south of Thebes, in about 1260 BC. The distance from the temple facade – guarded by four enormous seated statues of the pharaoh – to the building's farthest end was an impressive 55m (180ft). The design and execution of the Abu Simbel temple was so accurate that twice a year, in mid-February and October, dawn sunlight flooded through the gateway, bathing the statues at the farthest end in light.

Rameses II also contributed to the temple complex begun by Amenhotep III at Luxor, adding a forecourt and pylon, in front of which rose two monumental obelisks. One of these now stands in the Place de la Concorde in Paris.

The reign of Rameses II was the final high point for ancient Egypt. His successors struggled, with varying success, to defend their realm against increasingly powerful external enemies. Rameses III, who took the throne 30 years after his namesake's death, was the New Kingdom's last great ruler, but he wore himself out trying to secure his borders against raiders from the north. He had internal enemies too, and in 1162 BC fell victim to a palace coup. The nation survived for another millennium before becoming a province of the Roman empire, but Egypt's glory days were over.

A warrior ruler
Rameses III, ancient Egypt's last great ruler, spent much of his reign fighting off Egypt's enemies. He is depicted in many military scenes in the wall paintings of his mortuary temple. Other frescoes show victory parades.

ASIA

In the land of jade – China's early cultures

Before the first cities developed in Mesopotamia, skilled craftsmen in southern China were creating beautiful jade objects, while artisans in the north, already masters of the potter's wheel, were producing splendid ceramic vessels.

China has been inhabited for hundreds of thousands of years, as proved by the discovery, in 1929, of Peking Man – remains from a branch of *Homo erectus*, a precursor of the modern human species, *Homo sapiens*. Yet it was only as the last Ice Age drew to a close,

Precious jewellery
This valuable jade piece from ancient China's early days is known as a huang. It decorated a nobleman's apparel – the small holes near the top were for sewing it into place.

about 12,000 years ago, that the country began to assume anything resembling its future shape. Around this time northern China received a wave of migration from Central Asia, where the landscape was becoming increasingly arid and turning into steppe.

The new arrivals belonged to the Mesolithic era, or Middle Stone Age. They lived by hunting, fishing and gathering

plants and fruits, and they were adept at making stone tools out of flaked stone – axe-heads, scrapers and bits for boring. As their skills grew, they used sandstone, agate, opal and jade to produce finely finished tools, blades and arrowheads. They developed complex techniques to split stones under pressure; to shape the stones they used intervening materials to soften the blows. Similar tools have been found in Siberia, pointing to a common cultural sphere across much of northern Asia.

The peoples of the Mesolithic era assembled weapons and tools from several separate elements. These composite utensils had greater leverage and stability than the old hand-axes, simplifying many everyday tasks. Craftsmen were also shaping objects, including knives and spearheads, out of bone and horn, which similarly turned out to be an improvement on the stone tools they replaced.

The first village communities

Increased tool use and a growing understanding of the natural environment led China to experience its own Neolithic revolution as the Mesolithic era came to an end, paralleling the experience of other world regions. In China, as elsewhere, people who had previously lived as hunter-gatherers started to settle down in permanent communities. The first farming cultures appeared in China from about 6000 BC on. The best-known of these Neolithic cultures was first identified in 1921 by Swedish geologist Johan Andersson working in western Henan province, about 700km (450 miles) southwest of Beijing. Named the Yangshao culture after the village of Yangshaocun where Andersson made the first finds, it was dated to about 5000 to 3000 BC, showing that Chinese civilisation was much older than previously thought. The culture grew up along the valleys of the Huang He (Yellow River) and its tributaries, where extended families set up small village settlements that were independent and self-sufficient.

Migrating farmers

Hunting, fishing and gathering wild plants were still important for the Yangshao villagers, as they had been in the Mesolithic era. However, as the settlers discovered the possibilities inherent in cultivating land and raising livestock, they became farmers. The environment helped: the alluvial loess soil blown onto the lands around the Huang He from the Gobi Desert proved exceptionally fertile. Slash-and-burn techniques were used to clear the land, and then the villagers worked it with hoes, spades and digging sticks. They cultivated two types of millet, which was harvested with stone sickles and stored in underground storage pits.

No matter how good the yields from freshly cleared land, however, after a few years of cultivation the soil became exhausted and no longer produced sufficient crops to feed the community and their livestock. The settlers then had to abandon their village and start all over again. Driving their herds of pigs before them – and sometimes also cattle, sheep or goats – they moved to a new area of land, then settled down to prepare and cultivate it as before.

Yet the villagers did not forget the abandoned settlements, and sometimes their descendants would return many years later to reoccupy the old houses of their family clans. One such village was Banpo on a tributary of the River Wei, which went through four different phases of occupation. In the 5th millennium BC it covered almost 6 hectares (15 acres), a huge area for those times, and was home to some 500 people. A ditch 6m (20ft) wide and about the same deep protected the residents from enemies and wild animals. At the centre of the village stood a large communal building about 160m² (200sq yd), whose purpose is unknown. Surrounding it were about 45 smaller houses, built to round or square floorplans. Made of compacted mud, the dwellings were sunk into the

Mask memorabilia
This pottery mask from the Neolithic Yangshao period was uncovered in what is now Shaanxi province. The decoration is painted in red and black on a red background.

ground, and each had its own hearth. The
roofs were supported by wooden beams.

The burial ground stood outside the
village. Foodstuffs and tools were interred
with the dead, indicating that the villagers
believed in an afterlife. It is possible that
even at this early stage there were already
the beginnings of the ancestor worship
that marks Chinese culture to this day.
Archaeological finds, including figurines
of women and of androgynous beings,
suggest that fertility rites and animal
sacrifice were practised. Shamans –
mediators between the human and spirit
worlds – conducted the ceremonies, and
were also responsible for helping the
deceased on their final journey to join
their ancestors. Blood-red ceramic ware
decorated with skeletons frequently turn
up as grave goods.

Works of clay

The Yangshao culture is especially noted
for its pottery. Its Stone Age craftsmen
hand-fashioned bowls, pots and other
items out of clay coils. Simple items were
decorated with impressed lines or inter-
laced patterns, while more ambitious
works were often adorned with geometric
figures or stylised drawings of fish or birds.

As in other early cultures, the finest works
were often painted with clear cord-like
motifs, applied in red or black paint onto
the reddish brown clay. These patterns are
now considered the most characteristic
form of Yangshao ware.

The Longshan people

A new culture known to scholars today as
the Longshan emerged in northern China
around the middle of the 3rd millennium
BC. Once again the name comes from the
village – this time in Shandong province –
where relics of the culture were first
identified. The Longshan people lived in
permanent settlements and introduced the
potter's wheel, making it possible to create
delicately thin ceramics. Longshan pottery
was made from distinctive dark clay, and
the pots were highly polished to give
them a shiny appearance.

The Longshan era also saw advances in
other fields. Farmers learned new methods
of cultivation, and may even have begun
using manure to obtain better yields; at
any rate their fields remained fertile and
could be cultivated continuously, while
providing harvests that were more than
sufficient for the villagers' own needs. In
addition to millet the Longshan farmers

cultivated wheat, which had advantages over the older crop: its relatively large grains could be stored more easily, and the straw was useful as cattle fodder and as insulation. Knowledge of wheat-growing and seeds for planting appear to have reached China from the Fertile Crescent in the Near East. The Longshan bred cattle, sheep, goats, poultry and presumably horses, as well as dogs and pigs, both of which became increasingly important.

By Longshan times villages were protected by massive walls of compacted mud instead of a simple ditch. House walls were made of the same material, but now the mud was not simply smeared onto a wattle framework, it was applied in layers inside wooden shuttering before being tightly packed down.

Division of labour

The Longshan era was one of increasing specialisation and growing expertise in both agriculture and handicrafts. Knowledge of carpentry developed in response to the demand for permanent dwellings, and craftsmen working with bone developed filigree techniques to produce delicate hairpins and combs. The hand spindle – one of the most important developments in cloth-making – spread widely. Using distaffs and spindle whorls, Longshan weavers were able to spin strong, tear-resistant yarn suitable for making lightweight fabrics that dried out comfortably after becoming wet in the rain, unlike furs and leather.

People had come to accept the principle of the division of labour, and soon afterward the first social hierarchies

EVERYDAY LIFE

Fish and rice

When the Ice Age began to retreat, a warm, humid period set in between about 7500 and 3000 BC in East Asia. This provided ideal conditions for the development of Neolithic cultures. Dense vegetation covered the land, supplying food in abundance. Innumerable rivers, lakes and ponds in the region were well-stocked with various fish and other water creatures. Fishermen equipped with harpoons and sturdy nets went in pursuit of carp and sea fish, sometimes from boats. Natural water plants including lotus, reed mace, water chestnuts, rushes and wild rice supplemented the diet. The warm climate also encouraged the early development of agriculture: archaeologists have found traces of pollen from cultivated rice that are thought to be almost 10,000 years old.

began to develop. The class differentiation of the time shows up clearly in burials. Most graves of the period are small and contain almost no grave goods. In contrast, a smaller number of middle-ranking graves contain painted wooden coffins, ceramic pots, and ornaments of wood and stone. The elite were laid to rest in large burial complexes. Very few of these have been found, but those that have were richly endowed: paintings decorated the walls; bells and musical instruments made of wood and crocodile skin were there to provide entertainment on the journey into the afterlife; numerous ritual cauldrons stood ready for use.

These high-status tombs were not intended for farmers or craftsmen but rather for the shamans. Evidence of the connection is provided by the presence of grave goods made of jade, a stone that was not just highly valued but was thought to be imbued with a mystic force from which the shamans drew power. The more jade a shaman could call his own, the higher his status.

Fertility cults survived into the Longshan period from Yangshao days, but there were also new religious practices. Women lost some of their earlier cult status, while rising affluence boosted the standing of men; male descendants now took precedence in matters of

A face in jade
This early jade carving was probably made by craftsmen of the Liangzhu culture in the Yangtze Delta, a centre of excellence in the difficult art of sculpting this hard mineral.

Dragon bowl
In early China dragons symbolised the force of yang, representing male fertility. The creature on this Longshan bowl, made around 2500–2200 BC, holds a palm frond between its dense rows of sharp teeth.

inheritance. Longshan communities paid reverence to dead benefactors through an ancestor cult and they developed techniques for reading oracles to predict future events.

The power of the shamans

Shamans acted as tribal chiefs, controlling the political and military fortunes of their clans, as well as their religious life. They formed a leadership elite, overseeing neighbouring settlements from central power bases. Some controlled areas extending for several hundred square miles. Throughout the 2nd millennium BC, these small states, known to later Chinese historians as the 'ten thousand kingdoms', were constantly vying for supremacy in northern China.

Meanwhile in the south, another cradle of Chinese civilisation was developing. Here too Mesolithic and Neolithic societies grew up under religious and political conditions similar to those in the north. Rather than millet, however, rice was cultivated in irrigated fields along the course of the Chang Jiang (the River Yangtze) and in its delta, where water buffalo joined the other domesticated animals familiar farther north. Coastal dwellers lived in houses built out over the water on wooden piles.

Jade in art and ceremony

This region was particularly famous for its jade work, winning for China its ancient title of 'the Land of Jade'. The craftsmen of the Liangzhu culture, centred in the Chang Jiang Delta, were masters of the art and they inherited a long tradition. Jade was prized all over China, as the discovery of grave goods attests, but the oldest jade work yet discovered is from the Liangzhu area and dates back to about 5000 BC.

Jade is a fine-grained mineral and some types are harder than steel, so working with it made great demands on the craftsmen's abilities. The techniques they used, involving fairly basic tools and a great deal of patience, have not changed in principle to this day. Jade cannot simply be carved; it must first be sawn into slices which are ground and milled into shape and then polished. Liangzhu craftsmen worked with drill bits made of stone, wood, bone or even bamboo, which were rotated with the aid of a small bow. The finished works were polished with fine quartz sand, which gave them a soft sheen.

For their rituals, the shamans used jade utensils endowed with supposedly magical powers. These took two main forms: the cong, which was square in cross-section with a cylindrical hole in the middle, and the bi, a flat disc with a circular aperture. The cong symbolised earth while the bi represented heaven, and it seems likely that the shamans used chants and invocations to try to bring the earthly and heavenly powers into harmony.

Archaeological sites in the coastal province of Zhejiang have provided a colourful picture of late Stone Age ceremonies in which shamans sought to make contact with the heavenly sphere. They wore elaborate jade headdresses, bis and congs were tied to their hips and ankles, and they held magical jade axes in their hands. There were even jade particles embedded in the axes' wooden handles, which were topped and tailed by jade caps; small congs dangled from the hafts.

China's 'jade belt' stretched from the coastal regions east of Beijing to the province of Guangdong. Here, Stone Age peoples began the nation's long tradition of jade artistry. A ceremonial system grew up around the stone, with a complicated ethical framework. The history of the nation is so bound up with the precious mineral that the transition period between the Stone and Bronze Ages – known in other parts of the world as the Copper Age – is called in China the 'Jade Age'.

The Fertile Crescent

Eleven thousand years ago, people in the Near East were settling down to a farming life, setting in motion a revolution that would change the face of the world.

Fertility goddess
This ample female figure found at Çatal Hüyük probably represents the mother goddess who was believed to ensure the fertility not just of women but also of fields and animals. She is depicted here in childbirth, seated on a throne and flanked by two leopards.

A band of hunters travelling across the east Anatolian plateau in about 7000 BC might have stumbled on an unfamiliar sight. On a plain backed by mountains in what is now south-central Turkey, they would have seen a settlement of several hundred closely-packed rectangular buildings, unprotected by any surrounding wall, on the summit of a riverside mound. The walls of the buildings, each of which contained several rooms, were made of packed mud or air-dried mud bricks. The settlement dwellers used a white clay to render their houses inside and out; this coating was regularly renewed, possibly every year – some buildings had up to 120 separate layers. The dwellings were packed closely together and constructed without front doors; access was down a ladder from the flat roof above. This opening was the only way into the house, and it doubled up as a vent to take away smoke from the hearth and the baking oven.

Today this settlement is known as Çatal Hüyük, meaning 'forked hill'. Dating back to the latter years of the Palaeolithic, or Old Stone Age, Çatal Hüyük was one of the world's first towns, sheltering several thousand

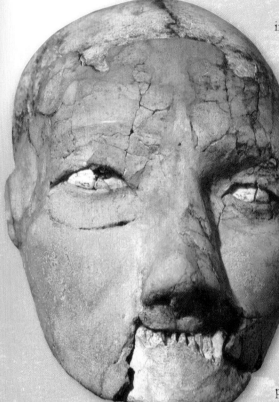

Masking the dead
This skull from Jericho was covered in plaster and modelled to create a lifelike appearance. Shells take the place of the eyes. These eerie mementoes were apparently portraits of the dead, kept for public display.

inhabitants. The cave-like structure of its houses has led some archaeologists to conjecture that the builders of the town may at some earlier time have been cave-dwellers.

The city of Jericho in Palestine would have presented a similar sight to travellers. Unlike Çatal Hüyük, however, Jericho was surrounded, from about 7500 BC on, by a 6m (20ft) high wall made of rubble. A stone tower stood guard over the enclosure; when the tower was unearthed in the mid-1950s, it still stood 8m (26ft) tall. Such sturdy defences imply that Jericho's citizens lived in fear of attack and therefore needed to protect themselves from enemies.

A land of plenty

Both Çatal Hüyük and Jericho lie on the edge of the Fertile Crescent, a well-watered region that runs in an arc across the parts of the Near East that are suitable for agriculture and stock-breeding. The Crescent stretches from Palestine on the Mediterranean coast up to Syria and eastern Turkey, then down the valleys of the Tigris and Euphrates rivers through modern-day Iraq.

Many environmental factors came together to make the Fertile Crescent particularly favourable for human settlement. Climate changes in the Near East following the end of the last Ice Age made an important contribution. Warmer weather led to increased rainfall, feeding rich vegetation that, in turn, supported abundant animal life. Large areas of the Near East that are now arid were then covered in forests and watered by rivers. Wild varieties of wheat and barley flourished there, alongside pulses such as peas and lentils. This abundant plant life supported wild sheep, goats, cattle and pigs, all of which were suitable for

domestication. In addition, there were gazelles and red and black deer for hunting. The Anatolian plateau near the top of the Crescent's arc sheltered another treasure: plentiful deposits of obsidian, a glass-like volcanic mineral that was particularly well-suited to being fashioned into cutting tools.

The agricultural revolution

Although the environmental conditions were clearly favourable, the precise circumstances that led to the creation of permanent settlements in the region are still not clear. The changeover from hunter-gathering to farming and stock-breeding did not happen suddenly, but took place over two or three thousand years. The pioneers of the move were most likely hunter-gatherer communities indigenous to Palestine and Syria, and during the early stages of the transition period they probably still lived mainly from hunting, while supplementing their catch by harvesting and processing wild species of grain. They built simple, round huts out of wood and stone, which they used as permanent habitations for at least part of the year. They also erected stone enclosures, presumably to pen wild goats and sheep – a first step towards the domestication of animals.

When the people of the Fertile Crescent started to settle down, their way of life changed irrevocably, and this revolution marked the start of the Neolithic period, or New Stone Age. This period is characterised archaeologically by signs of permanent settlements and the early beginnings of agriculture. By 7500 BC the transformation had spread across much of the Near East, and a network of villages dependent on agriculture and stock-breeding for their food supply covered the region. Soon after, the villagers added domesticated pigs and cattle to their sheep and goats. Hunting became steadily less important as the new food sources became more productive and reliable.

The early farmers tilled their plots with bent sticks that served as hoes, but ploughs came into use soon after cattle were domesticated, so providing the draught animals needed to pull them. Settlers also learned to conserve water resources. The first irrigation ditches were dug to the north of present-day Baghdad during the 6th millennium BC, reducing the people's reliance on the weather and opening up terrain that had hitherto been unsuitable because of insufficient rain.

Learning new skills

As agriculture and irrigation spread across the region, food production increased and with it the population that the land could support. Villages that had been home to just a few families grew into small towns with thousands of inhabitants.

Life in these spreading communities continued to revolve principally around agriculture and stock-breeding. A system evolved for preserving food surpluses. The inhabitants of Çatal Hüyük, for example, used large baskets or tanned hides to store their grain in central storage buildings. They also developed skills attuned to the changing lifestyle. They spun wool from their sheep into thread, then dyed the thread and wove it into fabrics that made warm clothing and durable blankets.

People continued to make their tools and everyday objects out of stone, wood, and bone as their ancestors had done, but they brought a new degree of technological expertise to the old, familiar tasks. They used flint, which could be sharpened to produce a fine cutting edge, to make knives, daggers, spear points, boring tools and arrowheads. They carved bowls out of wood, and used

basic joinery skills to make small boxes. Bone was sharpened to produce sewing needles and awls.

Çatal Hüyük's residents were also fond of making jewellery and other personal adornments. They fashioned imaginative, artistically worked chains, pendants and rings from various types of stone, as well as from ivory, bone and shells, and they could admire the results of their handiwork in obsidian mirrors.

A mysterious holy place

Conventional wisdom holds that the agricultural surpluses built up through the spread of farming were fundamental to the growth of cities. Stored reserves of grain meant that people could be spared from working in the fields for part of the year. Instead they could be employed on large-scale building projects, such as digging irrigation ditches or constructing temples, that were fundamental to the development of large urban communities.

A mud brick from Jericho
The bricks that built ancient Jericho, like this one, were created by mixing wet mud with chopped straw. This raw material was shaped in wooden brick moulds, then the bricks were laid in the sun to dry. The indentations helped to bond the bricks to the mortar.

A Stone Age town
Çatal Hüyük in southern Turkey, one of the world's very first towns, was sited on this mound rising almost 20m (60ft) above the surrounding plain. The overall area measures about 450 x 300m (1500 x 1000ft).

Hunting deer
This detail from a wall painting in Çatal Hüyük dates back 8000 years. It shows tiny human figures working together to bring down a huge stag.

building project might have been just the incentive needed to persuade hunter-gatherers to make the shift from simply harvesting wild grains to deliberately culti-vating them, thereby ensuring a constant source of food. If this was indeed the case, then the agricultural revolution might have started as a by-product of the human urge to unite and build.

The invention of pottery

Once people had secured the basic necessities of life, new perspectives and possibilities opened up before them. Their view of the world began to change, providing an impetus for new inventions. The use of mud and clay as building materials led to a breakthrough discovery of the New Stone Age: the invention of pottery. Clay vessels first appeared in the Near East sometime around 7000 BC. They were initially made simply by fashioning lumps or coils of clay into the desired shape and leaving the finished product to dry in the sun. By the 4th millennium BC, however, potter's wheels had come into use, and pots were being fired in purpose-built kilns to produce much stronger finished items. Early ceramics were decorated with scratched-line drawings or else were painted with pigments such as ochre or malachite, creating new possibilities for artistic expression.

The profound significance of this invention can be seen in the influence that it had on mythology. Several Near Eastern creation myths ascribe the origins of humankind to a divine potter, who created the first humans out of a lump of clay and then breathed life into them.

Mysterious wall paintings

The same artistic urge that led people to decorate pottery also found expression in

Recently, however, an extraordinary archaeological find in southeastern Turkey has challenged this view, raising the possibility that temple-building itself might have provided the first impetus towards large permanent settlements. On top of a rocky plateau called Gobekli Tepe, excavators have unearthed a stone sanctuary with columns up to 3m (10ft) high, decorated with animal reliefs of serpents, lions, bulls, foxes and cranes. The sanctuary complex measures 100m (325ft) across and was surrounded by a circular wall.

The crucial feature about this shrine is its date: it was constructed as early as 8500 BC, which predates the arrival of settled agriculture in the region. Yet it could not have been built without considerable communal effort. Given that only stone tools were available, archaeologists estimate it must have taken at least 500 workers months of labour to cut and shape the heavy stone blocks, each weighing between 10 and 20 tonnes, then transport them to the building site nearby. The workers would have needed a substantial supply of food – a considerable challenge for a hunter-gatherer community. Some scholars have suggested that such a painting. A number of colourful and varied wall paintings can be seen in Çatal Hüyük: hunting tableaux, geometric designs that possibly imitate textile patterns, even a schematic diagram of a town that may be Çatal Hüyük itself. There are also mysterious scenes that may have mythical significance: a view of vultures circling above headless bodies, for example, appears to show a burial ritual. Vulture skulls, along with those of foxes and weasels, were sometimes embedded in wall reliefs. Researchers assume that buildings decorated in this fashion were sanctuaries or shrines.

Çatal Hüyük's artists also expressed themselves through sculpture. Many small, usually female figures have been found made in a variety of materials: limestone, pumice, alabaster and fired clay. With their characteristic heavy breasts, broad hips and large thighs, the statuettes are thought to have been connected to the cult of a fertility goddess. Çatal Hüyük was far from unique in displaying such creativity. People all over the Middle East were producing human and animal sculptures at this time. Almost lifesize human figures, thought to represent gods or ancestors, have been found in Jordan.

However, there is little hard evidence to indicate the social structure of these early towns. It remains unclear whether they supported a priestly class or any similar elite. In some parts of the world, such as Europe's Atlantic seaboard, there are signs of large-scale building activities coinciding with the arrival of agriculture; this was the age of the menhir, the barrow and the stone circle. In the Fertile Crescent, however, major construction projects such as ziggurats are associated with the next phase of development – the growth of the temple cities of Sumer and Akkad.

Even so, baked clay seals found in Çatal Hüyük suggest that personal possessions may have begun to play a role, pointing to a degree of social differentiation. Seals decorated with geometric patterns were pressed into damp clay to mark vessels and other containers as a way of designating ownership. The trend was no doubt encouraged by the fact that Çatal Hüyük was a major trading centre, exporting obsidian extracted from the volcano of Hasan Dag 135km (80 miles) to the east. Obsidian was much in demand for making mirrors, knives and jewellery, and it was traded over great distances throughout the Neolithic period.

Mastering metal

From about 6500 BC on, a new material that would have enormous significance for future humankind made its first appearance at Çatal Hüyük. This was copper. Use of this versatile metal spread so rapidly across the Near East over the next thousand years that some prehistorians speak of this period as the Chalcolithic, the 'copper-and-stone' period. In fact, stone very quickly lost the central role that it had occupied for so many hundreds of thousands of years in the manufacture of tools and utensils. The mastery of metal had far-reaching consequences both socially and culturally. When the New Stone Age finally came to an end in about 4500 BC, the foundations were already in place for the creation of the first advanced civilisations.

Earthenware storage
Nomadic hunter-gatherers had little use for containers that could break, but for settled farmers pottery was ideal for storing food and drink in their granaries and homes.

PAST VOICES

Interior decor – New Stone Age style

The inhabitants of Çatal Hüyük liked to decorate the walls of their houses with elaborate murals. Their artists worked mainly in ochre, but also had access to red, brown, blue, green and yellow pigments, derived from a variety of different minerals.

They painted the walls of their living quarters mostly with simple geometric patterns, but the town's many shrines and cult buildings were adorned with far more elaborate decorations. There are vibrant hunting scenes, with people shown touching and moving among the prey animals. And plaster models of bulls' heads with enormous horns were hung on the painted walls, perhaps the popular symbols of a fertility cult.

Sumer and Akkad – the first city civilisations

The first cities, the birth of writing, the earliest legal codes and the invention of the wheel are just some of the ways in which the early civilisations of Mesopotamia made their mark.

As the 3rd millennium BC was drawing to a close, Persian Gulf traders who sailed their ships a hundred miles up the River Euphrates were met by an impressive sight. On the fringe of the delta marshes, the walls of the city of Ur rose up before them. Sophisticated harbour facilities and palaces lined the shore but were overshadowed by the three-tiered ziggurat, a stepped temple, towering high above their heads and visible from afar.

The temple complex surrounding the ziggurat was the city's heart. In its precincts were the city's principal place of worship, dedicated to the moon god Nanna, and a second temple (known as Giparu) where Nanna's wife Ningal was venerated, alongside dwellings for the priests and priestesses. Here, too, stood the king's palace and the treasury.

The city's residential districts spread out from this ceremonial centre, densely packed around wide boulevards and narrow alleys. The citizens lived in a confusion of flat-roofed houses, many of which had an inner courtyard and an upper floor. The streets were a hive of industry, loud with the din of craftsmen's workshops and taverns where local people and foreigners mingled. In the city's two walled harbours, ships from Magan (modern Oman) and Meluhha (in the Indus Valley) unloaded cargoes of exotic goods.

The city of Ur owed its prosperity to King Ur-Nammu, founder of the 3rd Dynasty of Ur (reigned 2111–2094 BC), and his successors who ruled until 2003 BC. After a period of unrest, Ur's rulers had succeeded in unifying the city-states of Mesopotamia under their rule, making Ur the capital of a large empire.

Seedbed of civilisation

Sumerian civilisation itself was already old by the time that Ur-Nammu rose to power. The first signs of an independent culture had begun to appear in southern Mesopotamia as early as about 3500 BC. We still do not know precisely when Sumer was first populated, or where the Sumerian people's original homeland might have been, although speculation places it to the east or northeast, in modern Iran. What is known is that the new arrivals encountered an existing population that put up little resistance and was quickly overwhelmed.

The Sumerians lived by arable and livestock farming. Their most important crops were several types of grain – notably barley and wheat – although pulses such as peas were also grown. They also grew vegetables, date palms and fruit trees, and raised animals, including cattle, sheep, goats and pigs for food and donkeys as beasts of burden.

The rivers and extensive marshlands of the delta provided fish, but because of the lack of reliable rainfall, the construction

This magnificent gold bull's head decorates a harp that was found in one of the royal tombs of Ur. The bull symbolised power and fertility.

and constant maintenance of irrigation ditches was essential. Through these, water from the Euphrates, Tigris and their tributaries was channelled to the fields.

By 3000 BC a number of settlements had sprung up that soon became powerful city-states, each ruling over the lands that surrounded it. Among the most important were Ur, Umma, Kish, Nippur, Eridu,

The magnificence with which Sumer's early rulers surrounded themselves is best seen in the richly appointed graves of the Royal Cemetery of Ur, dating from about 2600 BC. The splendid artefacts unearthed from its tombs reveal the skill of Sumerian craftsmen in fashioning metals, wood and stone. They included musical instruments inlaid with shell, jewellery made of gold and precious stones, golden vessels and weapons, as well as the famous engraved golden helmet of King Meskulamdug, hammered and chased to fit the contours of the royal head. A sinister aspect of the burials was the practice of human sacrifice: the entire royal guard and entourage were forced to follow their master into the afterlife by drinking poison.

City-state rivalry

From the world's oldest surviving historical records, as well as from monumental inscriptions and other artefacts, it can be seen that the city-states were already vying for power as early as about 2500 BC. Kish was one of the first to rise to prominence, and it retained its special prestige even in later times when real power had transferred to other cities.

The enemy's fate
A detail from the Stele of the Vultures shows Ningirsu, patron god of the city-state of Lagash, dressed in royal garb and holding captured prisoners of war in a net. The net is closed by a lion-headed eagle, a symbol of death.

Lagash, and Uruk. Each was ruled by an *en* or *ensi* ('lord' or 'city prince'), probably supported – at least in the early period – by some form of council of elders.

However, unlike Egypt's pharaohs, the *en* was not regarded as a god, although he held the supreme priestly as well as secular office. This enhanced his exalted status even further and associated it with the divine sphere. An *en* whose power encompassed several city-states bore the title of *lugal* (literally 'great man'), a synonym for 'king'.

An early monument, the Vulture Stele, prepared for King Eannatum of Lagash in about 2470 BC, vividly illustrates the art of war at the time, and provides uncomfortable evidence of the harsh treatment meted out to defeated enemies. The king is shown in his war-chariot, leading his warriors into battle against the troops of the city of Umma. The Lagash soldiers are armed with lances; for protection they have copper helmets, metal-studded jerkins and rectangular shields.

The reverse of the stele shows vultures devouring the enemy dead – the scene that gives the stone its name. Yet Lagash's triumph was short-lived. Around 2450 BC, King Lugalzagesi of Umma finally gained undisputed control over his neighbour and rival Uruk, and then went on to establish a kingdom that embraced the whole of Sumer.

The layout of Sumerian cities

Despite their political rivalries, the Sumerian cities closely resembled one another. The main public buildings – the temple of the city's patron god and the king's palace – had a central position. The temple precinct was generally separated from the surrounding residential areas by a wall, divided into sections by projecting battlements. A similar, larger wall surrounded the entire city; on occasions (as in the case of Uruk), this was also equipped with projecting bastions. According to tradition, the building of the walls of Uruk was the work of Gilgamesh, a semi-legendary king, who through their construction united the formerly separate districts of Kulaba and Eanna into a single, large, urban area.

The principal building materials in ancient Mesopotamia were air-dried mud bricks, which were simple and cheap to produce. Fired bricks were available, but because of the large amount of expensive fuel it took to make them, these were only used for cladding important buildings such as palaces and temples. The most significant temple was that of the city's own patron god, which was raised on a terrace made of mud bricks above the surrounding buildings.

By the time of the 3rd dynasty of Ur, this high terrace, which was reached by an open flight of steps, was raised even further by the addition of a number of step-like platforms, on the uppermost of which the shrine itself was located. In this way the ziggurat, Mesopotamia's most distinctive architectural form, came into being.

Several million bricks were needed to construct a ziggurat. Layers of rush matting were laid at intervals among the courses to level the structure and ensure its stability. For additional strengthening, bitumen was used as a binding agent, and at regular intervals thick hawsers woven from rushes were pulled diagonally through the terrace and anchored to the external walls.

Single-storey temples were also constructed alongside the towering ziggurats, and they too had their own set pattern of construction. From the ziggurats' highest points priests watched the night sky and made astronomical observations that helped them to draw up calendars fixing the seasonal round.

Gods for all walks of life

In the temples, priests and priestesses paid homage to hundreds of different deities. After the king himself, the chief officiant was an individual known as the *en*-priest, who headed a hierarchy of lesser officials whose job it was to perform the daily

---

EVERYDAY LIFE

Potter's wheel or cart wheel – which came first?

One of the most important Sumerian inventions was the potter's wheel. Early models were in use from about 3500 BC. Before that, potters had fashioned their pots and containers by shaping lumps of clay with their hands. The new devices speeded up the task and also encouraged the division of labour.

It remains unclear if the potter's wheel provided the inspiration for the development of wheels on vehicles. These may have evolved out of the rollers placed under the sled-like carriages that were used in Sumerian religious processions. Some of these sleds had semicircular recesses cut into the runners, presumably designed to take the end of a log or other cylindrical object; the niches would have done away with the need to repeatedly replace the rollers under the sled as it moved forward. A revolving axle of this type may well have been a prototype of the wheel.

The first carts were relatively crude two or four-wheeled vehicles with solid wooden wheels whose rims were studded with copper nails. The earliest known examples, vividly depicted on the famous Standard of Ur, were used as war chariots. Donkeys or onagers (crosses between wild asses and domesticated beasts) were used as draft animals. Horses only became widespread in Mesopotamia shortly before 2000 BC.

The Sumerians were long credited with the invention of the wheel, but in recent years, fresh archaeological evidence from the Caucasus and Europe has led some scholars to question this view. Wheeled vehicles, it now seems, were in use elsewhere from early times, suggesting either that the new technology spread from Mesopotamia more rapidly than previously thought, or that the wheel was invented almost simultaneously in several different places.

A game for eternity
This boardgame was found in a king's tomb in the royal cemetery of Ur, no doubt intended to help the ruler while away his long hours of leisure in the afterlife.

rites and sacrifices. The climax of the ceremonial year came in the New Year celebration, when the king was carried to the temple in solemn procession, to be met by a high-ranking priestess playing the part of the goddess Inanna. A text from the time of King Schulgi describes their encounter: 'The crown and the magnificence of his garb radiated from the king's head, and Inanna was entranced…' The couple then performed ritual sexual intercourse in the temple, acting out a so-called 'sacred marriage' that was intended to guarantee the fertility of the land. The model for this rite was an ancient myth of death and resurrection in which Inanna's deceased husband Dumuzi returned to Earth from the underworld for a six-month period each spring.

As goddess of love and desire, Inanna was one of the most prominent deities in the Sumerian pantheon. She was linked with the planet Venus, the evening star, yet at the same time had a martial aspect, obvious in her symbolic animal, the lion. A hymn in her honour proclaims: 'My father gave me the heavens… He gave me war… He gave me battle.' Other significant Sumerian gods were Enlil, god of the air, Enki, the water god, Utut the sun god, Nanna the moon god, and An, the lord of heaven.

Farmers, craftsmen and scribes

In early Sumerian times almost all the cultivated land belonged to the city temple and was administered by the king, the gods' representative on Earth. He was responsible for the tilling of the fields and for the welfare of the livestock, as well as for ensuring that maintenance work was carried out on the irrigation ditches. The farmers and herders who actually worked the land either delivered their entire harvest to the temple or, as tenants, handed over a large part of it; in return they were furnished with everything they needed from the temple storehouses.

In the cities, skilled artisans and craftsmen also worked mainly for the king and the temple; among their ranks were artists, bronze founders, leather workers, carpenters and stonemasons. Other activities such as spinning, sewing, weaving, basket-making and pottery were mostly carried out at home, predominantly by the women; some households no doubt specialised in a particular skill, exchanging goods with their neighbours. The lowest social class was made up of slaves, mostly prisoners of war. Since many of them came from the mountainous regions to the east, the pictogram for 'slave' consisted of the symbol for 'man' or 'woman' combined with that for 'mountain'.

The elaborate bureaucracy needed to run the temples could not have functioned without a system of writing and an educated class of scribes. These officials recorded harvest yields and herd sizes and kept account of the deliveries made to the temple warehouses, as well as of the rations handed out to the people and to important state officers.

Another Sumerian invention was the cylinder-seal – a small stone marker embossed with a distinctive image, usually of gods or mythical scenes. The seals were rolled on the damp clay of jar stoppers to provide proof of possession. Cylinder-seal markings were also imprinted on clay tablets bearing cuneiform messages as proof of the identity of the sender.

The birth of Akkad

Shortly after 3000 BC a new ethnic group entered the Sumerian melting-pot. Semitic settlers moved into Mesopotamia from the Syrian desert to the east. The newcomers became known as Akkadians,

a name taken from the capital city they eventually founded. There appears to have been no major clash between the Sumerians and the Semites; rather, the two peoples intermingled, so that by 2600 BC some rulers of Sumerian cities already had Semitic names.

Eventually an Akkadian came to power in his own right as ruler of the city of Kish. His origins are shrouded in mystery; legend tells that, like the Biblical Moses, he was abandoned as a baby in a rush basket in a river, and was found and raised by a farmer. After seizing power he took the name of Sargon – in the Akkadian tongue *Scharrukin*, or 'the true King' – and reigned from 2340 to 2284 BC.

Gradually, by sheer force, Sargon subjugated all the other Sumerian city-states. In time he even overcame his arch-rival Lugalzagesi, the king of Umma and supreme overlord of all Sumer. Sargon defeated Lugalzagesi's forces in a number of battles and the king himself eventually fell into Sargon's hands. The humiliated ruler came to an ignominious end, cruelly paraded in front of the Temple of Enlil at Nippur with his hands and neck shackled in a wooden harness.

The world's first empire

Key to Sargon's victories were the Akkadian warriors, who were skilled in the use of bows and arrows. Sargon deployed them against the unwieldy

The ziggurat of Ur
The restored temple of the god Nanna is the best-preserved of the Sumerian ziggurats. The monument was rebuilt at least seven times in its history. It originally stood 25m (80ft) high.

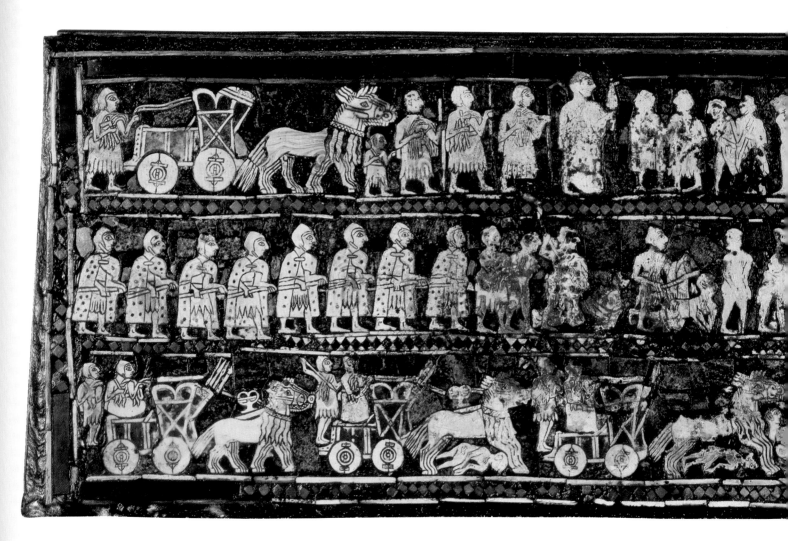

The Standard of Ur
This small wooden panel, inlaid with nacre and lapis lazuli, shows a king of Ur inspecting naked and bound prisoners of war. A panoply of infantrymen and chariots line up below.

Sumerian formations to deadly effect. In a relatively short time he extended his grip over the whole of Mesopotamia, founding the world's first empire. The Akkadian realm included the upper reaches of the Tigris, in what is now eastern Turkey, and stretched from the Zagros mountains of Persia as far west as the Syrian coast. From there, according to some accounts, Sargon may even have crossed to Cyprus; however, this seems improbable and is most probably a later embellishment.

In the course of his campaigns Sargon conquered many cities, forcing their rulers to pay him tribute. He used these funds to extend and beautify the capital he founded at Akkad in central Mesopotamia. On his death he bequeathed the city and the empire to his successors, but the dynasty proved to be relatively short-lived, holding power for little more than a

century after Sargon's demise. The best-remembered of his successors was his grandson Naramsin (reigned 2259–2223 BC), who had himself deified while still alive, assuming the title 'Ruler of the Four Corners of the Earth'. On a victory stele, later carried off to Susa in southern Persia, Naramsin is shown wearing a horned helmet, headgear hitherto reserved for the gods. At his feet lie dead and dying enemies, mortally wounded by his arrows. Behind him stand his victorious warriors.

External threats

After Naramsin's death, the Akkadian empire soon fell into decline, shaken by internal insurrections and palace revolts. Semitic nomads – the Amurru or Amorites – encroached on its borders from the west. In its weakened state, it fell prey to the Gutians, a mountain people

The 3rd dynasty of Ur

Utuhengal (2116–2110 BC), the ruler of Uruk, then emerged as Sumer's new champion, finally expelling the Gutian mountain-dwellers from the Mesopotamian flatlands. He installed his brother Ur-Nammu as governor of Ur, and in time this ruler (2111–2094 BC) took on the mantle of sovereignty, building up a new empire that eventually extended over all Mesopotamia. Under this 3rd dynasty of Ur, the region experienced what historians have called the 'Sumerian Renaissance' – a final flowering of its indigenous art and culture.

The renaissance was short-lived, as the Sumerian language was increasingly supplanted by Akkadian, a Semitic tongue implanted across Mesopotamia in the wake of Sargon's victories. From about 2000 BC onwards, Sumerian became a largely ceremonial language, rather like Latin in medieval Europe, preserved in religious ritual but rarely used in everyday life.

Even so, much survived from the world's first urban civilisation. Stories of Gilgamesh and the Great Flood, and of the goddess Inanna and her dying lover Dumuzi, were passed down to succeeding cultures. The Akkadians and their Semitic successors, such as the Amorites, identified their own gods with those of the Sumerian pantheon, many of whom continued to be worshipped, but with new Akkadian names. Inanna became Ishtar, for instance, while the Sumerian sun god Utu was venerated in later times as Shamash. The Sumerians had shaped the first great age of Mesopotamian civilisation, but its last two millennia were to be the era of the Semitic peoples.

A respected ruler
Made of diorite, this seated statue represents Gudea, one of the last rulers of Lagash. The inscription on his robe praises him as the builder of a temple to Ningirsu, the city's patron deity.

from the Persian uplands. Akkad was not only plundered but razed to the ground. The destruction was so extensive the site was never resettled (which was the common practice) and in time came to be forgotten; its exact location is still not known to this day.

After Akkad's collapse, Lagash came to the fore among the Sumerian city-states. It is best remembered not so much for its warrior kings as for a peacefully inclined ruler, Gudea (2143–2124 BC). Surviving statues depict him as a great builder; one shows him cradling the plans of a newly constructed temple in his lap. In his inscriptions, Gudea boasted of his construction work and of an extensive network of trade contacts: 'Magan, Meluhha, Gubin and Dilmun all brought their tribute; their ships brought building timber to Lagash.'

Flourishing cities of the Indus Valley

An Indus king or priest?
This soapstone bust of a man wearing a patterned toga and headband comes from the ruins of Mohenjo-Daro in Pakistan. The carefully tended beard and general air of authority have led historians to assume he was a high dignitary in the civil or religious spheres.

In the 3rd millennium BC, the Indus Valley in what is now Pakistan had cities with advanced plumbing and a thriving economy. After 600 years, the civilisation that built them disappeared almost without trace.

In 1865, British engineers building a railway from Lahore to Multan in what is now northern Pakistan needed ballast to line the track. They found a convenient source in a large mound that had been first noted by English explorers four decades earlier. The mound had in fact been investigated by Sir Alexander Cunningham for the Archaeological Survey of India in 1856. He noted that it contained the ruins of a substantial town, which he named Harappa after a nearby village, but as his interest was chiefly in Buddhist relics, he passed on, leaving the mudbrick ruins to be mined by the railway builders.

A formal survey of the site was begun in 1914, but was interrupted by World War I. By that time that systematic excavation got under way at Harappa, in 1921, an Indian archaeologist called R.D. Banerji had started work at another site – Mohenjo-Daro, some 600km (375 miles) to the southeast on the lower course of the River Indus. Like Cunningham, Banerji expected to find Buddhist remains; what he turned up bore a startling resemblance to the discoveries being made concurrently at Harappa.

In the course of the 1920s, the penny finally dropped. Both Harappa and

Mohenjo-Daro had been great cities, founded at a time of previously unimagined antiquity. A seal found at Harappa proved identical to one unearthed in a Mesopotamian temple dated to 2300 BC. The truth gradually dawned that, around 2500 BC, one of the world's earliest civilisations was thriving in the Indus Valley region. It subsequently took its place, alongside Mesopotamia and ancient Egypt, in the roll call of the world's first urban cultures.

Elephant seal
Indus Valley traders made much use of baked-clay seals like this one, often decorated with pictures of animals. The meaning of the characters inscribed on them is still unknown.

City planning

Mohenjo-Daro and Harappa were strikingly similar in their layouts. Each had a palace that stood in a fortified area known as the citadel, which was raised on an artificial mound of rubble high above the residential part of town. Here, the secular and spiritual head of the city, perhaps a priest-king, had his residence. Anyone looking out across the city from the palace would have noticed its grid layout, as regular as a chessboard. The main roads ran strictly north–south and east–west.

A special feature of Mohenjo-Daro was the Great Bath, situated at the centre of the citadel. Fed and drained by a mains water supply and surrounded by a hall of columns, it almost certainly served some religious purpose. Almost as impressive was the main warehouse area. It is still possible to admire the 27 separate silos, built in three rows on an east–west axis, with foundations standing almost 5m (16ft) high and a raised brick floor to provide ventilation for the stored grain. Much of the harvest of the surrounding fields and villages must have ended up here to fill containers of such a size.

Like Mohenjo-Daro, Harappa did not simply grow but was laid out to a plan. It too had a citadel and a lower town with its own separate fortifications. Here too the citadel housed the civic buildings: assembly halls, administrative offices, places of worship. Harappa's granaries stood beside the citadel and the grain-store workers lived nearby, in small but comfortable terraced houses connected, barracks-like, to their place of work.

Home comforts for the wealthy

Both cities had a wealthy upper class of merchants and their families. These were the people – together with the leading landowners – who organised and took

The city of Mohenjo-Daro
Up to 35,000 people lived in Mohenjo-Daro, in brick-built houses which were often two storeys high. They were overshadowed by the raised citadel, the town's administrative centre.

part in the religious festivals and parades that enlivened urban life, taking advantage of the opportunities they provided to display their wealth and power.

The cities' religious leaders also played a part, dressed in multi-coloured robes and bedecked with precious jewellery. Women spectators must have cast envious glances at their splendid outfits, for they too liked to adorn themselves with bracelets, necklaces, neck rings and beautifully crafted belts. Such items often featured a delicately worked fig-leaf motif; the people of Harappa venerated the fig tree as a symbol of fertility, and images of its leaves abounded.

Also popular with Indus Valley citizens were tiny female figurines, often only 10cm (4in) tall, made of clay and decorated with delicately-shaped chains and other jewellery. Or, to decorate a living room, they might acquire an elegant statuette of a dancing-girl, cast in bronze.

Exotic dancer
This elegant dancing girl, naked except for a necklace and an array of armlets, stands about 11cm (4½in) high. The figurine is one of the few bronzes found at Mohenjo-Daro.

Such miniature works of art gave citizens a chance to show off their wealth, although ostentatious displays of riches were avoided.

Well-to-do citizens lived in the comfort of multi-storey houses built of fired mud bricks. These buildings were square or rectangular and were constructed around an enclosed inner courtyard. Many had their own water supply, and were equipped with bathrooms and brick-built toilets that connected up to an extensive mains drainage system. Less affluent residents drew their water from wells distributed across the city.

Prosperous merchants lived close to the warehouses where their goods were stored. Nearby too were the studios of the craftsmen who produced the objects that were traded. Cotton fabrics, bronze tools and brownish-red carnelian beads were all popular items exported as far as distant Mesopotamia. There was also considerable demand abroad for luxury items made from silver, turquoise and lapis lazuli. In the warehouses, Indian ivory was stored beside high-quality hardwoods brought down from the hills and locally grown rice and aromatic spices. The traders used scales and sets of stone weights that were meticulously checked to ensure accurate measures. Ships from Indus Valley ports regularly plied the shores of the Arabian Sea and Persian Gulf, and comfortably-off citizens must have waited impatiently for their return, eager to see what exciting new goods had been brought back from a successful journey.

The life-giving river

At the heart of the Harappan Culture was the River Indus, the vital artery that provided the conditions for the rise of an advanced culture. Its abundant fish supplied a crucial source of protein for people living along its banks, while the regular spring flood, fed by meltwater from the Himalayas, spread out each year over the fields, bringing minerals that acted as natural fertilisers. By the mid 3rd millennium BC, local residents were already building artificial irrigation channels and raising levees for protection against the high water.

At the same time, the Indus and its tributaries provided natural highways for communication and trade. Boatmen in reed vessels carried goods back and forth throughout its catchment area, from the delta right up into the Himalayan foothills. Enterprising traders from the Indus Valley cities also travelled farther afield, venturing up the Persian Gulf. Texts from Akkad in Mesopotamia name ports in Bahrain and Oman together with a certain Meluhha as trading partners; Meluhha is thought to have been the twin cities of Sutkagen-Dor and Sotka-Koh, now inland but at the time prosperous Arabian Sea anchorages on the western borders of the Indus Valley culture area.

Far-flung outposts

The influence of Harappan Culture spread well beyond the Indus Valley itself. It stretched across a vast region from the foothills of the Himalayas to the Arabian Sea and from the eastern borders of Iran to the headwaters of the Ganges near modern New Delhi, covering a total area of about 1.3 million km² (500,000 square miles). In the north, its influence reached into Afghanistan, a source of gold and lapis lazuli. In the south, the port of Lothal was an important trading centre at the head of the Gulf of Cambay, just 300km (200 miles) north of modern Bombay.

Although Mohenjo-Daro and Harappa were almost certainly the main urban centres, archaeologists have investigated over 150 other sites in the region of which at least half a dozen deserve the title of city. Kalibangan was an important centre about 500km (300 miles) east of Mohenjo-Daro. Closer to hand were Kot Diji and Amri, which lay on the Indus only 150km (100 miles) downstream. Mohenjo-Daro's influence is particularly evident in ceramics recovered from this site. Initially, Amri's potters painted their wares with geometric motifs, but over the centuries the style gradually changed until they were producing exclusively red and black ware of a style closely associated with the metropolis. At the same time, Amri's population diminished; one residential mound was completely abandoned, perhaps because its citizens deserted it for the greater attractions of the city's bigger neighbour.

■ The Indus Valley culture
● Indus Valley cities

EVERYDAY LIFE

A love of small things – terracotta toys

The archaeological record of the Indus Valley shows that its inhabitants loved small objects. Instead of monumental statues, they left behind diminutive figurines or groups of figures, together with tiny beads and seals the size of postage stamps.

The figurines, which are rarely larger than the palm of one's hand, were carefully modelled out of clay and then painted. Female figures wear short skirts with wide belts that emphasise their shape. Their hair is artistically coiffured – curled, braided, or put up in a fan shape – and decorated with flowers, clasps or bands. In the past, the statuettes were taken for mother-goddess figures, particularly as some are breast-feeding babies. Yet most were found in places that suggest their owners simply threw them away. As a result, they are now generally thought to have been girls' toys – the dolls of their time. Miniature teams of water-buffaloes and carts that have been found may have been toys for the boys.

Two-wheeled cart
A terracota female figure rides in a cart drawn by a pair of water buffaloes.

Elsewhere, too, there is evidence that the smaller settlements diminished as larger cities became more powerful. Their expansion may have involved social upheaval or even local wars. The inhabitants of Kot Diji, which lay about 50km (30 miles) from Mohenjo-Daro, certainly felt the need to protect their town with a substantial fortified wall. Kot Diji was eventually destroyed by a catastrophic fire of unexplained origin. Survivors may well have migrated to the ever-expanding Mohenjo-Daro.

The fate of Kalibangan

Kalibangan – which was founded as early as 2900 BC and was already well established long before the expansion of Harappa – suffered a similar fate. The city was built in the form of a parallelogram aligned to the north and protected by an outer wall. The houses were made of mud bricks that had been dried in the sun or fired in kilns. In about 2650 BC, however, some sort of catastrophe struck the city, which was abruptly abandoned for unknown reasons. For half a century or more it seems to have been left completely deserted. It was perhaps no coincidence that Harappa, situated 250km (150 miles) to the north, first rose to prominence at about the time of Kalibangan's collapse. Harappa had an efficient administrative apparatus far in advance of that of any of the other cities in the

A small masterpiece
Only 9.5cm (3½in) tall, this red sandstone torso from Harappa is modelled with an astonishing anatomical accuracy and attention to detail that prefigures the sculpture of classical Greece.

POINT OF VIEW

Mohenjo-Daro's end – massacre or natural disaster?

Mystery still surrounds the final fate of Mohenjo-Daro. Archaeological excavators have found about 40 corpses left unburied and untended in the site's upper layers – evidence that was initially taken to suggest that the city must have come to a violent end. Yet the numbers were small for such a large metropolis; it seemed hard to imagine that it would have relied on so few defenders to protect it.

Now most historians look to environmental causes rather than invasion or attack by enemies to explain the final demise of the Indus Valley culture – not least because other sites in the region that were also abandoned at around the same time show no signs of external force.

region. Additionally, its rulers had experienced troops at their disposal.

When Kalibangan was eventually rebuilt, the work was carried out in the Harappan style. A citadel rose on the ruins of the deserted city, and a separate residential area was created, still parallelogram-shaped but much larger than before. Both parts of the city were separately fortified. This community survived to the end of the Indus Valley period – about 1800 BC.

One of the outstanding characteristics of the Indus Valley civilisation is its well-developed sense of order. Throughout the area of its influence, standardised weights and measures were in use. All the bricks used in Kalibangan's construction measured 40 x 10 x 20cm (16 x 4 x 8in). The width of the roads was also fixed, according to their importance, at either 3.6m (12ft), 5.4m (17ft), or 7.2m (23ft) – just as they were in Harappa.

Among the most intriguing discoveries at Kalibanagan are traces of fire altars; seven were laid out on a small hill 100m (330ft) east of the residential quarter. Others have been found in the citadel itself and at other Indus Valley sites. These finds challenge the conventional wisdom that fire altars arrived in India with Aryan invaders from central Asia who arrived only after the collapse of the Indus cities. Now some scholars suggest that sacrificial rites involving fire may have been native to the subcontinent long before.

Undeciphered symbols

For all the archaeological breakthroughs that have been made, many questions remain unanswered about the religion, government and society of the Indus Valley culture. Everything known comes from studying the excavations, for the Indus Valley's script – which was in use for several centuries – remains undeciphered to this day. Several hundred symbols have been identified, impressed into thousands of tiny clay tablets, that may have been used to label trade goods in transit.

The tablets were marked by pressing inscribed seals onto the wet clay. The seals themselves are square-shaped and usually made of soapstone. In addition to writing symbols, they also bear images of animals or fabulous creatures, some of which may depict local gods of whom nothing certain is known. However, there are elements represented on the seals that link up with later religious traditions, such as the images of fig leaves – sacred fig trees still guard the approaches to many Indian villages. A horned god shown surrounded by animals – a rhino, a buffalo, a tiger, an elephant – calls to mind the Hindu god Shiva, who was also often represented as a lord of the animals.

A lucrative sea trade

Many such seals have been found in the port of Lothal, along with huge numbers of stone beads and utensils used in various trades. The finds confirm that Lothal was an important trading centre, where both raw materials and finished goods from the Indus Valley crossed paths with goods arriving from abroad. The city of Lothal was founded in

Civilised society
The Indus Valley cities are famous for their advanced drainage systems, with covered drains and water conduits. A high standard of workmanship is also seen in their domestic pottery.

A practical ornament
Jewellery was clearly popular with the residents of the Indus Valley cities – and not solely for adornment. They used decorative brooches like this to hold their cotton clothing in place.

about 2200 BC, when the Harappan Culture had already reached its zenith. In its layout, the port followed the traditional Indus Valley grid pattern. Its most striking feature, however, was a massive basin – 129m (420ft) long, 8m (26ft) wide and 5m (16ft) deep – equipped with a sluice gate for regulating water levels. Archaeologists believe that it was a dock for seagoing vessels, making it the first such facility known to history.

Lothal was inevitably affected when the Indus Valley culture fell into decline, although for a time it seems to have been cushioned from the blow. Perhaps it was temporarily reprieved by its far-flung network of trading partners; even when food became scarce elsewhere in the region, Lothal's inhabitants may have been able to acquire provisions from overseas.

Supply problems

The situation was very different in the inland cities, where the inhabitants had always been dependent on local farmers to fill their giant grain stores. As long as crops flourished in the agricultural hinterland, there were few problems. From about 1900 BC, however, rainfall drastically decreased and the harvests began to fail, sporadically at first and then with worrying regularity.

As the grain deliveries faltered, the rulers of the cities must have become increasingly desperate in their attempts to feed the citizens, on whose labours the

very survival of the communities depended. One way of bolstering supplies might have been through armed force and territorial aggression, but there is no surviving evidence to suggest that militarism was on the rise at this time. It is even possible that the generally peace-loving disposition of the cities' inhabitants may have contributed to their eventual downfall.

The final decline and fall

In spite of all the speculation surrounding its fate, the final collapse of the Indus Valley culture is still shrouded in mystery. Some researchers have suggested that tectonic upheavals along the coast may temporarily have blocked the Indus off from the sea, causing its waters to back up and submerge the cities under devastating floods. Certainly, some of the smaller sites seem to have been abandoned very suddenly. In one house, archaeologists found a meal left half prepared, just as though the cook had momentarily slipped out of the room.

In Mohenjo-Daro itself, silting may have caused the river level to rise, subjecting the city to ever more frequent flooding and undermining the foundations of many of the houses. The situation may have been made worse by deforestation along the upper course of the Indus, for large quantities of firewood were constantly required to feed the furnaces of the region's brickworks. The valley farmlands may also have been overgrazed as human and livestock populations grew.

Whatever the underlying causes, the great cities of Mohenjo-Daro and Harappa had ceased to function as urban centres and disappeared by about 1800 BC. In the space of barely 100 years, their populations drastically declined, houses and canal systems were abandoned and fell into ruin, and all the trappings of urban civilisation were lost. For all its sophistication and technical expertise, the Indus Valley culture had vanished almost as if it had never been.

Mighty Mesopotamia – Babylon and Assur

For more than a millennium Babylon and Assur vied for supremacy in northern Mesopotamia, between them creating the greatest empires the Near East had ever seen.

Babylon rose to become one of the most famous cities of ancient times, yet its birth was far from the most promising. It took place at a time when the cities of Mesopotamia were under attack and the old power bases were beginning to shift.

The attackers were nomadic desert tribesmen who spoke a Semitic, rather than Sumerian, language. The inhabitants of Mesopotamia knew them as Amurru, the people from the west; today we call them Amorites. Many had long been settled in the region between the Tigris and Euphrates rivers, earning a living as labourers, slaves and mercenaries.

But around the year 2000 BC their compatriots began to conduct large-scale raids from the Syrian desert. Border fortifications were overrun, and before long the constant assaults were causing serious difficulties in provisioning the cities of Mesopotamia. Grain supplies ran short and prices soared.

Meanwhile, the last king of the 3rd dynasty of Ur, Ibbisin (2027–2003 BC), was at war with Elam, a powerful kingdom situated in what is now southwestern Iran. In time the Elamites gained the upper hand, conquering Ur and taking Ibbisin off into captivity. With this defeat, Ur's demise was inevitable, and the city-states of Mesopotamia once more locked horns in a struggle for supremacy, from which the cities of Isin and Larsa finally emerged victorious.

Amorite tribal chiefs took advantage of the confusion to seize control of several city-states, among them the relatively insignificant city of Babillu on the River Euphrates. Thanks to its

God save the king
This bronze figure was found at Larsa, 250km (150 miles) downstream from Babylon. It bears an inscription indicating that it was presented as a votive offering to the god Amurru to beg protection not just for the donor but also for the king, Hammurabi. Incense was burned in the small receptacle at the front.

A Babylonian home
Mesopotamian houses were almost always fashioned from clay, like this model. Built of air-dried mud bricks, they often had an upper storey.

Religious sacrifice
This fragment of a mural once decorated the royal palace at Mari, on the Euphrates River upstream from Babylon in what is now eastern Syria. A larger-than-lifesize figure, representing a king or a god, leads a procession of priests, one of whom holds a sacrificial ox by a nose-ring.

consonance with a term in the Akkadian language, the pre-Sumerian name of this city would in time be interpreted as meaning 'Gate of the Gods'. Its Greek form was Babylon, and as such it would be remembered as one of the greatest cities of antiquity.

Palaces by the Euphrates

Babylon's rise to glory at the heart of a great empire began in about 1792 BC with the accession of King Hammurabi. By combining military campaigns and diplomatic initiatives, in the course of a 43-year reign Hammurabi succeeded in extending his sovereignty over most of Mesopotamia. He installed governors in several of the conquered cities; others were persuaded to accept Babylonian overlordship, and offered up tribute to acknowledge their subordinate status. Sadly nothing is now left of Hammurabi's palaces and temples amid the ruins of

Babylon. However, the excavated remains of a structure built at almost the same time – by King Zimrilim at Mari on the middle reaches of the Euphrates – give a clear indication of how early Babylon's great public buildings might have looked.

The complex at Mari was 120m (400ft) long by 200m (650ft) wide, covering a total area of 2.4 hectares (6 acres). Many different rooms clustered round a stuccoed inner courtyard. They served a variety of purposes, for the palace was not just the home of the king and his court but also an administrative centre and a warehouse for storing valuable trade goods – for example, tin ingots, which were vital for producing bronze.

The interior walls were decorated with brightly coloured murals depicting mythical scenes and sacrifices to the gods; one shows the war goddess Ishtar bestowing kingship in the midst of a paradise landscape filled with palm trees

and mythical animals. The king's throne room sheltered behind massive wooden doors. Other rooms served as offices for senior administrative officials and as living quarters for the royal family; some were used to store administrative archives in the form of inscribed cuneiform tablets. There were kitchens, store rooms and bedrooms, and a bathroom with ceramic bathtubs, connected to a drainage system of clay pipes, catered for the physical comfort and hygiene of the palace's inhabitants.

The king as law-giver

In the throne room of the palace in Babylon, Hammurabi would have received the homage of vassal princes and accepted gifts from diplomatic envoys. Here he no doubt framed the laws that were chiselled into the famous stele now preserved in the Louvre Museum in Paris, the world's earliest surviving comprehensive legal code. At the head of the carved tablet the king is shown receiving the insignia of royal authority from the sun-god Shamash, who is seated on a throne; below them, the various articles of the Code of Hammurabi are carved in stone.

But Hammurabi was far from the first Mesopotamian monarch to compile a law code. Older texts of this type have been recovered dating back as far as the time of King Ur-nammu of Ur, 300 years earlier, although only in fragmentary form. Codifying laws not only created a framework for a city-state's growing population, but also helped to forestall their commercial exploitation.

While earlier legislation rarely, if ever, prescribed the death penalty or corporal punishment – fines were generally preferred even for serious crimes – Hammurabi's laws were considerably harsher. They were largely based on the principle of an eye for an eye, meting out heavy sentences even for what would now be regarded as relatively minor offences. One law proclaims: 'If a man's wife is caught sleeping with another man, the pair shall be tied together and thrown into

the river.' However, it goes on: 'If the husband chooses to spare his wife, the king may similarly spare his subject.'

Whether such punishments were actually carried out is unclear. Professional judges sentenced the guilty, who were usually tried outside an entrance to the palace known as the Justice Gate. Even so, the king himself remained the highest legal authority in the land, and he was often called on to pass judgment in person.

Babylon society

The bulk of Babylon's citizens lived in mud-brick houses, densely packed together, a far cry from the luxury of the royal palaces. These simple buildings sometimes collapsed, burying their occupants. Hammurabi's code indicates that, in such cases, the builder of the faulty structure should himself be put to death if the owner of the house was fatally injured.

By Hammurabi's day, the ownership of property in Mesopotamia was much changed from Sumerian times. Although the king and the temple remained the major landowners, much more of the land was in private hands than before. Many tenant farmers and small landowners now ran the risk of falling into debt if harvests failed, preventing them from paying their rents or their bills. Worse still, the downward spiral of indebtedness could eventually lead to enslavement for those who found themselves hopelessly bankrupt.

Babylonian society was broadly divided into three classes: free citizens (*awilum*) – so called because they were free from all direct obligations of servitude; bondsmen (*muschkenum*); and slaves (*wardum*). The highest priestly caste, army commanders and top officials were recruited from the

The Stele of Hammurabi
Preserved now in the Louvre Museum in Paris, the stone tablet bearing the laws of the Babylonian ruler Hammurabi is topped by this capital showing the ruler himself, dressed in a toga-like robe and wide-brimmed hat. He is paying homage to the sun-god Shamash, supreme ruler of heaven and earth, who sits enthroned holding a sceptre and ring, the insignia of power. The lower part of the 2.2m (7ft) basalt tablet contains the text of Hammurabi's laws incised in cuneiform script.

ranks of the free citizens. So too were most scribes, for learning cuneiform was, even for Babylonians, a difficult and time-consuming undertaking. Scribes were trained in special schools – surviving texts describing Babylonian school-days suggest that teacher–pupil relationships may not have radically changed in the intervening centuries.

Astronomy to serve the gods

Once settled in Babylon, the Amorites were soon assimilated into the indigenous culture, having been well prepared by long previous contact with the Mesopotamian city-states. Even in matters of religion there was little conflict, except that the newcomers introduced the cult of their own tribal deity Amurru and added the weather-god Adad to the already extensive Sumerian pantheon.

A more significant development in the long term was the growing importance of Babylon's own god, Marduk, whose fortunes prospered with the city's rise to imperial status. Initially an insignificant figure, Marduk came to be venerated as the greatest of the gods in the latter half of the 2nd millennium BC, largely thanks to Babylon's political supremacy.

The most important religious event in the Babylonian year was Akitu, the New Year festival, which was held at the spring equinox. The ceremonial high point came when the king visited the city's main temple to enact a sacred union with the goddess Inana. The Akitu festival was a glorification of spring, celebrating the renewal of nature in the hope of rich harvests to come.

Like the citizens of all the world's early civilisations, Babylonians were deeply anxious about life's uncertainties. They ascribed illness, suffering and failed harvests to the influence of evil demons. Among the most feared of these malign creatures were Pazuzu, lord of the wind-demons, who could induce fevers, and the dreaded 'Seven', of whom it was said, 'They know no pity or mercy, and heed no prayers'. Amulets were the first line of defence against malevolent powers, but people placed even more trust in omens, which indicated if evil was afoot and also revealed the will of the gods. Studying the entrails (especially the liver) of sacrificial animals was a popular form of divination performed by a caste of specialist priests known as *baru*.

Other priests studied the movements of stars and planets to divine the will of the gods. From the roofs of temples and the upper levels of ziggurats they observed the night sky, calling it the 'heavenly writing tablet' on which the gods spelled out their intentions. One fruit of their observations was the zodiac, whose twelve constellations were first listed by Babylonian astronomers. The priests linked the signs with the times of people's births, and so created the earliest horoscopes and originated astrology.

Science, myth and literature

Other fields of knowledge pursued in Babylon included medicine, which was still closely bound up with magic: incantations and prayers were chanted whenever patients took healing potions in order to make the remedies effective.

The science of mathematics was already ancient by Hammurabi's day, for mastery of figures had been needed from early times both for measuring farmers' lands and for quantity surveying, reckoning the amounts of building materials required for construction projects. Babylonian arithmetic was based on a system that revolved around the number 60. Its legacy to the modern world can still be seen in the 60-second minute and 60-minute hour, as well as in the division of circles into 360 degrees.

The Babylonians made major advances in mathematical theory. In geometry, for instance, their mathematicians discovered the principle of Pythagoras' theorem long before the Greek thinker bequeathed it the name by which it is known today.

Babylon also had a vibrant literary culture, much of which revolved around ancient legends of the gods. The world's oldest literary classic, the *Epic of Gilgamesh*, had its roots in earlier, Sumerian times – Gilgamesh himself was a real-life ruler of Uruk in the 3rd millennium BC – but the version that has come down to modern times was compiled in Babylon almost a thousand years later. The Babylonians also prepared early dictionaries, listing words in their own and foreign languages, and drew up catalogues of plants and animals and gazetteers of cities, mountains and seas. Other lists gave the regnal dates of kings, fleshed out with short commentaries on the principal events of their reigns.

Yet for all the many branches of knowledge that they pursued, the Babylonian world view was determined by myth. Their priests and thinkers conceived the cosmos as a sphere divided into two halves. The upper part was made up of the vault of heaven with the stars embedded in it; the lower one was taken up by the underworld. Between the hemispheres lay a saltwater ocean known as Tiamat, upon which the flat Earth floated like an island. Beneath the Earth was another ocean, which the Babylonians called Apsu; the god Ea ruled over this subterranean freshwater aquifer.

The Kassites in Babylon

Hammurabi's successors soon had their hands full warding off the attacks of the Kassites, from the Zagros mountains of western Iran. Initially the invaders were driven back, but gradually more and more of them settled in Babylonian territory. The final blow, however, came from an entirely different quarter when, in 1595 BC, Hittite forces under their ruler Mursilis I swept down on Babylon from the uplands of Anatolia and sacked the city, dethroning Samsuditana, the last king of Hammurabi's line. The Hittites themselves soon withdrew to deal with trouble at home, but the Kassites took advantage of the power vacuum that they

Beast of burden
Because of their great value, horses were rarely used as pack animals like this one. Most Assyrian trade caravans made use of donkeys; later, donkeys were supplemented by mules and camels.

The death of Huwawa
Although the hero Gilgamesh was a central figure in Mesopotamian myth and literature, images depicting him are extremely rare. This Babylonian terracotta relief shows the killing of the forest monster Huwawa, guardian of the western cedar woods, by Gilgamesh and his companion Enkidu, illustrating a key episode in the *Epic of Gilgamesh*.

off to Susa, the Elamite capital. A similar fate awaited the last Kassite king, Enlil-nadin-achi, who conducted a fruitless last-ditch defence from 1159 to 1157 BC. With his defeat, Babylon entered a period that would see its imperial ambitions eclipsed for centuries to come, but the city's years of greatness were by no means over – the Neo-Babylonian Empire of Nebuchadnezzar lay more than 500 years in the future.

Assyria in the ascendant

Babylon was not the only northern Mesopotamian city to exert a decisive influence on the destiny of the Near East in the 2nd millennium BC. Assur was situated on the River Tigris, some 350km (220 miles) to the north of Babylon. Almost insignificant in the 3rd millennium BC, it came to prominence in the 2nd millennium as the capital of the long-lived Assyrian empire.

Assur owed its rise in large measure to its favourable position at the crossing point of several trade routes. From the Assyrian heartland, a merchant could journey east into the Iranian mountains, south down the Tigris toward Babylon (which lay at a point where the Tigris and Euphrates rivers were only 50km/30 miles apart), or westward into northern Syria and Anatolia.

Like Babylon, Assyria owed its rise to a period of Amorite rule, in its case under King Shamshi-Adad I (1815–1782 BC). Shamshi-Adad himself never lived in Assur; his capital lay to the west, in the city of Shubat-Enlil. However he rapidly extended the lands under his sway, building an Assyrian empire that would cover all of northern Mesopotamia. His power was further strengthened by his control over key trade routes.

There is evidence of the extent of Assyrian trade at this time in the surviving

had left behind, and for the next four centuries or more, Kassite kings held the reins of power in Babylon.

Under the Kassites, Babylon remained a significant power, maintaining diplomatic contact with other players on the Middle Eastern stage from Asia Minor to Egypt. Kassite princesses married pharaohs, although Babylonian demands for Egyptian princesses for their own rulers to wed went unanswered. Instead, Egypt sent gold, which the Kassites needed in large quantities for their extensive building projects. When it failed to arrive promptly, letters of complaint were fired off to the Egyptian court, including one from King Kadashman-Enlil (c.1374–1360 BC): 'If you do not send any gold, then I will not be able to finish the works that I have begun… How can I complete the building I have started?'

In time, constant wars with Assyria, a rising power to the north, as well as with Babylon's southern neighbour Elam, fatally weakened the Kassite realm. Two disastrous Elamite invasions – one under King Shutruk-Nachunte and the other led by his son Kudur-Nachunte – precipitated the final downfall of the dynasty. In the ensuing devastation innumerable treasures and artworks were plundered and carried archives of Kanesh, far to the west in Anatolia (now Asiatic Turkey). In trading post settlements such as the one at Kanesh, colonies of expatriate Assyrian merchants traded with the local people for textiles and for tin, supplies of which were vital for bronze-making and may have come from as far as today's Uzbekistan, reaching Assyria via Iran. Anatolia's most important export was copper. The Assyrian traders at Kanesh lived in their own enclave, called an *arum*, outside the city walls, within their own jurisdiction. Many business letters, accounts and contracts have been preserved, testifying to the commerce that was carried on there.

Rivalries among neighbours

Shortly after 1800 BC, trade contacts between Assyria and Kanesh ceased. One reason may have been the rising power of the Hittites, whose empire was based in eastern Anatolia; another was the waning power of the Assyrian empire itself. In the centuries following Shamshi-Adad's reign, Assur was reduced to little more than a small trading community, overshadowed not merely by Babylon and the Hittites but also by a new power, the kingdom of Mitanni, centred in eastern Syria. This situation finally changed with the accession of King Assur-uballit I (1365–1330 BC), who managed to revitalise Assyria as a major power. His successors held out against the Hittites and conquered Mitanni, once more uniting all of northern Mesopotamia under Assyrian rule.

The middle Assyrian empire

Assyria's rise inevitably brought it into conflict with Babylon. Under Tikultu-Ninurta I (1244–1208 BC) it launched a major assault on the southern metropolis, which they sacked and razed to the ground. In an inscription commemorating the victory, the Assyrian king boasted: 'In the midst of a skirmish, I was able to seize [the Kassite] King Kashtilash with my own hands … and dragged him as a

prisoner in chains before my lord Ashur.' Like Marduk before him, Ashur, the god of Assur, rose to prominence with the city he represented, becoming the leading deity in the entire Assyrian pantheon.

The last great king in this middle phase of Assyrian power was Tiglath-pileser I (1114–1076 BC), whose reign saw the city of Assur enjoying an architectural renasissance. The king endowed it with elaborate new fortifications, including gates carefully positioned to protect access into the city. Visitors approaching the town could see from far off the great ziggurat of Ashur towering high above the walls. Many other temples were also constructed at this time, notably a unique, double ziggurat surmounted by twin

temples dedicated to the gods Anu and Adad. The money to pay for all this building activity came partly from trade, but also from an influx of war booty and tribute paid by defeated enemies. Yet this period of Assyria's greatness was also doomed to fade. Assyrian power waned soon after Tiglath-pileser's demise, not to rise again for a further 200 years.

The world's oldest city plan
This clay map, of about 1300 BC, was found to tally closely with the actual layout of Nippur, which was revealed when the city was excavated by archaeologists in the late 19th century.

The Hittites – empire-builders of Anatolia

For 400 years the Hittites ranked among the leading powers of the ancient Near East, after Babylon and Egypt. Apart from their prowess as warriors, they were effective diplomats and developed an ingenious legal system.

Ritual drinking vessel
The relief pattern on this silver goblet in the shape of a deer shows a sacrificial scene. Living in a land rich in mineral ores, the Hittites were the foremost metalworkers of their age.

Rulers did not always have to be scrupulous with the truth – or so Egypt's Rameses II must have told himself. Sometimes events needed to be presented in the most favourable light. The pharaoh had just returned from a military campaign in Syria in which he had hardly covered himself in glory. Under no circumstances must his subjects learn that he, the master of the Nile, had not won the decisive victory they expected, earning himself due honour and renown. And he especially could not afford to admit to defeat at the hands of Egypt's old enemy from the north, the powerful Hittite nation.

So the ruler saw to it that the regal inscriptions that decorated his capital of Luxor proclaimed a victory that had never happened. Bulletins and battle scenes carved on temple walls described a largely imaginary triumph. A poet named Pentawer, perhaps writing after Rameses's death, in the reign of his successor, Merneptah, would even write an epic describing the king's godlike heroism, winning himself a place in literary history as one of the first-known masters of the enduring art of political spin.

A memorable battle

The battle that Rameses took such pains to present in a positive light took place in about 1275 BC. It was fought outside Kadesh, an otherwise rather undistinguished town in northern Syria that found fame only because the Egyptian and Hittite forces happened to encounter each other there.

The Battle of Kadesh has gone down in the history books as the most important military engagement of the entire 2nd millennium BC. Its outcome assured the Hittite king Muwatallis II, its true victor, a reputation as a military commander and strategist of genius.

One reason for the battle's place in history is simply the fact that extensive source material has survived describing the background to the encounter. The Egyptians and the Hittites had long been vying with one another for control of Syria and Palestine, and repeated clashes had taken place between their armed forces. But Kadesh put everything that had gone before into the shade. Prior to the

The rock sanctuary of Yazilikaya contains many reliefs depicting gods. This one shows a procession of male deities clutching scimitar-like swords.

battle Rameses, a young ruler eager to prove his military worth, insisted (at least in his public pronouncements) that his powerful army would bring the Hittites to their knees. In private, however, the Egyptian pharaoh had great respect for his opponents. Stories of their fortitude and toughness abounded.

A growing empire

The Hittites had recorded a string of famous victories over a period of centuries, and no one in Egypt, or indeed in the entire Near and Middle East, was unaware of their impressive military record. Under a succession of energetic and ambitious kings, foremost among them Suppiluliumas (1345–1320 BC), the Hittites had built a sizeable empire: as well as their homeland of Anatolia (today's Asiatic Turkey), they ruled over northern Syria and upstream areas of Mesopotamia. They had raided the Mesopotamian heartland as early as 1539 BC, when a Hittite expedition led by King Mursilis I had sacked even the mighty city of Babylon, bringing about the downfall of the great dynasty established by King Hammurabi. In the west, the long arm of Hittite power reached to the Mediterranean coast.

Changeable relations

In his preparations for the campaign Rameses no doubt took confidence from the fact that Egyptian forces had emerged victorious from the last major battle between the two armies, coincidentally also fought at Kadesh, a couple of decades earlier. On that occasion the pharaoh's great predecessor, Thutmose II, had proved convincingly that the Hittite army was far from invincible.

After the clash there had been a period of rapprochement, for the Hittites were not just brave warriors but also skilful diplomats – a faculty that stood them in good stead in the tortuous power politics of the Near East. Suppiluliumas had even

formed a temporary alliance with Egypt. In the time of troubles following the death of the heretic pharaoh Akhenaten, an unidentified Egyptian queen – possibly Akhenaten's widow, Nefertiti, or the wife of his deceased successor, Tutankhamun – wrote to Suppiluliumas seeking to marry his son, who would thereby have become pharaoh on her death.

The plan came to an unfortunate end, however. The Hittite prince travelled to Egypt but was killed in mysterious circumstances on his arrival, triggering a fresh period of tension and fighting between the states. According to an inscription drawn up on the instructions of Mursilis II, brother of the victim: 'My father became enraged, prepared for war, and attacked Egypt. He smote down their foot soldiers and their charioteers.' Rameses must have been turning all these matters over in his mind as he marched north towards the fateful encounter.

A cunning stratagem

The new Hittite ruler was Mursilis's son, Muwatallis II, who was waiting for Rameses in Syria. Muwatallis had a profound respect for the military prowess of his Egyptian adversary, and so decided that, rather than risk a pitched battle with an uncertain outcome, it would be wiser to employ subterfuge and deceive him.

Muwatallis called on the services of an undercover agent, who was instructed to have himself taken prisoner by the Egyptians. The spy's job was then to feed them with false information so that Rameses would be misled about the true position of the Hittite army – to reveal, falsely, that it was much further north, around Aleppo. The plan worked perfectly. On hearing the new information Rameses confidently advanced with his elite troops, just as Muwatallis had anticipated, without waiting for his main body of infantry to catch up with him.

Rameses' gullibility almost brought about his downfall. The Hittite army was lying in wait at Kadesh, spoiling for

An unconventional form
Standing about 50cm (20in) high, this elegant Hittite ewer was used for pouring out religious libations. Made of clay, its polished, reddish-brown glaze echoes the burnished sheen of metal vessels.

action. Even so, Muwatallis was clever and cautious enough not to launch a head-on attack. Instead his forces performed a pincer movement, separating the vanguard and rearguard of the Egyptian force, and so cutting Rameses off from even more of his troops. Only then did the Hittites close in on the Egyptians, who were now split in two.

The Egyptians were taken completely by surprise – so much so, that they were hard-pressed to defend themselves. But then the tables suddenly turned. Flushed with success, the Hittites fell on the camp where Rameses had spent the previous night, and proceeded to burn and plunder indiscriminately. This diversion gave Rameses the opportunity to mount a counterattack.

With his chariot-borne shock troops Rameses managed to break through the Hittite lines, so the two parts of his vanguard were able to link up once again. Contrary to later propaganda, however, he did not then stand and fight. Happy to have avoided total disaster, he retreated to join the rest of his army and then went back to Egypt.

A divinely sanctioned peace

The Battle of Kadesh was extremely costly for both nations, and in its wake both the Hittites and the Egyptians lost their appetite for war. Muwatallis's successor, Hattusilis III, negotiated an historic peace accord with Rameses (who would remain in power for a remarkable total of 67 years until his death at about the age of 90). The text of the treaty – the earliest known in history – has been preserved in two separate versions, one drafted in Egyptian and the other in the Akkadian language of Mesopotamia.

In the florid language of diplomacy at the time, the signatories agreed not to attack one another and to settle their conflicting claims to Syria amicably. In addition, the two reconciled antagonists

The Lion Gate of Hattusas
Sculpted lions still guard one of the main entrances to the ancient Hittite capital of Hattusas. The regal beasts are carved into the massive stone blocks that served as doorjambs.

BLACK SEA

Hattusas

Miletus

KINGDOM OF MITANNI

ASSYRIA

Euphrates

Tigris

Kadesh
1275 BC

MEDITERRANEAN
SEA

Damascus

Tyre

Babylon

Nile

EGYPT

■ **Hittite heartland**

■ **Greatest extent of Hittite kingdom**

➤ **Hittite expansion**

True to the treaty, no further conflicts flared between the two powers in the half century or so that remained before the final collapse of the Hittite kingdom in about 1200 BC. A couple of years after the treaty was concluded, peaceful relations were consolidated when Hattusilis gave one of his daughters in marriage to Rameses. And the friendly relations that developed between the nations brought other benefits. On one occasion, when the Hittite lands were threatened by famine, the pharaoh threw open his grain stores and sent vital supplies to his new ally.

Rediscovering a lost culture

For a long time, the history of the Hittites was shrouded in mystery, despite the prominent role they had played among the major powers of the ancient Near East. They are mentioned several times in the Old Testament of the Bible, where they are called 'Hittim', but until late in the 19th century, almost nothing was really known about them.

Then in 1905 the renowned German archaeologist Hugo Winckler led a team on extensive excavations of the ruined Hittite capital of Hattusas in central Anatolia. The site would eventually yield an archive of some 25,000 clay tablets inscribed in cuneiform script in the Akkadian language. These documents gave researchers vital insights into Hittite history and their religious and cultural life.

The Hittites migrated to Anatolia sometime around 2000 BC. They initially established their capital at Kussar, but the royal court moved to Hattusas in about 1600 BC. The Hittite kings wielded extraordinary power, combining in the one person the roles of high priest, commander in chief of the army and supreme judge. To reflect the glory of this office, they set out to make Hattusas into a fitting backdrop for their activities.

The first impression on approaching Hattusas was of a massive double wall surrounding the city. This signalled to

concluded a pact against all internal and external enemies and drew up regulations governing the mutual extradition of refugees. According to the carefully worded terms of the treaty, no one who was repatriated in this way needed to fear any sanctions or violent retribution: 'Their transgressions will not be held against them, their tongues and eyes are not to be cut out, neither shall anyone sever their ears or feet, and their homes with their wives and children are not to be destroyed.'

The text concluded with the hope that both parties would abide by the spirit of the agreement, in which case the two kings could rest assured of the blessing of both the 'thousand gods' of the Egyptians and 'thousand gods' of the Hittites. The same gods were also expected to ensure that each monarch would 'remain healthy and thrive, along with his houses, his lands, and his servants'.

Royal jewellery
This seal ring shows a winged deity standing on the back of a leopard, which is flanked by two lions. It was used to authenticate signatures and as a mark of ownership.

potential invaders that any attempt to storm the capital was doomed to failure. The king himself lived in an extensive palace, built on a monumental scale which was no doubt intended to overawe anyone who saw it.

City of the gods

Visitors to Hattusas must also have been impressed by the city's many temples, particularly the Great Temple dedicated to the weather god Tarhun and his wife, the sun goddess Istanu. The couple played a central role in Hittite religion; their main shrine was located in the central Anatolian city of Arinna. Below Tarhun and Istanu were many other gods, each of them with close connections to natural phenomena. The Hittites worshipped not just the sun, moon and stars, but also springs, rivers, woods and cliffs, all of which had their own deities. And each divinity was given a fitting form, mostly human.

This crowded pantheon demanded due respect, so priests and scribes laboured earnestly to provide believers with invocations singing their praises. One surviving prayer, designed to win the favour of Istanu, may be typical: 'O sun goddess of Arinna, you are most sublime. In your honour, my goddess, only the Hittites erect mighty temples – moreover, there is not a single temple dedicated to you in any other country. Only in the land of the Hittites are regular festivals and sacrifices conducted solemnly and properly in your honour – moreover, no such observances are made in any other country. Only in the land of the Hittites do you have temples decorated with gold and silver, and no such temples exist anywhere else.' Hittite priests evidently made exclusivity an important part of their national cult.

A successful administration

To have played a leading role in the Near East for as long as they did, the Hittites must have had special qualities. It is thought that several different factors contributed to their success. War and diplomacy were vital, but so, too, was social discipline. Practically everything was regulated in their lands. Countless clay tablets bear witness to a legal system with a vigilant eye for detail and a bureaucracy that was almost modern in its extent. To take a single example, surviving records spell out the course of action to be taken if one citizen wounded another seriously enough to disable him, albeit temporarily: 'Then he must care for his victim, and lend him a servant to work in his house for as long as it takes for the victim to recover. And when he is on his feet again, he is to be given six silver shekels, as well as having his doctor's fees paid.'

Other provisions specified penalties for the theft of beehives: 'If a person should steal two or three beehives, then he is liable for a fine of six silver shekels. And whoever steals a beehive containing no bees is liable for a fine of three silver shekels.'

Yet even the most elaborate legislation could not prevent the Hittite empire eventually disappearing from history's main stage. Very little is known of the exact circumstances, but its collapse came at a time of internal crises and spreading famine that coincided with the mass migration of displaced eastern Mediterranean tribes, known from Egyptian records as the Sea Peoples. Central royal authority crumbled in these turbulent times, with only a few outposts of Hittite culture surviving in southeastern Anatolia and northern Syria. These remaining neo-Hittite enclaves finally disappeared in the 8th century BC, swept away by Assyrian conquerors.

Ceremonial weapon
The rich ornamentation and blunt blade on this Hittite axe-head indicate that it was never intended as a battlefield weapon. It was probably used in rituals and religious ceremonies.

Cult of the ancestors – China's Shang dynasty

Through military skill and a strictly organised state system, the kings of the Shang dynasty secured their rule over northern China. They bequeathed the cult of ancestor worship to their successors.

For years the peasants who farmed the land around the town of Anyang, near northern China's Huang He river (the Yellow River), sold bones and tortoiseshells that turned up in their fields to city apothecaries, who ground them up to use as ingredients of traditional Chinese medicine. Eventually, the local authorities banned the unofficial trade, by which time experts in antiquities and ancient scripts had joined the traditional healers in the market for bones. What attracted the interest of these collectors were the symbols scratched on the relics. Scholars had already amassed about 200,000 oracle bones and had begun to interpret the signs. The message they read was unequivocal: the Shang dynasty, which had previously been considered semi-legendary, really had existed.

The inscribed characters that the linguists had so carefully deciphered had turned out to be early Chinese pictograms, and they reproduced the names of kings who were already known from ancient records. Surviving king lists recorded that, between the 16th and 11th centuries BC, 30 rulers recorded by name had reigned for 17 generations over the

first advanced civilisation on Chinese soil. The bones showed there was nothing mythical about China's Shang dynasty. More than a millennium before the start of the Christian era, Shang rulers were firmly in control of a substantial kingdom.

The Shang dynasty grew out of China's Neolithic cultures, particularly that of the Longshan, named after a village in Shangdong Province where its artefacts were first found. In the Longshan period northern China was fragmented between a large number of small, warring local states, known today as the '10,000 kingdoms'. Sometime in the mid 16th century BC, one of the competing rulers, an ancestor of the Shang, succeeded in subjugating enough of the neighbouring states to form a unified kingdom. Later rulers expanded his domain, enlarged by fresh conquests, into the Shang kingdom.

Cities of substance

The Shang rulers built their first capital of Ao near Chengzhou on the lower course of the Huang He river. The city covered an extraordinarily large area for those early times, stretching over some 3.2km² (1.2sq miles), surrounded by a wall almost 7km (4 miles) long. The remains of this barrier still stand 9m (30ft) tall in places; its foundation is 22m (72ft) deep, reaching down to 35m (115 ft) at the corners.

The wall was made of compacted mud built up in layers about 8–10cm (3–4in)

Symbol of power
Bronze axe blades from Shang times were often richly decorated. Such blades have been found in royal tombs near sacrificial remains, suggesting that they may have been used to execute the victims.

This elaborate bronze wine vessel in the form of a fantastic, tiger-like creature may have been used to serve wine to Shang kings in sacrifices to the ancestors. The tiger was a symbol of courage and fearlessness.

A sacred vessel
Food offerings for dead ancestors were prepared and kept in bronze vessels like this one. The tripod form recalls similar clay models dating from the preceding Neolithic period.

thick. No-one knows for certain how long this defensive wall took to build, but researchers have estimated that it would have taken a workforce of 10,000 men some 18 years to complete the job. The figures, rough though they are, give some idea of the amount of manpower that the Shang kings could call on, even in the early centuries of their rule.

The final Shang capital of Yin, near present-day Anyang, served as the seat of power for the dynasty at its peak from the 13th to 11th centuries BC. By that time the royal palaces extended over a 400km (250 mile) stretch of land parallel to the lower course of the Huang He. The royal residences were constructed of clay and calcitic limestone plastered over a wicker-work foundation – a humble building material for such magnificent and elegant edifices. In contrast, the majority of the population lived in semi-subterranean dwellings, built down into the soil for insulation; these also served as places of work. Some lived a troglodyte existence in caves and pits. The houses typically measured about 4m (13ft) across, and access was from above, down steps.

A stratified society

The hugely contrasting living arrangements suggest just how much society had changed since the egalitarian days of the Neolithic period. A strict hierarchy had developed. At the top was the Shang king – the only individual who could truly be described as free –

surrounded by his immediate family and a broad stratum of aristocrats from collateral dynastic lines. The state was organised around, and for, these few.

It was Wu Ding, the 21st Shang ruler, who led his clan to a peak of power and prosperity and built up the modest settlement of Xiaotun near Anyang into the splendid city of Yin. Wu Ding owned the lion's share of the land, granting estates to his 64 wives, to his sons and other princes, as well as to deserving higher civil servants and governors. He had absolute power in matters of state, including the power of life and death over his subjects. Wu Ding and the other Shang kings secured this monopoly not just through complicated marriage alliances but also by appealing to the authority of their ancestors, who were thought to exercise the same sort of hegemony in the afterlife as they enjoyed in the world of the living. The ruler combined secular and religious supremacy in his own person.

The voice of the oracle

One of the king's duties was to consult oracles about future events to ensure that his actions were in accordance with his ancestors' will. When Wu Ding was informed that his favourite wife, Fu Hao, was pregnant he turned to a soothsayer named Que to find out, first of all, whether the child would be a boy or a girl. The bones at first indicated that the birth would be propitious, but the royal couple needed more reassurance, so there were several more consultations over the course of the pregnancy. As time went by the predictions became more uncertain, even negative. Finally, the diviner turned again to the first bone, which had looked hopeful, but this time the reinterpretation proved unfavourable – a reading that was finally confirmed when Fu Hao gave birth not to the male heir Wu Ding had hoped for but to a girl.

Rulers consulted oracle bones on many matters besides family affairs. They sought advice on the likely outcome of hunts, decisions about employees, foundations of cities, wars, weather and harvest prospects, as well as to learn the will of the highest god, Shangdi.

In early Shang times the diviners were courtiers chosen by the king. Over time, however, the ruler became increasingly involved in the business of prediction, dispensing with the need for soothsayers. At the same time, the process of reading the future became more stereotyped and impersonal, and the bones increasingly predicted only good news. Perhaps that seemed natural enough, for there was little at the time for the Shang rulers to fear: they stood at the head of a huge imperial machine and their enemies were far away. They had little cause for concern, so long as they continued to enjoy the goodwill of their ancestors and the gods.

Dwelling places of the ancestors

To keep their influential ancestor spirits happy, the Shang rulers offered up elaborate sacrifices and erected temples, which they often sited directly above their own tomb complexes. When planning and building a palace enclosure, the quarters assigned to the ancestors took precedence even over the monarch's own living space.

The first stage of ancestor worship began with the funeral of a dead ruler, which was expected to reflect the status and wealth that he had enjoyed in life.

The 13 royal tombs that have been excavated near Anyang are startling in their scope and splendour. They take the form of shaft graves oriented toward the north-east; some have a cruciform plan. Two (sometimes four) ramps, each 15–20m (50–65ft) long, lead down to a pit 12m (40ft) deep, covering in all about 140m^2 (1500sq ft). The labour involved in construction must have been immense. The monarch's coffin was laid to rest in a wooden burial chamber that occupied the bottom layer of the pit. After a reign of 59 years, Wu Ding himself was probably buried somewhere in the area.

A treasured wife

Archaeologists found the resting-place of Wu Ding's wife Fu Hao in 1976. For once they beat the tomb raiders and were able to excavate an intact site. They found grave goods of the highest quality, reflecting Fu Hao's high rank and prestige.

Laid to rest
As these excavated graves near Anyang clearly show, wealthy and powerful individuals were sometimes buried with their chariots – and with the horses that once drew them. In a few cases, the charioteers too were forced to accompany their masters to the grave.

BACKGROUND

The oracle bones of the Shamans

For advice on the correct course of action to take for the well-being of their state, the Shang rulers sought advice from higher powers – from their ancestors, from the innumerable minor deities that controlled the forces of nature, and from the supreme god, Shangdi.

The media through which the spirits made their views known were oracle bones – normally either tortoise shells or the shoulderblades of cattle. In all, tens of thousands of animals

must have died to keep the diviners supplied.

Once the bones had been cleaned and cut to size, they were marked with a number that was used to identify them when they were later stored in the state archives. In preparation for a consultation, the diviner scored a number of holes or grooves in the back of the bone and then applied heat, causing cracks to form. He then used the shape, size and location of the fissures to reach his conclusions.

The results of a consultation – including the question posed, the date, the interpretation, and sometimes even the actual outcome – were engraved on the bones, which were bound together and preserved in pits in the temple area. Markings on oracle bones are the earliest direct evidence of literacy in China; the basic structure of the Chinese written language evolved from these marks over the course of the 12th and 11th centuries BC.

Symbols that speak
Around 3000 different characters have been identified on oracle bones. So far, about 1000 of these have been deciphered, thanks largely to the fact that many of the old signs still correspond quite closely with present-day Chinese ideograms.

achievements, and in hope of her future support from the afterlife, he saw to it that she was buried with fitting honours. Some 2000 precious objects of jade, bronze, bone, semi-precious stone, ivory and pottery accompanied her to the grave, along with more than 6000 cowrie shells – the currency of the time. Such riches were meant to ensure that she would continue to enjoy the luxury to which she was accustomed. Weapons were also included in her tomb, a mark of her role as a military commander: they included six bows and over 90 daggers.

Blood sacrifice

Fu Hao's grave goods also included four huge bronze axes that she herself may well have wielded during her lifetime. These might have come to her as tribute from a subject tribe, or perhaps they were gifts from Wu Ding in thanks for special services; one of them is inscribed with her name. The axes were probably not weapons of war but ritual implements used for animal and human sacrifices. Archaeologists studying Fu Hao's tomb found evidence of sacrifices performed on the entrance ramps during its construction. The remains of 16 people and a dog were found in the burial chamber itself.

Through evidence from oracle bones and other sources scholars have formed an idea of the extent of human sacrifice under the Shang. Between 1395 and 1123 BC, 12 rulers sacrificed more than 13,000 people. Servants and prisoners of war were buried alongside kings and their close family members, while confidants and followers were laid to rest in splendid tombs close by. Wu Ding's reign not only

Frightening features
This bronze mask from Sanxingdui, 1000km (600 miles) from Anyang, has holes in the forehead and sides that were probably used to hang it for display during cult sacrifices.

She was, it seems, a remarkable woman who must have ranked among the most outstanding personalities of ancient China. Evidence on oracle bones suggest that she was not just a royal wife and mother but also an active military commander, who led at least two expeditions against neighbouring states and tribes. Wu Ding entrusted her with her own estates, including responsibility for the harvest and stock. He also appointed her to carry out certain religious rituals of immense importance for the state. Other wives of Wu Ding also performed state duties, and later Chinese tradition praises his wisdom in bucking established convention to share power with capable women – one reason for the success of his long reign.

Fu Hao's death came as a heavy blow to the king. In recognition of her

represented the political, economic and cultural zenith of the Shang dynasty but also its most bloodthirsty era, combining religion and state power.

Once the body had been interred and the burial pit filled with earth, the focus of ancestor worship moved to the shrine where the dead person's memory was preserved. Traces of a large rectangular building above Fu Hao's tomb are thought to come from just such a structure, the oldest to have survived from Shang times. Family members would have gone to the sanctuary to pray for Fu Hao's well-being in the afterlife and to seek her advice and help. They directed their veneration to a tablet bearing the queen's name – the souls of dead ancestors were thought to enter these tablets whenever sacrifices or ceremonies were performed, allowing contact to be made between the two worlds. Fu Hao received a new name, Mu Xin, after her death, but continued to receive all the reverence that had been paid to her in life.

There was a strictly observed hierarchy in the ancestor cult, just as there was at the Shang court where rules governing dynastic marriages and the order of succession were laid down. Forebears in a direct line of descent to the existing ruler ranked highest; other relatives enjoyed lesser honours. Every year, the king and a prominent member of his clan carried out five main rituals – the Drumming, the Feather Dance, Wine and Meat, Millet, and the Great Harmony. These rites included offering human sacrifice to the supreme god, Shangdi, as well as to lesser deities and to the ancestors themselves, who kept the gods company in death.

Food and drink were also offered to the ancestors in their shrines. Beef, mutton and dog were prepared in giant bronze kettles or cauldrons, with millet and other cereals. Once the aroma had satisfied the appetites of the dead, winning their favour for the individuals who had prepared the meal, the food itself was eaten at banquets by family members and their guests.

Expensive feasting

Ancient texts describe the feasts of the Shang rulers and their courtiers. Fu Hao herself may have presided over the preparation of sacrificial banquets, directing servants and choosing the vessels in which the meat should be cooked. Guests came from far and wide, and included both clan members and outsiders. Under the benevolent eye of the royal couple they were served with heaped platters and goblets filled with wine, while toasts and good wishes echoed around the hall.

Strict rules of protocol governed these festive pledges. As the host, Wu Ding would descend from the high table to rinse out a goblet for the use of a selected guest, who stood waiting patiently, facing the east. Host and guest ascended the steps together, one politely allowing the other to go ahead. While the guest waited, the king filled the goblet with warm wine laced with aromatic herbs and pronounced a formal toast. The guest then returned to his place, sat down facing north, and bowed. Finally, a speaker announced to the king, 'The spirits have enjoyed their food and drink. They will eternally provide you with good provisions.'

Too much good wine

The Shang evidently set great store by sacrificial offerings of wine – almost three-quarters of all the vessels found in Fu Hao's tomb appear to have been designed for this purpose. An entire guild was charged with producing the wine used for the sacrifices, and a variety of kettles, jugs and other vessels were used for storing, warming, pouring, decanting and drinking the fermented millet brew. So much liquor flowed at Shang ceremonies and feasts that in later

Fit for a queen
This ivory beaker with an intricate inlay of turquoise is one of two that were found in the tomb of Queen Fu Hao. The ivory came from elephants hunted in the dense forests along the Huang He (Yellow River).

times the downfall of the Shang kings was blamed on misuse of alcohol.

After the dynasty's demise, the rulers of the succeeding Zhou regime forbade courtiers from drinking wine on pain of death.

Most of the vessels that accompanied Fu Hao into the afterlife were made of bronze. Chinese craftsmen had started working the material in the late eolithic period, but bronze-casting reached a peak of artistry and creativity under the Shang. Metalworkers devised their own techniques, creating clay models into which they cut elaborate decoration and detail. These moulds were prepared in ceramic workshops and so finely finished that little extra work had to be done after the final casting. In this way, Chinese bronze-work can be seen as an ingenious adaptation of the sophisticated techniques used by the New Stone Age potters.

To prepare the bronze itself, lead, tin and copper ore were melted down and purified, then cast into ingots. These were transported in carts to foundries where they were converted to molten bronze. Human, animal or water power was used to work the bellows that kept the fires hot enough for the smelting process.

The social pyramid and work on the production line

From about 1600 BC, ritual bronzes were often mass-produced to meet the huge demand from the Shang royal household and the upper class. By that time, division of labour was firmly established in a society that was organised on strict hierarchical lines. Economic activity was structured with one principal goal in mind: to supply the aristocracy and their ancestors with the tribute of food, ceramics, jade, weapons and tools – not to mention animal and human sacrifices – that they craved.

The ancestor cult was the great undertaking of the Shang Bronze Age. Even so, the living wanted to enjoy their share of luxury in the here and now, and to supply their needs the Shang rulers created a strictly controlled kingdom with a clear order of rank. Beneath the king and his immediate family lay a broad-based stratum of civil servants, military men and civic dignitaries, many of them from clans related, if only distantly, to the Shang line. This ruling establishment formed a tight, interrelated network that helped the inner royal circle to govern.

Influential civil servants supervised work in the royal factories, overseeing the craftsmen who supplied goods for the upper class. In all, there were about 300 of these factory managers keeping an eye on production, checking the quality of the finished goods, planning raw-material requirements, and maintaining records in an early form of bookkeeping to present their accounts to the court.

Thousands of craftsmen and workers in a wide range of professions slaved to satisfy the demands of the upper class. There were shield and flag-makers, jade cutters, carpenters, archivists, scribes, porters, traders, weavers, potters, various specialists in manufacturing and finishing bronze – and executioners. It is assumed that workers passed on the skills of their trade from father to son. Workshops were sited outside the city boundaries to reduce pollution and the risk of fires in residential areas. Labourers lived at their workplaces with their families, under the eye of the supervisors, and were not allowed to leave

Exotic motifs
Shang ritual flagons often had elaborately decorated lids. The crested-bird design on this example was cast using techniques learned from southern China, far from the Shang heartland.

without permission. Food and all the other basic necessities were brought in.

Bronzeworkers occupied a special position because of the high prestige of their craft. They were free to live and work at home, rather than being confined to the underground pits where many other labourers spent their days. But the increasing division of labour also brought disadvantages for them, reducing the amount of control each individual had over the finished product. Their status gradually diminished over the Shang period from that of artist–craftsmen to something more like factory workers.

Farmers and agricultural labourers were also strictly supervised. Teams of workers slaved on the royal estates and those of the nobility in order to supply food for both the living and the dead. The luxurious living standards in the Shang cities rested wholly on their work. They mostly cultivated millet, but wheat and rice were also grown, probably with the help of irrigation. Cattle, sheep, pigs, horses, water buffalo and dogs were reared for food or for sacrifices – some served as draught animals before they were killed.

The art of war

One way that livestock entered the Shang domains was as booty won in military campaigns. The dynasty's rulers waged constant warfare on neighbouring city-states and tribes from the heartland of the North China plain. At least 115 separate vassals, ranging from conquered neighbouring states to semi-independent local rulers, offered tribute to the Shang

Sitting bear
Shang craftsmen produced many decorative jade pieces. Sculpted figures of animals, like this bear, were popular as jewellery and highly favoured as grave goods. Bears were a symbol of strength and courage.

overlords in Yin. Rebellions in the border regions were quickly put down by armies 3000 or even 5000 strong, armed with fearsome bronze arrows, axes and spears, and protected by helmets and shields.

Shang commanders also learned lessons from the mounted nomads to the north, from whom they borrowed the use of horse-drawn chariots. It took the Shang some time to turn the innovation to their advantage: chariots with spoked wheels had to be built, and horses and drivers trained – no easy task, as the charioteers had to learn to steer their bucking vehicles over rough ground in a kneeling posture, with two other warriors on board. In time, however, the chariot companies, organised in five squadrons of five vehicles each, became an important element of Shang military power.

An abrupt end

After the death of Wu Ding and Fu Hao in the 11th century BC, luck seemed to desert the Shang. Their vassal states and one-time allies turned against them, and hostile forces moved steadily closer to the capital, Yin. Stuck in their rigid rounds of hierarchy and ritual, the kings continued to spend more time and energy than they could afford on preparing tombs for themselves. Eventually the important Zhou clan defected, and in about 1050 BC the Zhou chief Wu Wang attacked Yin from the west with a powerful military force. Once across the Huang He river, he destroyed the Shang army, bringing the dynasty to an abrupt and violent end.

The Phoenicians – seafarers and traders

The Phoenicians were unmatched as seafarers and canny traders. They were also responsible for one of the world's most significant cultural developments – the alphabet.

Imagine the scene as a sleek, state-of-the-art Phoenician ship cut slowly through the sea off the southern coast of Sicily, looking for the perfect place to make a landfall. Its crew, seated on their oarsmen's benches, dip and raise their long oars in a hypnotic, harmonised rhythm. Suddenly a cry rings out from the captain as he spots a small offshore island. Here they can set out their goods, and before long the locals, driven by curiosity, would make their way across from the mainland and start to trade with them.

Similar scenarios must have been played out many times in the course of the 2nd millennium BC as resourceful Phoenician traders sought out new markets around the Mediterranean's shores. But who were these merchant venturers, and what drove them to embark on their long, often dangerous voyages?

The Phoenicians formed part of the Semitic Canaanite people, who were indigenous to the Levant – the eastern Mediterranean coastal region. Their homeland was the Lebanese seaboard, where the port of Byblos (today the village of Jubayl, north of Beirut, stands amidst its remains) rose to prominence as early as the 3rd millennium BC,

Under sail
This highly detailed relief from a sarcophagus, now in the Archaeological Museum of Beirut, shows the advanced design of Phoenician cargo ships, rigged out with large sails and steering oars.

establishing close trading relations with Egypt. The main cargo on the Egyptian ships was cedarwood from the Lebanese mountains, which was prized as a building material in the timber-poor Nile Valley.

By the following millennium, other ports such as Tyre, Sidon, Beirut and Ugarit (now in southern Syria) were also engaged in this thriving trade. Many pieces of Egyptian jewellery have been found in Phoenician royal graves, providing clear evidence both of the large profits made by the merchants and of the strong Egyptian influence on the art of the region. For a time in the second half of the millennium Egypt even claimed sovereignty over Phoenician cities.

Eyes to the sea

The layout of the ports followed a set pattern, which was also adopted all around the Mediterranean when the Phoenicians began their push to establish trading colonies. They were situated either on rocky headlands or on offshore islands with sheltered bays suited for the construction of harbour facilities. One important reason for Phoenician

The ruins of Byblos
Byblos, in present-day Lebanon, was one of the ancient world's most important trading ports. The Greeks imported Egyptian papyrus for paper-making through Byblos, and they adopted the city's name as their word for 'book'. In this way, it eventually gave its name to the Bible.

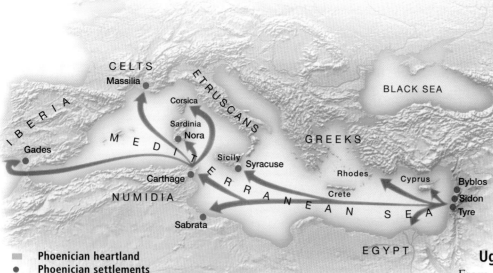

Phoenician heartland
● **Phoenician settlements**
➡ **Trading routes**

since the Phoenicians were the Greeks' arch-rivals for control of the Mediterranean trade routes. Even so, the Greeks never denied that their competitors were formidable traders: '... and the Phoenicians stayed on the island for a whole year, buying and carrying on board untold quantities of goods.'

Ugarit: a centre for trade

From about 1500 BC, Ugarit, on the site of Ras Shamra (near the modern Syrian city of Latakia), became important as the most northerly of the Phoenician ports. It owed its pre-eminence to its favourable position at the meeting place of trade routes to Anatolia, eastern Syria and Mesopotamia. It had a merchant fleet of 150 ships that plied the whole eastern Mediterranean coast, from the southern shores of modern Turkey by way of Cyprus, the Aegean Islands and Crete to Egypt. The city had all the features that were to become characteristic of Phoenician urban centres. Traders and visitors from all over the ancient Near East thronged its streets, among them Hittites, Egyptians, Hurrians from what is now eastern Turkey, and Babylonians.

expansion was the lie of the land in their Levantine homeland itself. Behind the narrow coastal strip rose the Lebanese mountain chain, making further expansion inland impossible, so the Phoenicians could only turn their gaze toward the sea.

Phoenician purple

The term 'Phoenician' can be traced back to the Greek *phoinikis*, used to describe a purple robe. This came from the dye the Phoenicans used to colour the precious textiles that were one of their most sought-after exports. In Greek literature, the Phoenician people were characterised as shifty and unreliable; Homer's *Odyssey* portrays them as treacherous kidnappers. Such depictions were no doubt biased,

International script
This clay tablet from Ugarit bears the state seal of a Hittite king. Cuneiform script was used across the ancient Near East to write down a wide variety of different languages.

The Alphabet

Practical merchants as they were, Phoenicians soon came to realise that writing in complicated hieroglyphs or traditional cuneiform script was not particularly convenient for business purposes. As early as the start of the 2nd millennium BC, an alternative writing system, syllable-based and derived from Egyptian demotic script, was developed in Byblos.

The first true written alphabet, in which every character was represented by a separate

phoneme, was probably invented by Phoenicians in southern Palestine in about 1700 BC, and was similarly based on Egyptian models. This principle was adapted in Ugarit some 200 years later, when the individual curved symbols were replaced by cuneiform characters. This modified cuneiform alphabet disappeared with the city's demise 300 years later. In other Phoenician centres, a modified 22-character alphabet was established by about 1200 BC.

The Greeks adopted this Phoenician script from the 9th century BC onwards, with one crucial alteration. Some of the sounds employed in the Phoenician language did not exist in Greek. Accordingly, the Greeks used the redundant characters representing them to render vowel sounds, which were not written down in Phoenician. The result was a complete alphabet that provided the model for the Latin script that has come down to modern times.

In its workshops, craftsmen fashioned delicately carved ivory tablets to adorn thrones and bed frames, along with precious bowls of chased gold and silver. One surviving example is decorated with an embossed design of a hunter on a war chariot shooting wild boar with arrows.

Ugarit's ruler was a merchant prince, most likely supported (as was later the custom) by a council of influential merchants. In the temples the citizens principally worshipped the gods El and Baal, along with three goddesses Ashera, Astarte and Anat. El was the supreme deity and ruler of heaven; Baal, a weather god who appeared under a number of guises and names, was also the guardian deity of cities. The city-god of Tyre was Melqart, who was worshipped there under the name of Baal Melqart. A stele from Ugarit shows Baal wearing a horned helmet and swinging a cudgel, the symbol for thunder. The goddesses Ashera, Astarte and Anat resembled one another so closely as to be almost indistinguishable. They were primarily fertility and love deities, but Astarte and Anat also had warlike aspects, so war booty was offered up in the temple of Astarte.

Confident merchants

Shortly after 1200 BC, Ugarit was razed to the ground during an invasion by the so-called 'Sea Peoples' and was never reoccupied. Although the other Phoenician ports also suffered during this invasion, they quickly recovered and went on to occupy an even more powerful position than before. The rival cities of Tyre and Sidon now took centre stage, to such an extent that for foreigners the very word 'Phoenician' became synonymous with the inhabitants of the two ports, even though their own citizens generally regarded themselves as Canaanites or identified themselves exclusively with their own home town.

An Egyptian story of about 1100 BC, relating the adventures of an envoy named Wenamun, paints a clear picture of the

self-confidence of the Phoenician merchant princes at the time. Wenamun was despatched to Byblos to purchase timber, needed to build the sacred barge of the Egyptian god Amun. However, his money was stolen at some point en route and he eventually appeared destitute before Zakerbaal, the ruler of Byblos. Even so, he imperiously ordered that the wood be made ready with the words, 'Your father did so, your father's father did so – and so must you!' Zakerbaal responded unambiguously 'I am neither your slave, nor the slave of the man who sent you!' Wenamun only got his wood once he had raised the necessary cash – which tells much about the Phoenicians' way of doing business, not least on their unwillingness to grant credit.

Alien motifs
This winged Sphinx, with its Egyptian-style headdress, is actually a Phoenician product that was found in the treasury of King Ahab of Israel. In Egypt the Sphinx is male, but in the Levant it took on female characteristics.

Mistress of the animals
This ivory box lid, found in the harbour at Ugarit, shows a Minoan or Mycenaean goddess flanked by two mountain goats. It may have been intended for export to Greece.

Opening the Mediterranean to trade

In the wake of the Sea Peoples' incursion, the balance of power in the Near East shifted dramatically, resulting in the partial collapse of the complex trade network that had been built up in the course of the preceding Bronze Age. In their search for new sources of raw materials and fresh markets for their goods, the Phoenicians started, from about 1000 BC onwards, to venture ever westwards along the Mediterranean coastline. Their ships gradually advanced farther and farther along the North African coast, while also making landfalls at Malta, Sicily, Sardinia, the Balearic Islands and on the southern coast of the Iberian peninsula.

To begin with, they did not go far inland; the expeditions were on a small scale and operated from temporary bases.

The main Phoenician move towards colonisation, in which major cities were established, only began in about 800 BC, although ancient sources claim that Cadiz (Gadir in the Phoenician tongue) may have been founded as early as 1100 BC by traders from Tyre.

Advances in seafaring

The cornerstones of Phoenician expansion were shipbuilding and navigation. The seamanship of their mariners was already renowned in antiquity, as were their ship-building skills; they are thought to have been the first people to use the keel, which made their vessels considerably more seaworthy than the flat-bottomed hulls that had previously been used.

The earliest known Phoenician craft was the sleek *pentekontor*, or 'fifty-oar ship', which was about 25m (80ft) long. It was equipped with a mast and a rectangular sail as well as with oars, so that even when the wind dropped it could make steady progress through the efforts of 25 rowers plying their oars galley-like on each side of the vessel. A flute player ensured the oarsmen kept time. The ship's officers – captain, mate and helmsman – completed the crew, along with a ten-man team to hoist and lower the sails. In an emergency, they could cover more than 200km (125 miles) in a 24-hour period. The *pentekontors* were primarily deployed in war and for courier services.

The workhorses of the merchant fleet were broad-beamed cargo ships, around 30m (100ft) long and 7m (23ft) wide, which could transport large consignments of merchandise. These vessels, too, were equipped with a mast and sail; their prows were often decorated with a carved horse's head. They carried a crew of around 20 seamen, and could cover about 100km (60 miles) a day, depending on their cargo.

Because of the high risk of shipwreck, commercial shipping only put to sea between March and October. In general, even the experienced Phoenicians preferred to stay in sight of the coast in order to seek shelter in case of storms, and at nightfall they liked to drop anchor off an island or in the lee of a promontory. Even so, they occasionally ventured on open-sea routes where all sight of land was lost. At night on these voyages they navigated by Ursa Minor, which contains the Pole Star; in ancient times, this constellation was known in their honour as the Phoenician Star.

The luxury trade

Trading voyages to little-known lands far across the sea were costly ventures that had to be financed either by the king, the temple or by rich ship-owners. The principal Phoenician export commodities were precious purple textiles dyed with a substance extracted from two species of snail, *Murex trunculus* and *Murex brandaris*, which at that time were found in abundance along the Phoenician coast. Other sought-after goods included cedarwood furniture inlaid with ivory, chased silver, bronze and gold dishes, brightly coloured glass vessels, fabrics, jewellery and weapons.

In exchange, foreign ships docked each day in the Phoenician ports bringing goods from across the Mediterranean world. From Cyprus came copper and from Anatolia tin; Spain supplied silver as well as more copper, Egypt sent linen and papyrus, while from the African interior came gold, ivory and precious stones.

If they were attacked, the Phoenician cities defended their independence fiercely but, because their only interest was in trade, they harboured no territorial ambitions of their own. As a result, they were at pains to foster good relations with the rulers of neighbouring empires. In the last quarter of the 2nd millennium BC, Assyria consolidated its supremacy over

EVERYDAY LIFE

The luxury of ivory

Ivory carving was an important part of Phoenician craftsmanship. Tablets made as open-work artefacts or carved reliefs were used to decorate furniture or walls, sometimes in combination with materials such as glass, precious stones or gold leaf. Phoenician craftsmen also produced little ivory boxes, crafted in similar fashion. The influence of the Aegean world and of Egypt is evident in the motifs employed: sphinxes and gryphons feature alongside small palm trees and human figures. Much sought-after as trade goods, or as war booty, these artefacts have been found in Assyrian palaces and throughout the Middle East.

northern Syria, and in the course of one campaign the Assyrian King Tiglath-Pileser I (1114–1076 BC) advanced as far as the Phoenician coast. The Phoenicians diplomatically welcomed him, and the ruler noted in his victory inscription: 'I arrived on Mount Lebanon. I had cedar trees felled and carried off to build the Temples of Anu and Adad... I received tribute from Byblos, Sidon, and Arados... I made the crossing from Arados, which lies on the coast, to Symira in the land of Amurru on board ships from Arados...'. In the course of this last voyage, the king used a harpoon to slay 'a nahiru, which they call a sea-horse' – perhaps a dolphin.

King Hiram of Tyre (969–936 BC) also maintained good relations with his neighbours, judging from the Old Testament Book of Kings, which tells how he supplied King Solomon of Israel with building timber and craftsmen for the Temple at Jerusalem. Solomon, in return, provided him with wheat and olive oil.

However, this was not the limit of the two monarch's cooperation. Solomon dispatched ships, built and manned by Phoenicians, from the Red Sea port of Ezion-Geber to the land of Ophir, most likely modern Yemen or Somalia. According to the Biblical account, the expedition took three years, and the voyagers returned with gold, silver, ivory, sandalwood, precious stones and monkeys. At the time the Phoenicians still enjoyed undisputed dominance in long-distance trade, but their monopoly of the sea routes would increasingly be challenged by the Greeks in the centuries to come.

Lord of the weather
This bronze statuette of the storm god Baal shows him with one arm raised, ready to hurl a bolt of lightning.

Philistines and Israelites – the struggle for Palestine

Starting out as an insignificant band of nomads, the Israelites fought to establish a homeland for themselves in Canaan. Before long they were strong enough to take on the feared Philistines, and succeeded in founding the first Hebrew kingdom.

King David – a royal musician
A detail from a floor mosaic shows David, who became king of Judah and Israel after Saul, charming wild beasts by playing the harp. Dating from late classical times, the image comes from the synagogue at Gaza.

As early as 1950 BC, Palestine had been seen as a land of plenty: 'It was a fine land… There were figs and vines there, wine flowed in greater abundance than water, and it was rich in honey and oil. All manner of fruit grew on its trees. There was barley and wheat, and any number of cattle…' According to Biblical tradition, the Israelites had just such a vision in mind when they left Egypt with Moses at their head 600 years later, setting off in search of the Promised Land.

For the Semitic nomads who since Middle Kingdom times had journeyed to graze their herds on the fringes of the fertile Nile Delta, the rich land of Egypt must have seemed like a paradise at times. The Egyptians, who adopted a mostly tolerant attitude to the migrants, knew them as *apiru*; the Babylonians had a similar term, *hapiru*, which they used to denote foreigners who earned a living as labourers or mercenaries. Anglicised, both terms equate to the Biblical 'Hebrew'.

In Egyptian texts from the time of Pharaoh Rameses II (*c.*1279–1212 BC), *apiru* are mentioned as undertaking construction work on royal building projects. The reference obviously recalls the Biblical story of the Hebrews' servitude in Egypt, although it still remains uncertain whether the *apiru* of the text and the Biblical Hebrews were in fact the same people. However, it is certainly historically possible that a group of just such migrant labourers fled into the wilderness of Sinai under an Egyptian-born leader named Moses around the middle of the 13th century BC. They would have had good reason to make a detour into the desert to avoid the border guards policing the main coastal route, who would otherwise have arrested them.

From Sinai the wandering tribes made their way to Palestine, arriving in separate groups at different times. There, in the highlands to the west of the River Jordan, they joined with other nomadic people of Aramaic origin who had come from the east. In this mountainous region the Israelites initially went unmolested, settling the land in twelve separate tribes. This peaceful situation does not seem to have lasted for long. The first non-Biblical mention of 'Israel' occurs on a stele of Rameses' successor Merneptah (1212–1202 BC), who briefly reasserted Egyptian control over Palestine: 'The princes have been vanquished and sue for peace! Canaan, with all its wickedness, has been conquered; Ashkelon has been led off into captivity…Israel has been made barren and brings forth no more seed…'

This depiction of Solomon's temple in Jerusalem is part of a series of wall frescoes created in the 3rd century BC for the synagogue of Dura-Europos in Syria. It is now in the National Museum in Damascus.

Egyptian overlords
This Egyptian relief shows Canaanites and Libyans pleading for mercy following the Egyptian conquest of their lands in the 13th century BC. They were obliged to pay tribute to the pharaohs of Egypt's New Kingdom.

Settling in Palestine

Palestine was divided at the time between a number of independent Canaanite city-states. Each one was centred on a fortified capital, strategically located to dominate the surrounding villages, whose people tended the fields and raised livestock to keep the citizens fed. Within three or four decades of Pharaoh Merneptah's reign, however, the Sea Peoples descended on the coast. These migrating tribes, who were probably also responsible for the collapse of Mycenaean Greece and the Hittite realm in Anatolia, swept into Palestine, putting an end to the Egyptian presence and challenging the Canaanite city-states. One group, the Philistines, settled the southern coastal lands, having come to an understanding with their Egyptian neighbours. There they formed a confederation of five cities: Gaza, Ashkelon, Ashdod, Ekron and Gath.

Even in their inland mountain retreats the Israelites were not unscathed by the turmoil. They now found themselves facing a complex and challenging political situation, in which they were vying for land not just with the newcomers but also with earlier Canaanite settlers. While their initial arrival in Palestine may have passed off peacefully, conflicts now began to erupt and the Israelites found themselves at a disadvantage. The Bible tells of their strategies to overcome this: surprise attacks, espionage, subterfuge and secret incursions into the Canaanite cities.

These methods were essential as the Israelites could not engage in battle on the plain, where the Canaanites and Philistines had an inbuilt military advantage. The Old Testament points out that their armed forces were equipped with war-chariots, which the Israelites could not match.

A unifying faith

The key factor uniting the twelve tribes of Israel was their belief in the god Yahweh, or Jehovah. The concept of Yahweh probably started as a local deity from the Sinai region, adopted by the Israelites as a patron in the course of their wanderings in the desert. As was customary with nomads, they prepared a mobile shrine for their god, housing it in a special tent; this wooden receptacle became famous as the Ark of the Covenant.

In their first years in Palestine, the Israelites were strongly influenced by Canaanite religion, identifying Yahweh with El, an indigenous sky god, or with the weather god Baal. They were also influenced by local customs in constructing the Tabernacle to house the Ark of the Covenant, endowing it with *massebas* – ritual standing stones that derived from an ancient fertility cult. The Tabernacle is thought to have originally been located in the town of Sichem, but it was moved several times before finding a permanent home in a specially built temple at Shiloh.

At this time the Israelites were still divided into tribes, whose chiefs were supported by councils of elders. In times of crisis, the people turned for help to temporary leaders known as 'judges'; these individuals have given their name to an entire era of Israelite history between 1200 and 1020 BC, the so-called ' Time of the Judges'. They were not judges in the modern sense of the term – the judiciary in fact played a subordinate role – but

rather were military and political commanders, probably elected for a specified term at meetings of the tribal chiefs held in the Tabernacle. Famous judges included Ehud, Gideon and Deborah; her election shows that women could occupy high office at the time, perhaps reflecting the influence of the priestesses who played an influential role in Canaanite society.

During Deborah's term of office, the Israelites won a decisive victory over the king of Hazor and his general, Sisera, at Mount Tabor. Gradually, the Israelites were carving out a secure power base for themselves in Palestine.

The struggle for power

Yet the battle-hardened Philistines remained the Israelites' principal foe. They owed their strength partly to overseas trade, which enabled them to import the materials needed to produce armaments. By the late 2nd millennium BC, iron had begun to supplant bronze as the metal used for weapons and tools, and the Philistines, thanks to their network of foreign contacts, quickly learned how to work it. In contrast the Israelites, cut off from the coast, had neither the ores nor the expertise needed to match their skills.

And so the Israelites found themselves facing their most formidable challenge. The Philistines were well armed, with an elite chariot force drawn from the ranks of the aristocracy. They had quickly adjusted to their new homeland, even adopting the cult of the Canaanite god Dagon. They had won control over several Canaanite towns and extended their rule into the interior. It was only a matter of time before the two peoples found themselves at war.

The two armies finally met in about 1050 BC at Ebenezer, near the modern city of Jaffa. The lightly armed Israelite forces stood no chance against the Philistine chariots and were duly routed. The Philistines even captured the Ark of the Covenant, which the Israelites had

TIME WITNESS

How accurate is the Bible?

The Biblical Old Testament is our only written source for the early history of the Israelites. The oldest section is the Pentateuch, consisting of the Books of Moses – Genesis, Exodus, Leviticus, Numbers and Deuteronomy. It contains the most ancient oral and written traditions, possibly dating back to before 1000 BC.

The earliest parts of the Old Testament were probably written down by about 900 BC, with other books being added over the next 400 years or so. The various parts were finally brought together in the last centuries of the pre-Christian era. As a result, the Biblical account of early events – particularly those that occurred between 1200 and 900 BC – must be read with a degree of caution as the written text is not contemporaneous with the events or deeds it describes. Even so, the Old Testament is believed often to accurately portray the conditions prevalent at this time.

For the period after 950 BC, much of the information in the Old Testament has been borne out by non-Biblical sources, such as archaeological discoveries.

Sacred smoke
The Israelites burned incense during religious ceremonies in earthenware vessels like this one. The tall, hollow bases pierced with holes encouraged the circulation of air.

carried with them into battle, taking it in triumph to Dagon's temple in Ashdod. To add insult to injury, they raided the Tabernacle at Shiloh, which they looted and destroyed. The whole of western Palestine was by now firmly under Philistine control.

The Israelites responded to the crisis with a new-found show of unity, coming together under a single ruler. In about 1020 BC, Saul from the tribe of Benjamin, was anointed as their leader, to general acclaim. Saul scored some initial successes over the Ammonites in the east, and even managed to expel the Philistines from a few areas, among them his own home town of Gidea. He raised a small standing army and surrounded himself with a close circle of warriors, among them his sword and shield-bearer David. But as Saul grew older, the support he had at first enjoyed started to wane and he also fell out with David. Against this discouraging backdrop, a Philistine counter-offensive was not long in coming. The two armies met at the foot of Mount Gilboa, near Jezreel. This time the Israelites were vanquished and Saul and his sons were killed.

A warrior king

After the split with Saul, David raised a guerrilla band of outlaws and adventurers and took to the hills. He lived by raiding and extortion, honing his fighting skills. At one point he even offered his services to the Philistines, but they were suspicious of his motives and rejected the offer. At the same time he courted the leaders of the southern tribes with gifts. The strategy paid off when they elected him King of Judah in the year after Saul's death. A short time later, he persuaded the northern tribes to acknowledge him as their ruler, too, and reigned jointly over Judah and Israel.

The Philistines immediately declared war, but David was familiar with their fighting methods and now had at his command a tried and tested fighting force made up of well-armed, battle-hardened professionals. So he was able to drive the enemy back to their original borders. These victories, which had begun even while Saul was still alive, provided the background to his legendary confrontation with the Philistine champion, Goliath.

For his new base, David chose Jerusalem, located at the time in the territory of the Jebusites. He conquered the city and established it as his capital. With its officials and court, Jerusalem outwardly resembled the centres of government of neighbouring Canaanite princes; even the palace was constructed with the help of craftsmen from the Phoenician city of Tyre. David's personal bodyguard consisted of a cosmopolitan collection of mercenaries, some from the Philistine lands and others from even farther afield in the eastern Mediterranean.

To consolidate his grip on the throne, David had the Ark of the Covenant – which had evidently been returned to the Israelites, or perhaps a new one made – brought to Jerusalem in a solemn procession: 'Thus did David and all the people of Israel carry the Ark of the Lord up to the Temple amid loud jubilation and the blowing of the ram's horn'.

Yet the lives of ordinary people were little changed under the new regime – they tilled the land and tended livestock as they had always done. The typical

Israelite dwelling was a square house of air-dried mudbricks with several rooms and a colonnaded inner courtyard. A calendar based on a lunar month of 29½ days marked the passage of the year. Small tablets carved from bone, indented with three rows of 10 holes each, helped people to count off the passing days.

Through his military campaigns David turned Israel into a significant regional power, extending its grip over the neighbouring Ammonites and Moabites and the Aramaic state of Damascus. In temperament, the king showed himself to be pragmatic and sometimes ruthless; the Old Testament records how he sent the Hittite mercenary leader Uriah (Urija) to a certain death so that he could have Uriah's wife.

King Solomon's peace

On David's death in about the year 965 BC, his son Solomon acceded to the throne. A ruler in the oriental mould who loved pomp and ceremony, the new king set about reaping the benefits of his predecessors' rule. He maintained good relations with his neighbours while also fostering contacts with far-flung regions, recorded in the celebrated visit to his court of the Queen of Sheba – probably Saba, in modern Yemen.

Solomon quickly built up the bureaucracy and put the population at large to work on a massive building programme. In cities all around the country, among them Hazor, Megiddo and Gezer, palaces and fortifications were refurbished and grain warehouses, stables and chariot-making foundries were set up.

The magnificence of Solomon's own residence in Jerusalem – called 'The House of the Forest of Lebanon' – was surpassed only by that of the huge new temple he commissioned on a rocky outcrop that later became known as the Temple Mount. The temple was built over a period of several years under the supervision of master-builders sent by King Hiram of Tyre.

Solomon's name has come down through history as a byword for wisdom, and yet Old Testament accounts of his reign indicate that his extravagance and the ostentatious splendour of his court tried his subjects' patience. Towards the

end of his reign, his policy of using forced labour on building projects sparked open revolt against his rule. Fresh trouble broke out after his death in 926 BC, and the unified monarchy collapsed. The kingdom divided once more into the separate states of Israel and Judah.

Goddess of fertility
These tiny, full-bosomed statuettes of the Canaanite goddess Astarte were found on the coastal plain of Palestine where the Philistines lived. Made of clay in the 8th century BC, they stand less than 15cm (6in) high.

The peopling of the earth

The human race almost certainly originated in East Africa, where our australopithecine ancestors are known to have lived at least 6 million years ago. The genus *Homo* made its first appearance around 2 million years ago. Not long afterwards, groups of hominids started to fan out from their African homeland in search of new food sources. These early migrants from the species *Homo erectus* are thought to have reached Southeast Asia via the Near East, and they may also have penetrated southern Europe.

A wide-branching family tree

A second wave of migration began about 800,000 years ago. As the early humans adapted to their new homes and to the various environmental and climatic conditions that they found, different subspecies and races developed, among them Java Man, Peking Man and, in Europe, *Homo heidelbergensis* and the Neanderthal race.

The rise of *Homo sapiens*

Meanwhile, in Africa, a new type of human evolved – one that would eventually spread out across the globe and supplant all the others. *Homo sapiens sapiens*, the modern human race, dates back to about 100,000 years ago. About 40,000 years ago the species reached central Europe and had arrived in Australia. America was the last continent to be populated – by settlers crossing from Asia via the Bering land bridge. The success of *Homo sapiens sapiens* in displacing all its rivals is due to the species' greater mental capacity and, in particular, its complex language skills.

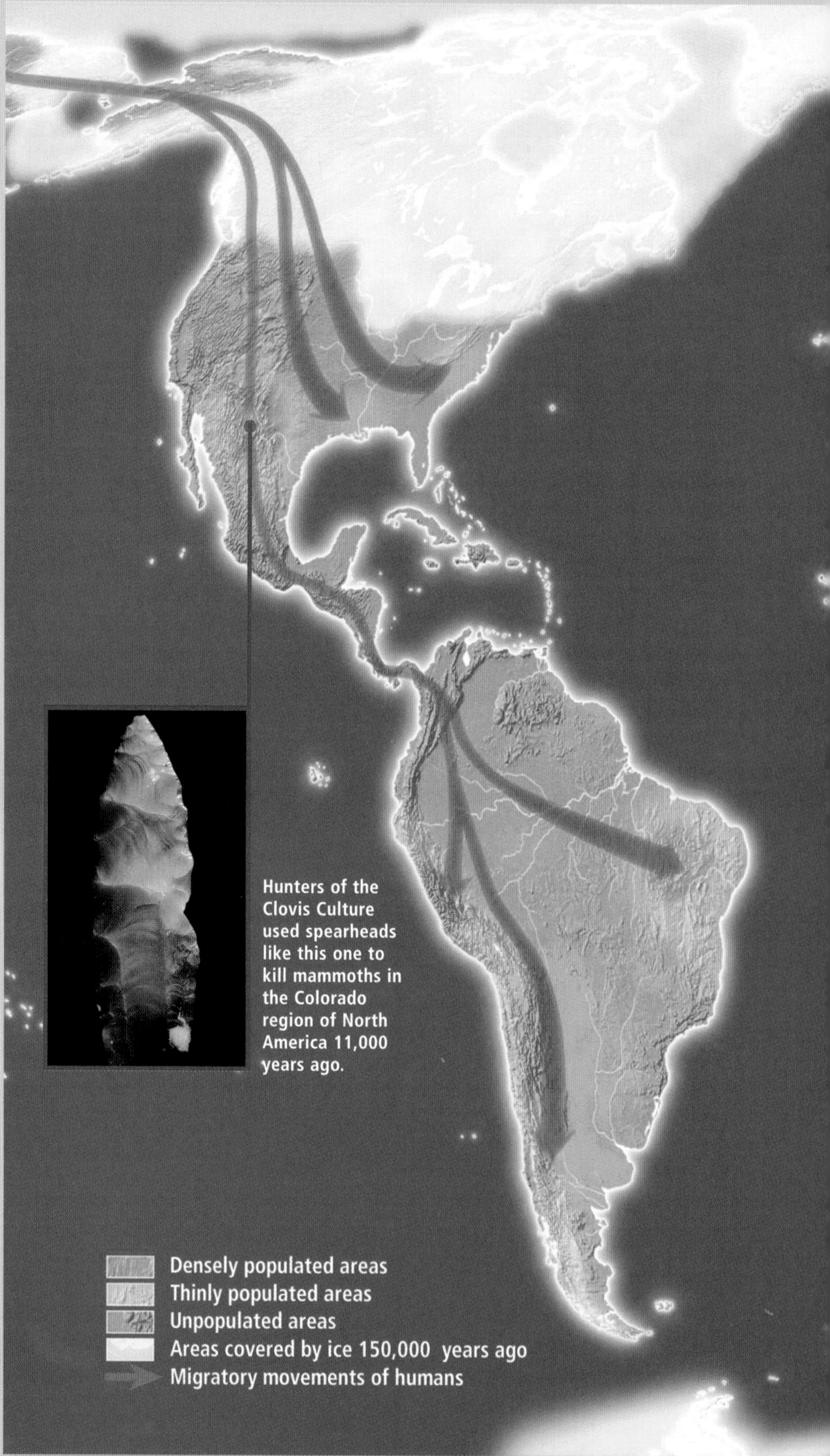

Hunters of the Clovis Culture used spearheads like this one to kill mammoths in the Colorado region of North America 11,000 years ago.

Densely populated areas
Thinly populated areas
Unpopulated areas
Areas covered by ice 150,000 years ago
Migratory movements of humans

Humans shaped the first sculptures out of clay. This bison, found in a cave in southern France, was made in about 15,000 BC.

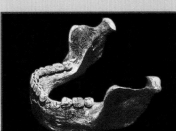

The earliest human remains found in northern Europe, including this *Homo heidelbergensis* jawbone, are about 600,000 years old.

Java Man belonged to the species *Homo erectus*. This skull dates back to about 600,000 years ago.

This australo-pithecine skull is 2.5 million years old. Such early hominids are considered the forerunners of *Homo sapiens*, the modern human race.

From about 12,000 years ago, aboriginal artists in Australia produced silhouetted hand images by spraying pigment onto and around the backs of hands pressed palm down on a rock surface.

First steps to art

The bison was one of the main prey animals targeted by hunters in Europe.

Over the course of evolution, the hominid line became distinguished from the anthropoid apes by its upright stance, vocal chords and increased brain capacity.

Human culture took a giant step forward in the latter part of the Old Stone Age, from about 40,000 to 10,000 years ago. This was a time when humans were beginning to shape the environment they lived in, and as they did so they began to feel a need to express themselves through art.

Art seems to have been an exclusive preserve of *Homo sapiens sapiens*. The number of works produced increased dramatically in the course of the last Ice Age as the ancestors of modern humans spread out around the world. The rock drawings and engravings they created still have a powerful impact today, as do the small human and animal figurines that the first sculptors carved out of mammoth ivory.

Community backing

Prehistory specialists believe that the early artworks had a magical purpose: by painting or sculpting the animal world, people may have hoped to ensure successful hunts, for example, or promote fertility and abundance. Some 17,000 years ago, in the caves of Lascaux in central France, talented Stone Age artists created stunning images of large game animals in vivid shades of ochre. The pictures cover the walls to a height of 6m (20ft) and show a keen eye for anatomical detail. Presumably, only specialist craftsmen, supported and fed by an entire community, would have had the time to develop their talents to create such works.

The growth of trade

A love of jewellery and ornament developed alongside the taste for art. Early humans bored holes in animal teeth and shells and strung them together to make necklaces and pendants. Such objects were often bartered over long distances, proving that different groups were already in contact and trading with one another.

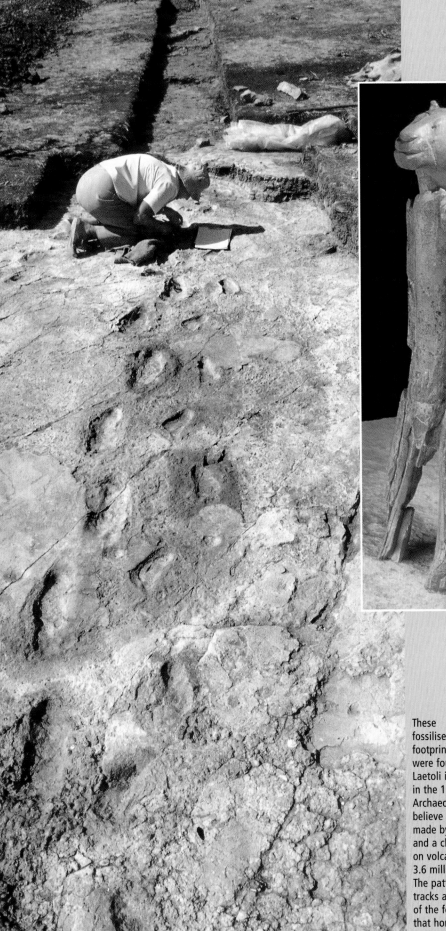

This ivory carving of a lion-man was found in the Swabian Alps, in the German province of Baden-Württemberg. It counts among the world's oldest sculptures, dating back about 30,000 years.

Approximately 25,000 years old, this female figure carved of mammoth ivory probably served as a ritual object for a fertility cult during the Palaeolithic period (the Old Stone Age). The massively exaggerated breasts and buttocks symbolised the fertility of the natural world and Mother Earth.

These fossilised footprints were found near Laetoli in Tanzania in the 1970s. Archaeologists believe they were made by two adults and a child walking on volcanic ash some 3.6 million years ago. The pattern of the tracks and shape of the footsteps show that hominids were walking fully upright by that time.

Fire – a necessity for survival

Hominids were working knapped stone fragments with sharp edges as early as 2.5 million years ago. The tools were used for cutting and scraping.

Prehistoric craftsmen made these leaf-shaped flint tools in the Thuringia region of central Germany some 30,000 years ago.

The symmetrical shape of this carefully worked hand axe was the result of careful planning and specialist skill. The development of such utensils, about 1.5 million years ago, marked a huge step forward in tool-making and made jobs like cutting up meat and severing tough skin or fibres much easier.

Along with the use of tools, the greatest achievement of early humans was the mastery of fire. The earliest archaeological clues that demonstrate the use of fire are the remains of charred bones found in Africa. These were found near some tools used by early hominids, probably of the *Homo erectus* species, that date from more than a million years ago. Initially, humans probably obtained fire by tending kindling that had been set alight naturally – by lightning strikes, for example – and by carefully preserving burning embers from one fire to the next. Gradually, they would have learned to make fire for themselves as required, with the aid of tinder and flints.

The first cooked food

Control of fire gave *Homo erectus* new ways of manipulating the environment. Flaming branches could be used to chase dangerous animals away from campsites – or to chase prey towards a trap. By cooking their food, early humans expanded their diet and increased their nutrient consumption. Not only were cooked meats and grains easier to digest, the heat also destroyed toxins and parasites. Smoked or dried meat could be kept for much longer than raw flesh, and could be available as a reserve in times when fresh game was scarce.

Campfire gatherings

Artificially created heat allowed humans to expand their geographical horizons, opening up regions that were previously uninhabitable because of the cold climate. Fire also had an important social function. A carefully tended hearth became the focus of every campsite – the place where the tribe gathered to share food, to tell stories and to exchange gossip. In this way, fire became one of the foundations of human social development.

Humans have been using heat to harden and fire ceramic vessels since at least 7000 BC.

About 12,000 years ago people were making awls and needles from the antlers of animals.

Hunting for food

In common with lions and other predators, hominids in savannah regions often ambushed prey at waterholes. They kept a close eye on the migratory movements and behaviour of their quarry, and concentrated on individuals that were easy to separate from the herd and – especially in the case of hippos or elephants – could be picked off without too much risk to the hunters themselves.

A prehistoric artist carved this stylised mammoth from an animal's shoulder-blade, shaping it according to the natural form of the bone. The mammoth's curved tusk can be seen beneath the hole bored to represent an eye.

Fish-tail daggers fashioned from flint were common in the Neolithic period (the New Stone Age). The narrowed handle made the tool much easier to grip and use.

These spearheads were carved out of animal bones about 30,000 years ago. The points were then inserted into long wooden shafts.

The availability of game animals was essential in drawing people into previously uninhabited regions. While the earliest hominids had a mainly vegetarian diet supplemented by occasional finds of carrion, their successors were forced to adapt to meat-eating by climate changes that caused increased drought and the spread of savannah grasslands. *Homo erectus* increasingly looked to hunting to provide a regular supply of food. Some have argued that the higher protein diet obtained through more meat consumption – as well as the greater culinary variety made possible by fire – probably contributed to the larger brain capacity of the species. At the same time, however, the honing of hunting tactics as they learned to pursue game in a planned way would have served to develop mental faculties.

The first weapons

Soon *Homo erectus* was using weapons as hunting aids, and was no longer so reliant on physical strength and endurance to capture prey. The earliest wooden spears date back about 400,000 years, suggesting that hominids were already skilled big-game hunters by that time. Using javelins up to 2.5m (8ft) long, they could bring down wild horses, forest rhinoceroses, forest elephants and bears. By that time, if not earlier, hominids were also catching fish.

Reaping the benefits of cooperation

Homo erectus also used missiles and stones for hunting, and brandished flaming torches to drive entire herds of animals into marshes and ravines. Such techniques could only be employed by groups of hunters working together. The need for cooperation encouraged early humans to live in larger groups, which, in turn, could only be fed by large-scale communal hunts. In this way, hunting fostered social cohesion, communication and strategic thinking.

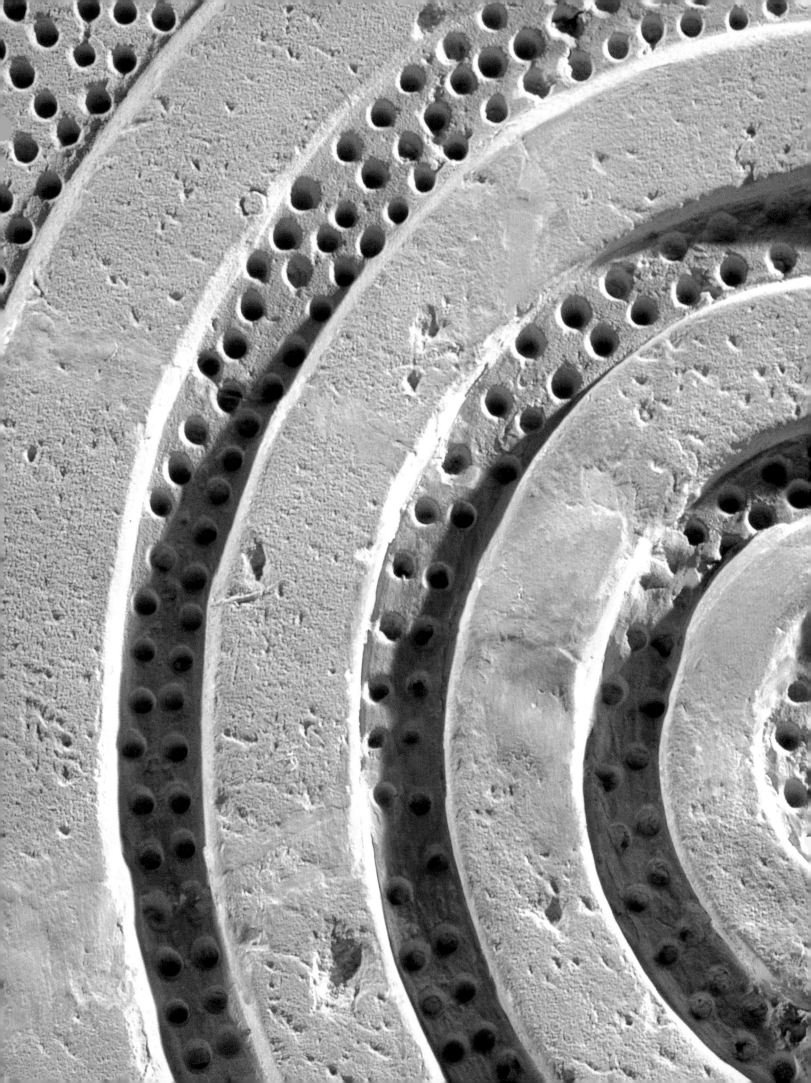

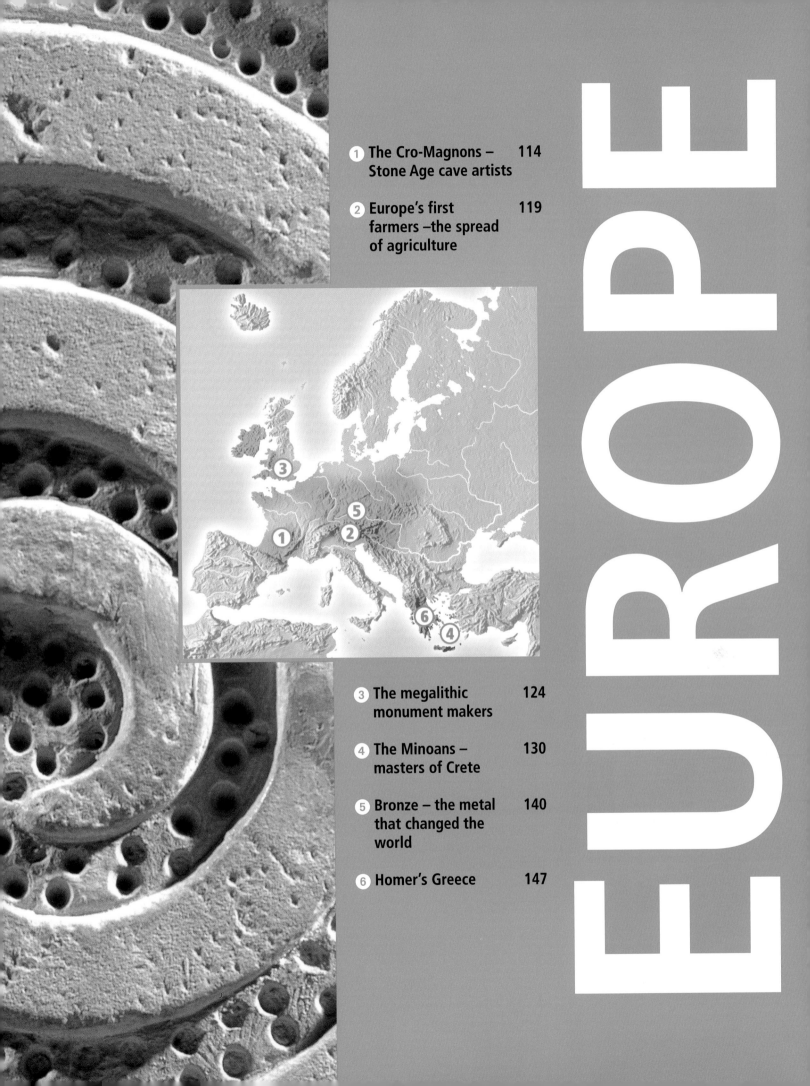

EUROPE

The Cro-Magnons – Stone Age cave artists

Our Stone Age forebears settled into new living spaces in southern Europe, where they began creating masterful cave paintings and exquisite sculptures – the earliest known art in the history of mankind.

Portrait from the past
Carved in mammoth ivory, this tiny female head from the French Pyrenees is about 25,000 years old, making it one of the earliest known depictions of the human face.

The artist laid down his brush, his task complete. For hours he had been perched on a ledge high up the side of a cave, painting by the flickering light from a torch. Now he took a good long look at the results of his labours. He was well satisfied with what he saw: the ochre-coloured bulls looked almost alive. Carefully but contentedly he clambered down to the cave floor, gathered up his utensils and left the cave.

Scenes similar to this must have taken place many times in what is now southwestern France and northern Spain, the centre of European cave art some 20,000 years ago. The artists were direct forebears of modern humans; all belonged to the species *Homo sapiens* rather than to the co-existent Neanderthal race. They and their peers are sometimes referred to as Cro-Magnons, after a cave in the Dordogne region of southwestern France in which their remains were first discovered in 1868.

The Cro-Magnon people had strong, well-muscled bodies, and from skeleton remains we know that some of them grew up to 1.8m (6ft) tall. They had considerably larger brains than the Neanderthals, and a high, narrow skull. Their skin was relatively light, the better to absorb the weak sunlight of these northern latitudes, which was essential for the production of vitamin D.

The ancestors of the Cro-Magnons had left Africa some 80,000 years earlier, moving across the Near and Middle East into Europe and Asia. Some groups had migrated to the Black Sea and from there up the River Danube into present-day Austria and the Swabian Alps. By about 40,000 years ago, their descendants had settled along the Mediterranean coastline of present-day France and Spain.

Masterpieces on cave walls

The chief legacy of these Old Stone Age peoples is their impressive art. Surviving examples include cave paintings in northern Spain – at Altamira, for example – and in southwestern France at such sites as Lascaux and Chauvet. They also carved human and animal figures out of mammoth ivory. Their small, portable statuettes have been found in southern France, in the Swabian Alps, near the Austrian town of Willendorf, and at Dolni Vestonice in the Czech Republic.

The first signs that the Cro-Magnon people left of their presence were simple palm and fingerprints imprinted on rock faces about 40,000 years ago. They graduated to line drawings and symbols scratched onto the walls of limestone caves, which were possibly meant to represent animal tracks. Soon afterwards the first pictures of animals appeared, usually of horses, bison or reindeer. Later, and far less often, humans were also

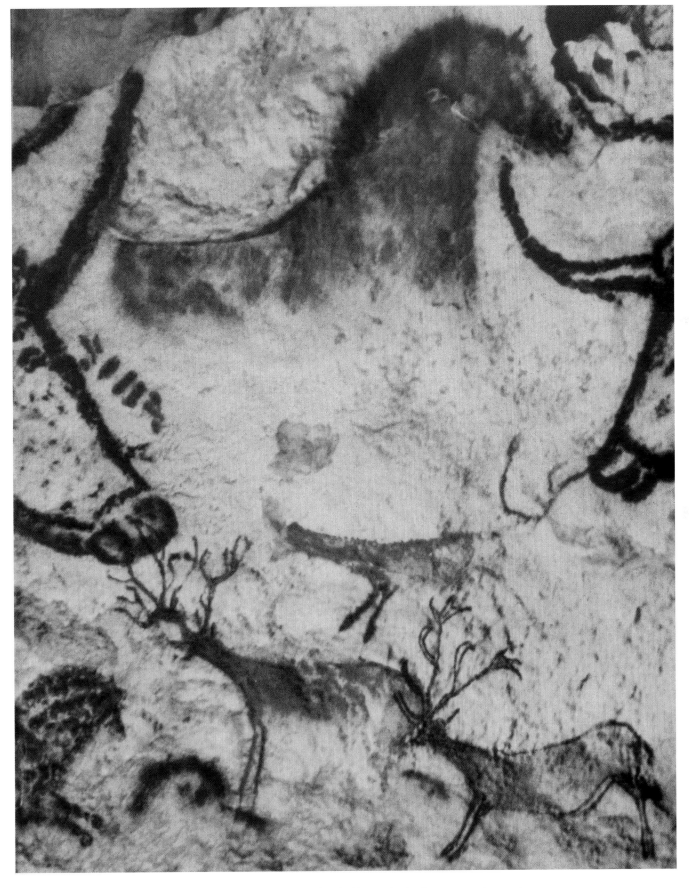

These stags in the cave of Lascaux in southwestern France were painted with over-sized antlers — no-one knows why.

Bringing animals to life
Paintings in Cro-Magnon caves reflected the wildlife of the surrounding region. Artists at Altamira in Spain mostly depicted bison, like the magnificent creature above.

depicted. The drawings, which are often astonishingly graceful and elegant, were done in a variety of different styles. The contours could be hard or soft; some are naturalistic in their representation of animals, while others are stylised; surface areas could be filled out in different ways.

Many of the animals were multi-coloured, and occasionally contours were created by applying colours of varying strengths. The results could be startlingly true to life. Even now, it is hard for people viewing the 300 or so images drawn and scratched into the limestone walls of the cave at Altamira in northern Spain to believe that these works are tens of thousands of years old.

A broad palette
The cave artists had a wide range of colours at their disposal. They obtained black from carbonised ivory, bone or wood; white from limestone; and green and blue from minerals. Burnt ochre yielded many variations of yellow and red. Most of the pigments were crushed and ground into a fine powder with the aid of grinding stones, then mixed with binding substances containing fats. They applied

the colours to the rock walls with their fingers, with spatulas, or with brushes made of hair or bits of fur.

Symbols of early religion?
Scholars still argue about the significance of the paintings. They seem to have been intended as something more than simple decoration, for most of the caves where they were created were not lived in. In addition to animal and hunting scenes, thought to be about 16,000 years old, the famous Lascaux cave in the Dordogne region of France contains enigmatic signs and symbols that probably indicate that the cave had some kind of religious significance. Further support for this view comes from the relatively inaccessible location of many of the paintings, which are often hidden in nooks and crannies in the rock; some can only be reached via a complicated system of underground passageways. Very often, the artists would have had to paint them lying flat on their backs, or supporting themselves against a rock wall, or they may have used an early form of scaffolding.

Some of the most puzzling paintings show humans wrapped in animal furs and wearing horns or animal masks on their heads. Researchers have not ruled out the possibility that Cro-Magnon hunters may have camouflaged themselves in this way when pursuing big game. Another possible explanation is that the figures represent shamans – intermediaries between the human and spirit worlds, who may have played a significant part in the religious life of Stone Age peoples. It has also been argued that the images themselves had a magical significance, and that the people who painted them were trying to influence the outcome of the hunt.

Everyday life in the Stone Age

To appreciate the achievement of the Cro-Magnon artists, it is necessary to remember the conditions in which they lived. The early migrants from Africa would have found a generally inclement climate in Ice Age Europe. Life was hard and full of privations, and most people must have been too concerned with the daily struggle for survival to have much time for art. The Mediterranean area where the Cro-Magnon communities flourished enjoyed relatively favourable conditions, with summer temperatures averaging around 15°C (59°F) – higher than anywhere else in Europe at the time. There was a rich variety of game available, which could be supplemented by fish from the local rivers and, for people living near the coast, by shellfish.

The Cro-Magnons were nomadic hunter-gatherers, like all the world's early Stone Age people. They lived in caves, in simple tents or in shelters constructed under rock overhangs. The Cro-Magnon area of southern France and northern Spain was well provided with limestone caves, yet they seem rarely to have used these as permanent dwellings – even if they may have occasionally sought shelter and protection in them during winter months.

Weapons and tools

In addition to creating works of art, the Cro-Magnons used their resourcefulness and intelligence to develop new tools and weapons. They perfected a special flint-knapping technique to produce extremely sharp flint blades, knives and spear heads. They fashioned stone chisels and various kinds of scrapers, and they improved on the traditional methods of working bone to make sharp-pointed awls and needles, which were used to sew clothes and tents out of animal skins. For thread they used tendons, dried gut, or thinly cut strips of leather. To prepare the furs and skins they used to make clothing, they would have used flint scrapers to strip the animal pelts of their fat, and then probably tanned them, perhaps using animal brain tissue or other substances.

Better hunting equipment

The Cro-Magnons also devoted considerable ingenuity to improving their hunting equipment. About 15,000 years ago they developed an extremely effective barbed bone harpoon that was not just useful for catching fish but could also be hurled by hunters from a spear-thrower to bring down big game such as reindeer, elk, wild cattle, bears and stags.

The invention of the bow and arrow was another important milestone. Early bows were made from boughs of yew, ash, pine or elm cut from the surrounding forests. They were strung with plant fibres, animal tendons or plaited gut. The arrows had flint heads, attached to smoothed wooden shafts. Meat from the slaughtered animals was eaten either raw or roasted over an open fire; so far, no vessels that might have been used for boiling or stewing food have been found.

Cro-Magnon people obtained most of their calories and protein from meat, but their diet also included tubers, berries,

An early relief
Cro-Magnon artists also created animal sculptures on rock walls. This hyena, crouched and ready to spring, was found in the cave of La Madeleine in southern France.

Figures of fertility

Mostly made from ivory or stone, the so-called 'Venus' figurines found at sites across Europe are between 27,000 and 18,000 years old. Unlike the realistic animal sculptures created by cave artists, the Venus figurines are highly stylized, with huge breasts, bulging buttocks and fat thighs. In most cases the head, arms and legs are only tentatively indicated, while the feet are missing altogether. Generally taken to represent pregnant women, the figures may have been credited with magical qualities in association with some sort of fertility cult. Their extreme voluptuousness – even obesity – is in marked contrast to early statuettes found in Siberia, which are characterized by their slender forms.

Venus of Willendorf
This carved limestone figure gets its name from where it was found – near the village of Willendorf in Austria. It stands just 11cm (4.3in) tall.

fruits and nuts. They may also have harvested wild grains and seeds, which could be ground up and mixed with water to create a doughlike paste; this could be baked as flat loaves on heated stones or in the hot ash of the campfire.

Art and fire

Campfires may have stimulated another breakthrough discovery that would have important repercussions for Cro-Magnon artists. At some early point, people must have noticed that the scorched loess soil beneath the hearths of their campfires always hardened into a solid mass. Someone, somewhere, then had the brilliant idea of using fire to bake small clay statuettes, like those found at Dolni Vestonice in the Czech Republic. The Dolni Vestonice sculptures were formed out of clay-like loess and fired like pottery – or at least heated to a temperature high enough to enable them to survive for more than 25,000 years. Cro-Magnon artists also made small figurines of bone, stone, wood and mammoth ivory. They took their subject-matter from the animals they hunted, including mammoths, woolly rhinos, horses and bison. Some of the earliest animal sculptures were found in the Vogelherd caves of southwest Germany; they are thought to be almost 40,000 years old. Human representations were mostly rare, with the notable exception of voluptuous female statuettes which have become known as 'Venus' figures. These have generally been interpreted as fertility symbols, but some have also argued that they provide evidence that women held a socially privileged or even dominant position at the time.

Language and society

Modern research suggests that the total population of southern France 20,000 years ago amounted to no more than two or three thousand people. By the end of the Ice Age, about 10,000 years later, that figure had increased threefold. It follows from the steady growth in numbers that members of different tribes and clans must have met up more frequently, with a growing need to be able to communicate with one another.

Drawings, symbols and hand signs could go some way to meeting the need for communication, but the most important tool for exchanging ideas was language. Anatomists who have studied Cro-Magnon skulls have no doubt that these people possessed the anatomical prerequisites for fluent speech, citing the upward curve of the palate and the dropping of the larynx as evidence.

Making music

It seems more than likely that these people sang as well as spoke. Archaeologists have recovered pipes made from hollowed-out bird bones that probably served as musical instruments. The craftsmen who fashioned them removed the jointed ends of the bones, leaving tubes that they drilled and polished smooth. No-one can be sure of the use the instruments were put to – some have suggested that they may simply have served as signalling devices for hunters to alert their companions to the presence of game. It seems more likely, though, that they were used to make music, either for rituals or simply for entertainment around the campfire at the end of the day.

The time of the cave artists came to an end, along with the Ice Age itself, about 12,000 years ago. With them, the nomadic lifestyle of the Old Stone Age also went from Europe. The Neolithic period that followed was to be characterised by the spread of agriculture, stock-breeding and permanent settlements, marking the start of a whole new chapter in human history.

Europe's first farmers – the spread of agriculture

After the end of the last Ice Age, from about 8000 BC, a new epoch dawned in Europe. Increasingly, people gave up the wandering lifestyle of hunter-gatherers to settle in permanent communities.

Imagine a scene in central Europe at the start of the Neolithic period about 10,000 years ago. A group of hunters has just come home from a successful hunting expedition. Content with their work but exhausted by the long trek, they are more than ready for a rest in some shady spot on the riverbank, where their women and children are waiting for them. Burned by the hot sun, the hunters have built up a terrible thirst, having found no water at all while hunting that day; for the want of suitable containers, they cannot carry water with them. Later, sitting by the campfire, refreshed with food and drink, perhaps some of the men start to question the continuous, energy-sapping wandering. If only they could settle down in their pleasant, safe riverbank campsite. But what would they live on?

The lifestyle of hunter-gatherers was independent and egalitarian, but it can rarely have been easy. The idea of a settled lifestyle held obvious attractions, particularly when the climate started to improve as the last Ice Age ended. The agricultural revolution began with a change in the hearts and minds of

Stone-Age knife
This flint-bladed dagger with a solid wooden handle was found in the belongings of the Stone-Age skeleton, Ötzi, uncovered in the Ötztal Alps. The 12cm (5 in) long scabbard was made of linden fibre.

Europe's oldest observatory

The complex at Goseck has been dated to c.7000 years ago. It served to determine the winter solstice and was also a cult gathering place.

Finds of bones reveal that the central space was used for sacrificial offerings, including human sacrifices.

The rising and setting of the sun on the 21st December can be observed exactly from the very centre of the circle.

Like a gun sight, the width of the gates in the palisade fences narrows from the outside to the inside, enabling precise observations of the sun's movements.

A bank and ditch surrounded the entire complex and served as protection against intruders.

human beings that led the wandering hunter-gatherers, over time, to wish to settle down. Over the ensuing millennia they took up a new life as farmers and stock-breeders, setting in motion the far-reaching social and economic changes that we now know as the Neolithic revolution.

The effects of climate change

When the Ice Age ended, temperatures climbed relatively quickly to present-day levels. Glaciers melted and the sea level rose, so that great stretches of low-lying land were flooded. Britain was separated from the continent at this time, and in about 7750 BC the waters of the Mediterranean broke through the Bosphorus strait into the Black Sea. The coastline of the Black Sea itself shifted

more than 1km (½ mile) inland, displacing shepherds and their herds from their settlements on the shores. The displaced tribes migrated up the River Danube towards central Europe, taking the knowledge of agriculture with them.

Evidence for this migration comes from the fact that the earliest traces of European agriculture are to be found in the southeast corner of the continent. Most of the early cultivated plants, like emmer wheat and barley, did not naturally grow in central Europe – they must have been brought in from elsewhere. The same applies to domesticated animals like sheep and goats, which also originated in the Near East.

The remains of early settlements, houses made of air-dried mud bricks, have

However farming first took root in central Europe, the crucial factor in its growth and development was the notion of gathering and planting seeds, grains and tubers. Villagers who took the trouble to plant seed were able to harvest the results of their efforts the following autumn and to store these provisions for the hard winter months ahead.

Observatories and other inventions

The seasons and, above all, the sun's course were vitally important for farming communities, and they adjusted their sowing and harvesting to fit the demands of the weather. Exciting proof that Neolithic peoples were keen sky-watchers came in 2002 when German archaeologists, working on a site at Goseck in the valley of the River Saale, unearthed what is believed to be Europe's oldest astronomical observatory. Dated to between 5000 and 4800 BC, the structure consisted of three concentric wooden palisades whose entrances were aligned with sunrise and sunset at the time of the summer and winter solstices.

Agriculture stimulated invention in other spheres, too, notably the development of new stone tools. People quickly realised that it was difficult to harvest grain with simple flint blades, so instead they developed the first sickles – curved pieces of wood or antler with a blade glued to the inner surface with pine resin. These new tools meant that bundles of cereals could be harvested much more easily.

Another innovation of the time was the polished axe blade. In the past, people had been content to split off hard flakes of flint and then chisel them down to the desired shape. Now,

Neat work
Hammers and axes were more effective and easier to make once craftsmen learned to attach the heads by boring holes in the shafts. Such new techniques quickly spread: these examples come from a variety of sites in Austria, Hungary and the Czech Repubiic.

also been found in southeastern Europe. The villages were home to 50 to 300 people – almost certainly too large for food requirements to be met exclusively from hunting and gathering edible plants.

At the same time that the first farmers were penetrating central Europe, the region's vegetation was adapting to the changes in climate. The warmer weather led to forests of oak, birch and elm spreading out across the land; hazel trees also flourished, as did grasses whose seeds could be collected and re-sown. Even without the help of external influences, a Neolithic tribe could well have worked out for themselves, on returning to an old campsite after a long period of absence, that seeds they had earlier discarded had sprouted and grown.

Ötzi – the man from the ice

Perfect insulators
The Iceman was dressed for mountain weather. His fur boots were lined with hay for insulation and tied with laces made of grass or leather.

In 1991, a couple hiking in the Ötztal Alps on the borders of Austria and Italy discovered a naturally mummified corpse in the melting ice of a glacier. Examination of the body subsequently revealed that it was more than 5000 years old, which meant that the dead man so dramatically brought to the world's attention had lived in the latter part of the Neolithic period.

The Iceman, as he soon became known, was about 30 years old at the time of his death. In keeping with the era and the climate, he was dressed in fur and leather. He wore a cap sewn from strips of fur and had a cape made of woven grasses that was more than 1m (40in) long. He carried various pieces of equipment in his pack: an axe, a bow and a deerskin quiver, a leather bag with diverse items, and a flint-bladed dagger which had a handle wrapped in animal tendons. The knife's scabbard was attached to his belt with a narrow strip of leather. Recently, fresh examinations have shown evidence of an arrowhead freshly embedded in the man's shoulder, indicating that he most likely died from wounds inflicted in a skirmish some hours before his death.

however, they learned to grind the blades on stone slabs. With these new axes, Neolithic farmers were able to cut down trees more quickly and with far less effort. There was increasing demand for tree trunks for various purposes. One of these was the construction of boats, which at the time took the form of dugout canoes that were hollowed from tree trunks and used for fishing.

Solid houses instead of huts

The main call for wood was for house-building. From about 7500 years ago, people in central Europe started exchanging their primitive mud shelters for more solid wattle-and-daub structures.

Massive communal dwellings also made an appearance, particularly in the coastal regions and along the banks of rivers. These large, rectangular structures were usually supported by five rows of posts, and were typically 40m (130ft) long and 5–8m (15–25ft) wide; sometimes they rose two storeys high. The walls were made of interwoven sticks or else of split lengths of hazel, birch or poplar. The whole structure was covered with damp clay or cow dung, which hardened when it dried. The roof was probably covered with reeds. In buildings with two storeys, the upper level could have served as a winter store for the cereal harvest and cattle fodder, while the ground floor was used as a

Permanent dwelling
In the early Neolithic period, villagers in central Europe built longhouses like these, with massive stone walls and low, reed-covered roofs. This reconstruction of a Neolithic hut is in Provence in southern France.

living and sleeping area. Cooking was done in dome-shaped ovens that stood on a fireproof base of stone or clay; the rest of the floor was covered with rough-hewn wooden floorboards.

The wattle framework could be erected in a matter of days, but finishing the house would have taken several weeks. Once they were completed, such houses could be expected to last for up to 40 years. Neolithic farming villages typically consisted of 30 or 40 of these longhouses. They were surrounded by ditches, walls and palisades, initially for protection from wild animals, although in later times they also helped to keep out human raiders.

People began to domesticate animals soon after the introduction of agriculture. Their first success was with pigs, as the animals could feed themselves by rooting around for food in the woods that surrounded most settlements. They were followed by cattle, sheep and goats. Dogs, which had been domesticated from wolves or jackals, at first proved useful as hunting companions. As the importance of hunting declined, they found a new role guarding herds and acting as watchdogs to warn off intruders or wild animals.

The birth of pottery

The most significant of the technological developments of the New Stone Age was the invention of pottery. Knowledge of ceramics spread across Europe from the Near East by about 4000 BC. By that time Neolithic homes no longer lacked basic household equipment; clay storage jars and water containers, jugs and cooking pots were all in plentiful supply.

The earliest vessels were made by kneading coils of clay into the desired shape. Later, craftsmen improved the technique by moulding the clay around a suitably sized, rounded stone so as to give the interior of the pot a regular shape. Rough edges could be smoothed down afterwards with a wet hands.

In central Europe north of the River Danube, ceramics were often decorated with incised bands. Because of this, the farming communities of the time (from 5800 to 4500 BC) have been called the Linear Pottery Culture. In contrast, people in Scandinavia and the Baltic region preferred to decorate their pots with combed lines and small, pitted indentations. They built their settlements near coasts, relying on fishing and hunting more than agriculture for their survival.

The flint trade

Trading in flint flourished in the Neolithic period. Flints can be traced back to their place of origin from their colour and composition, making it relatively easy to trace the trade routes that carried flint tools across Europe. A quarry near present-day Maastricht supplied customers within a radius of about 400km (250 miles). Scandinavian flint ended up deep in central Europe.

By about 4000 BC most people in Europe were living in permanent settlements. Working in organised groups, they could now embark on the great building projects that were to characterise the subsequent megalithic period.

Pots in all shapes and sizes
Neolithic craftsmen were the first to master the art of making pottery. They made vessels of various types for different purposes, and with many kinds of decoration.

The megalithic monument makers

The gigantic stone structures of the megalithic cultures hint at a preoccupation with the transitory nature of human life. Were these early megalith builders trying to defy death by creating works for eternity?

The farmer stood reverently with his goat in front of the mighty façade of the temple at Tarxien on the Mediterranean island of Malta. A pious man, he felt very insignificant as he passed through the immense outer and inner walls, made of huge blocks of stone, and stepped into a central courtyard flooded with light. Here, he handed the animal over to a priest for sacrifice. The priest cut the animal's throat with a flint knife and caught the blood in a tall stone vessel on the altar. The smoke from burnt carcassess, offered up in large, round firebowls, stung the farmer's eyes. Through the haze, he could only glimpse indistinctly the colossal statue of the Great Goddess, all of 2.5m (8ft) tall. Her voluptuous form promised fertility and life. Awestruck, the farmer would have loved to linger in front of the statue but, as usual, there was a great deal of activity in the temple. Swiftly the priests hurried him on through a labyrinth of chambers and passages, past finely chiselled animal reliefs and colourful, painted ornaments.

In one of the rooms at the very back of the third temple the faithful petitioner

The eye of the goddess
The spiral was often used as a decorative element on structures in Malta. In the temple district, the symbol marked the sacred chambers that only priests could enter.

finally received the oracle he had come to hear. He was surrounded by cool darkness. Anxiously he listened to the echoing voice of the priest, who addressed him from a neighbouring cell through a hole in the decorated wall. After he had heard the priest's words, the farmer bowed thankfully. He had received good news. In gratitude he handed over a clay vessel containing a food offering. The servants of the goddess should not go without.

Mysterious structures

This scene from the temple of Tarxien some 5000 years ago is an imaginary one, but it suggests, on the basis of the available evidence, how the people of Neolithic Europe may have celebrated religious rites. Many of their puzzling megalithic structures – the word itself derives from the Greek for 'big stone' – were built before the Egyptian pyramids. They can be found from Malta and Corsica to the Atlantic coast of Spain and Portugal, from Carnac in Brittany to England's Stonehenge and on up to the Orkneys. These monumental complexes are among the most impressive and mysterious legacies of early European history.

Hardly anything is known about the people who built them. They did not belong to a single homogenous 'megalithic people', but to many different groups, who bestowed a huge cultural diversity on Neolithic Europe. Although

The mighty stone circle of Stonehenge in Wiltshire is one of the most impressive monuments of the megalithic period.

An imposing place of rest
These megalithic tomb structures resemble giant tables. Some were hidden beneath earthen mounds, others were free-standing and clearly visible in the landscape. This one is known as the dolmen of Pedra Gentil and is in the province of Barcelona in Spain.

they expressed their religious ideas in different ways, there were some striking similarities, notably in the building methods they used to erect their great stone monuments.

The Great Mother goddess

Malta and its neighbouring island of Gozo are among the oldest centres of megalithic culture; the temple complexes there went up between 3800 and 2800 BC. Immense effort went into building them, for the colossal stones used in their construction weighed up to 57 tonnes. The toil involved reflected the intensity of the builders' religious beliefs. They venerated a Great Mother figure, whose broad hips, heavy breasts and voluptuous form represented life and fertility. Her cult spread from Palestine and Anatolia through the Mediterranean region

Typical grave goods
The people of the Bell Beaker Culture were skilled in making pottery. This wide-mouthed clay vessel decorated with straight and zig-zag lines is a typical example of the Bell Beaker style.

from the 5th millennium BC. Food and animal sacrifices were offered to her in the temples, and people consulted oracles to seek her advice.

A cult of the dead

The cult of the Great Mother goddess was closely bound up with ancestor worship. The people of Malta spent much time and effort digging graves out of the bedrock in order to bury their dead in the lap of the Earth, thereby symbolically returning them to the Great Mother. The giant necropolis at Valetta had several storeys of burial chambers, halls, passages and stairs going down to a total depth of 10m (30ft). Over the course of the centuries 7000 people were laid to rest there in small tomb chambers cut from the rock. Priestesses who took part in the burial rites sought to make contact with the deceased in the afterlife. At night they would sleep in special chambers beside the tombs, seeking advice from the ancestors in their dreams. Very similar complexes are found in Sardinia.

Large numbers of people must have cooperated to create such cemeteries. Clans and villages must have come together to pool their labour under the supervision of experienced architects. Joint projects of this type only became possible once the hunter-gatherer groups, that had long made up the population of Europe, had adopted agriculture and stock-rearing and settled down in permanent farming communities. Only then could they dedicate the time and effort needed for such large-scale building activities in one place. In Brittany, where the population surged in the 5th millennium BC, the transition to agriculture initiated a phase of cultural growth. No other region is as rich in megalithic structures as this north-western region of France. Brittany profited from its favourable position on the Atlantic coast. Mariners travelling up the coast from the Mediterranean brought artistic and religious influences with them from the Aegean world. Seafaring traders came in search of the greenstone axe-heads that Breton craftsmen made out of the local dolerite, a greenish form of basalt, which were traded as far afield as southern France, Alsace and Britain.

Dolmens and menhirs

The first great tomb monuments in Brittany were created between 3900 and 3000 BC. Several different types of structure evolved. The simplest was the dolmen, an arrangement of two or more upright stones topped by a capstone. Dolmens sheltered tomb chambers that usually contained just a single burial.

This basic design was subject to many variations. Some dolmens were extended to house multiple burials placed in side chambers giving off a central passageway. Passage tombs of this type could be reused and extended over generations. Those in the cemetery of Locmariaquer are particularly impressive: the capstone of one tomb measures 11.5 x 4.5m (37 x 15ft). Researchers still argue over how the builders transported such huge blocks of stone to the site. Presumably they were inched along on rollers – either specially prepared stone columns or tree trunks stripped of their branches.

The Breton monument-builders also erected menhirs – free-standing stone monoliths. Some were huge, and their raising must have been a dramatic sight. The largest of all – the 'fairy stone' of Locmariaquer – once stood 20m (65ft) high and weighed 350 tonnes, although it now lies toppled and broken into four pieces. To erect such a giant with only rollers and ropes, the workteam must have dragged the obelisk inch by inch up a specially built earthen ramp. The decisive

moment came when the stone was slowly lowered into position on the far side of the rise. Once the base was in place, men and draught oxen probably worked together to heave the menhir into a vertical position. No doubt spectators would have gathered to watch and must have cheered when the great task was finally accomplished.

Standing stones played a part in all megalithic cultures. They marked the location of important tombs, and were thought to have magic powers because the souls of the dead were believed to dwell in them. Some were decorated with religious symbols, or with images of ancestors or the Great Goddess.

Tombs for the elite

Only a society exhibiting a marked degree of status differentiation could have built the megalithic tombs. The vast amount of effort required to erect dolmens and menhirs meant they could not be built

Mysterious symbols
One of the most impressive passage tombs in Brittany can be found on Gavrinis, the uninhabited Isle of the Dead. A passage 13m (40ft) long leads to this rectangular burial chamber incised with decorative patterns.

for all the population, but only for a few outstanding individuals. Similar considerations apply to the tumuli – enormous mounds of stone and earth covering tomb chambers. The tumulus of St Michel at Carnac is one of the largest burial mounds in Europe, measuring 125 x 60m and reaching a height of 12m (406 x 195 x 39ft). In the stone-lined burial chamber beneath the mound, precious grave goods including jadeite axes and bead jewellery were found. Researchers know too little about the megalithic societies to determine whether the dead owed their elite position to noble birth, wealth or religious status.

The religious rites for funerals were probably carried out close to the burial sites. Such was most likely the case in the little Breton village of Carnac, not far from the burial field of Locmariaquer, where some 3000 standing stones are arranged in 13 rows extending over 6.5km (4 miles). The menhirs seem to stand guard over the village like an army of petrified soldiers, drawn up in parallel lines. They come in many shapes and sizes: the largest are 7m (23ft) tall, while the smallest, at about 50cm (20in), are barely visible in the thick grass. The rows lead to stone circles, many now destroyed, and to further tombs.

Menhirs on parade
The prehistoric builders of Carnac in Brittany arranged menhirs in 13 separate rows, laying out the standing stones in ascending order of size.

A pan-European phenomenon

In many parts of Europe besides Brittany, this megalithic phenomenon formed part of the rapid economic and cultural upswing that followed the arrival and development of settled agricultural communities. On the North German Plain, in Scandinavia and in eastern Europe, the peoples of the so-called Linear Pottery Culture – the name comes from distinctive zigzag or curved incisions with which they decorated their pottery – adopted megalithic architectural designs between 4300 and 2700 BC. In Germany and elsewhere, the great burial mounds they erected were called 'giant's graves' by later peoples who knew nothing of their making.

The megalithic culture also flourished in the British Isles. Scottish and Irish passage graves show striking similarities with Mediterranean burial sites. The domed burial mound at Newgrange in Ireland, which was probably built to house the bodies of a royal clan, can be seen from afar. The tomb's inner walls, and the numerous standing stones around it, are decorated with concentric circles, spirals, and eye and sun symbols that are strongly reminiscent of the designs found on Maltese structures.

Stone Age star-gazers

With no contemporary written sources to enlighten us, very little is known for certain about the intentions and purposes of the megalith builders. Instead, there is boundless speculation. Some researchers see evidence of a sun cult in the orientation of the monuments. Evidence for this view can be found at Newgrange, where on 21 December (the winter solstice) – and only then – the rays of the rising sun penetrate a narrow slit above the doorway and shine right down the passage into the burial chamber. Proponents of the solar cult theory suggest that at the darkest time of year it was particularly important for the sun's life-giving rays to reach the abode of the dead.

The relationship between the older traditions of ancestor worship, the Great Mother goddess and the newer sun worship remains unclear, but in the course of time the dolmens gave way to circular structures with banks and ditches. Tribal communities led by wealthy royal clans had settled in the Wessex area of southwest England by the middle of the 3rd millennium BC. The largest circular complexes were created under their aegis from 2500 BC, the most spectacular example being Stonehenge. This vastly impressive complex was constructed in different phases over a period of several hundred years. The earliest part consisted of a circular earthen bank and ditch 115m (380ft) across, with a main entrance that led to a banked pathway known as the Avenue. Later, two concentric circles of bluestones were built, probably around the year 2000 BC. The huge blocks of bluish-tinged dolerite and rhyolite were transported from quarries in Wales more than 200km (125 miles) away. In the last phase of construction, about 200 years later, an outermost stone circle of 30 mighty sandstone pillars connected by stone lintels was added. Other massive trilithons – arrangements of two upright stones with a third sitting across them as a capstone – were constructed in the centre of the circle, arranged in a horseshoe shape.

Right from the start, Stonehenge almost certainly had some astrological significance. The main entrance and the avenue extending from it are aligned with the sun at dawn on 21 June, the summer solstice. The positions of other stones are arguably also orientated to various other stations in the solar and lunar cycles. Overall, the arrangement of the stones appears to have been calculated very precisely, suggesting that the monument's architects were able to draw on a well-established tradition of astronomical observation.

POINT OF VIEW

The mysterious stones of Carnac

The stone rows at Carnac pose many unanswered questions. Some prehistorians insist that they were gigantic sightlines for observing the sun and other stars, while others have argued that the stone rows marked the positions of heavenly bodies. A recent theory holds that Stone Age astronomers devised a 16-month solar calendar. There is no firm scientific evidence for any of these theories, which presuppose a sophisticated knowledge of astronomy that may not have been available to people familiar only with the solar and lunar cycles. It seems more likely that Carnac was intended by its builders as a ceremonial site. Processions may have taken place along the stone rows to the tombs and stone circles at their ends. The complex was large enough to play host to crowds of several thousand people.

Standing stones
The background image shows some of the many menhirs at Carnac in Brittany.

The Beaker People

The solar significance of Stonehenge may be linked with a group known as the Beaker, or Bell Beaker, People. They arrived on the western fringes of Europe in the course of the 3rd millennium, spreading up the Atlantic and North Sea coasts and along the river valleys of northern and western Europe. Their culture got its name from bell-shaped, handle-less drinking vessels that have been found in graves alongside their dead.

Their living society greatly valued hospitality and was marked by sharp divisions in wealth. It was more individualistic than the earlier megalithic clans, which had concentrated on communal achievements. The newcomers introduced horses to the lands they settled, and were evidently more mobile than the farmers they encountered. They also brought with them knowledge of metal-working and of weaving. The wrist-guards, daggers and arrowheads that they fashioned hint at a warlike disposition. In time, the descendants of these people would replace the earlier megalithic cultures and go on to shape the further development of Europe.

Sleeping priestess
This clay figurine of a sleeping priestess comes from the necropolis of Hal Saflieni in Malta. It is thought to represent the custom of incubation, in which individuals spent the night in a temple hoping to obtain information or advice from the gods.

The Minoans – masters of Crete

Serpent goddess
This fine glazed figure found in the palace of Knossos depicts a goddess grasping a pair of writhing serpents. Serpents symbolised the Underworld for the Minoans.

Early in the 2nd millennium BC, a dazzling new centre of culture emerged on the Mediterranean island of Crete. Palace ruins and wall paintings still reflect the sophistication of Minoan society and their extraordinary artistic skills.

Until comparatively recent times, Minoan Crete was best remembered for a story told about it by the ancient Greeks. Once every nine years, they claimed, its ruler King Minos demanded that the Athenians pay him tribute in the form of 14 young people – seven youths and seven maidens. When they arrived at his palace they faced a terrible fate. They were forced to confront the Minotaur, a monster half-man and half-bull, who was the result of an unnatural liaison between King Minos's wife Pasiphae and a white bull. To hide his family's shame, Minos had commissioned the brilliant inventor Daedalus to design the Labyrinth, a complex maze in which the beast could be permanently confined. Thrust into the Labyrinth, the young Athenians were sacrificed to the Minotaur's cannibalistic appetites – until the hero Theseus volunteered to make the journey and managed to kill the creature in its lair.

Knossos – centre of power

This bloodthirsty tale does not sit well with the image of a happy and peaceful civilisation that has emerged from the archaeological excavations on Crete. These have provided abundant evidence of the Minoans' highly developed artistic sense and luxurious lifestyle. The old legends probably say more about the Greeks' lack of understanding of Cretan culture, which pre-dated and was very different from their own, and maybe also the envy that they felt in face of the long-lasting supremacy of the great island kingdom of the Aegean. The myths credited Minos as the legendary founder of Crete's maritime supremacy, and indicated that he resided in a vast palace at a place called Knossos. Modern scholars have given his name to the civilisation that flourished

POINT OF VIEW

Was there a King Minos?

According to Greek legend, Zeus, the king of the gods, took on the shape of a bull to abduct Europa, daughter of a king. He took her to his island home on Crete and fathered three sons by her, one of whom was Minos, the first king of Crete.

Minos is supposed to have ruled a great island kingdom with 90 towns under his control, and he duly gave his name to the Minoan civilisation. There is no historical evidence, however, that any such figure ever existed. More likely, Minos was a royal title, similar to the Egyptian 'pharaoh', and is not to be identified as a single person.

The Hall of the Double Axe in Knossos has been painstakingly reconstructed based on the evidence of fragmentary remains.

on Crete from 2600 BC, which is now generally considered to be Europe's first advanced culture.

The British archaeologist Sir Arthur Evans stumbled on the remains of Knossos in the early decades of the 20th century. The huge palace that he excavated was the unchallenged capital of the Minoan realm. Its ruins still give a clear impression of the importance the place must once have had, while the bewildering array of rooms give some clue as to how the myth of the Labyrinth may have started. Great halls and smaller living rooms were connected to one another by countless long corridors. The main residential area and the chief ceremonial halls surrounded a large central courtyard, measuring 50 x 30m (160 x 100ft), which also gave onto storerooms and workshops. Staircases led to the upper floors, while light wells provided ventilation and natural daylight for the lower storeys.

Palace servants kept a careful record of the goods that came and went in the storage areas; scribes painstakingly noted the contents of the many *pithoi* – the name given to the vast Cretan storage jars,

A walled labyrinth

It is easy to see how a visitor could have got lost in the palace of Knossos, which had some 1000 rooms scattered across wings that were anything from two to five storeys high. There were countless hallways and porticoes, and even ramps that were wide enough to accommodate wheeled vehicles.

Rectangular pits with stone covers were let into the floors of the storerooms.

The Throne Room and ceremonial rooms lay on the western side of the central courtyard.

An elegant staircase led to the royal suite in the upper storey of the east wing.

Wooden pillars painted bright red were a characteristic feature of Minoan architecture.

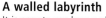

some of which were big enough to shelter a full-grown man. Armies of servants hurried back and forth along endless corridors. A corps of priestesses lived nearby in special sacred quarters, ready to carry out essential religious ceremonies.

The creature comforts that the Minoans enjoyed almost 4000 years ago, and the sumptuous luxury with which their state rooms were equipped, still astonish visitors to the palace today. Walls were decorated with brightly coloured murals depicting idyllic landscapes or lively scenes of everyday life. Some rooms were clad in precious alabaster panels. Bathrooms were equipped with earthenware tubs, and there was even a latrine flushed by running water. Pillared anterooms and double doors ensured that the palace remained pleasantly cool in the summer months.

Decorative hard hat
This Mycenaean leather helmet, decorated with boars' tusks, was found in a tomb at Knossos.

A hub of trade

Minoan Crete was evidently already prosperous by the time that construction began at Knossos, in about 1900 BC. Its wealth was based on trade, for the Cretans were the dominant mercantile power in the eastern Mediterranean at the time. They had laid the foundations of their success in the closing years of the preceding millennium, when Minoan mariners had used their navigational skills to establish contacts with other trading centres in the Cyclades, Sicily, Cyprus, Egypt and the Near East. The busiest ports at the time were those situated on the east coast of the island, which exported agricultural products – mainly olive oil, wine and grain – along with timber, weaponry, jewellery and ceramics. In return Cretan boats brought back copper, lead and obsidian, as well as sought-after ivory.

The economic upswing that ensued affected the whole island. At about the same time that construction began at Knossos, other palace installations were going up at Mallia to the east of Knossos and at Phaistos in the south. The contact with foreign lands that accompanied overseas trade brought side benefits in other fields, as the Cretan islanders absorbed new ideas and art styles from other cultures. From the Cyclades islands to the north they borrowed geometric patterns to decorate their ceramics. They learned the art of making stoneware from the Egyptians, and imitated Mesopotamian models when making jewellery and cylinder seals.

The Labyrinth of the Minotaur

The Labyrinth where the Minotaur lived has always had a hold on people's imaginations, even though there is no evidence that it ever actually existed. The word derives from the Greek *labrys* meaning 'double-axe', and double-axes like the one below, made of gold and precious stones, have been found in all the Minoan palaces. The axes also served as decorative pieces and were used as stonemasons' marks, particularly in Knossos. It is possible that the mythical Labyrinth is in fact the palace of Knossos itself, which did indeed have a mazelike interior.

The double axe
The double-headed axe was a sacred object to the Minoans.

Minoan craftsmen used the knowledge that their traders brought back to become masters metalworkers and potters. They produced attractive, wavy-patterned earthenware, as well as the eggshell-thin ceramics known as Kamares ware, the manufacture of which required the highest skills. Minoan products became sought-after export items. The port of Mochlos became an important centre, its harbour constantly packed with ships. Filigree jewellery from tombs in Mochlos give some indication of Crete's prosperity at the time; its wealthy merchants went to their graves adorned by pendants and chains in delicate floral patterns.

Busy traffic in the Aegean

Not content with visiting the eastern Mediterranean, the Minoans founded trading centres there – for example, on the islands of Kythera, Melos, Thera, Naxos and Rhodes. The everyday life of these Minoan settlements can still be glimpsed at Akrotiri on Thera, where the remains of an ancient port were excavated by the Greek archaeologist Spiridon Marinatos from the mid 1960s. The two and three-storey stone houses that he unearthed, built of rubble and clay rendered with lime and reinforced with timber, were packed close together in a maze of winding streets.

Generally, the ground floor of the house served as a workshop or a storage area for merchandise. The living rooms were on the upper storeys, which were accessible via stone stairs. Floors were covered with a glittering layer of compacted shells. The internal walls were coated in stucco and, in wealthy homes, were decorated with colourful frescoes. One work that has survived in particularly good condition is the 'Spring Fresco', a delightful mural that covers three walls of a room with a scene of flowering lilies, set in a volcanic landscape with swallows swooping overhead.

Akrotiri's gracious and happy lifestyle was brought to a sudden end sometime during the mid 2nd millennium BC. A devastating volcanic eruption caused half of the island to sink into the sea, burying the port itself under a thick layer of ash. The inhabitants barely had time to flee. Marinatos and his team uncovered living rooms abandoned just as their owners had left them – even down to the carbonised remains of uneaten foodstuffs, including barley and peas.

Tithes and regulation

The increased trading activity required tight central organisation, and was closely overseen from Knossos. The palace installations served not just as the ruler's residence and a focus of religious activity, but also as an administrative centre and a central storage hub. Cretan farmers had to provide a share of their crops as a form of taxation, and the tribute was collected and distributed from palace warehouses. Payment of this tithe was supervised by regional governors who lived on large estates scattered across the island.

The palace administration also regulated the manufacture and sale of luxury goods including jewellery and weapons, as the presence of numerous workshops in the immediate vicinity of the palace shows. Archaeologists excavating the palace and its close surroundings have found the studios of potters, ivory carvers, textile workers, stone and gem cutters, bronze-casters and jewellers. The craftsmen were supplied with their raw materials by the palace, and had to account meticulously for their use. They received free food handouts in lieu of pay.

Efficient administration

The rulers of Knossos had to devise a sophisticated bookkeeping system to keep pace with the booming economy and to keep track of the huge quantities of stock in their warehouses. Cylinder seals were used to mark goods in the Sumerian fashion, both to establish ownership and to acknowledge receipt or despatch. Large numbers of seals have

been found in Cretan palaces, displaying a wide range of motifs and shapes.

The ever-increasing demands of commerce also encouraged the Minoans in the development of their own written language. Busy scribes recorded details of goods and lists of names on countless small clay tablets. The script that they used was derived from a much older form of hieroglyphics and is known to scholars today as Linear A, but its symbols have still not been completely deciphered.

So far, the texts have provided very little information about Cretan history. Not a single name of a king, a dynasty or a god has come down from Minoan times. In marked contrast to the civilisations of Egypt and Mesopotamia, Crete seems not to have made its rulers the subject of a personality cult. From the lack of battle scenes in the island's many artworks, it can also be assumed that the Minoans were a generally peace-loving, unwarlike people.

Mysterious rulers

Scholars are still unsure as to who actually lived in the palace of Knossos. Some see it as a genuine royal palace, but others think it was the seat of a priestly elite, possibly housing a line of priestess-queens. A high-backed gypsum chair uncovered by Arthur Evans in 1900 has a regal air about it that led him to name the chamber where it stood as the Throne Room, although archaeologists since his time have argued that it could equally well have been a shrine. The walls on both sides of the throne are richly decorated with frescoes of griffins – fabulous creatures with the body of a lion and head of a bird – that were considered companions of the gods.

The adjoining suite of rooms (which include a bathroom) lends support to the theory that Minoan kingship was closely linked to religion, for the numerous paintings that decorate the walls have seemingly ritualistic themes. Processions of young men and women with long, curly

Life on the water
This fresco from Akrotiri on the island of Thera shows a Minoan boat. A man with a steering oar stands in the stern, while rowers propel the boat forward. The passengers relax under a canopy on deck and dolphins swim alongside.

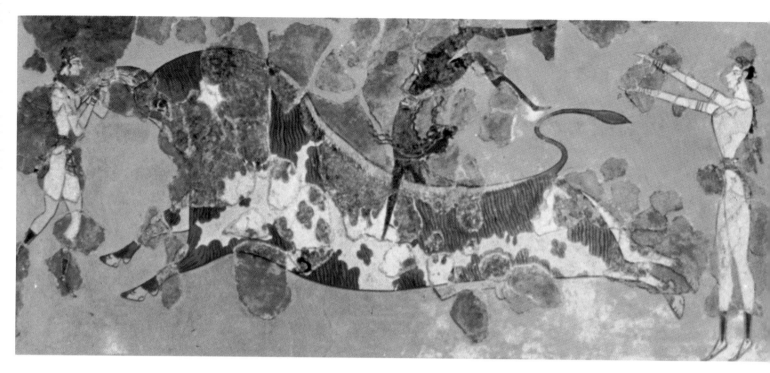

A dangerous sport
This fresco from Knossos shows a young man turning a somersault over a charging bull's back, while a light-skinned girl grasps its horns ready to repeat the performance.

black hair are depicted bearing offerings of food and drink. The almost life-sized, figures are arranged in two rows, one above the other, and show no trace of age or infirmity, perhaps indicating a beauty cult. Their pace is measured, their faces dignified and relaxed. The men wear only short loincloths, the women wear wide, layered skirts and tight bodices that leave the breasts exposed. Musicians accompany the processions. The overwhelming impression is one of affirmation and a positive attitude to life – a characteristic that has led observers to conclude that the Minoans were a happy, well-adjusted people who for the most part lived in harmony with their gods and with nature.

Powerful women and symbolic bulls

Another feature that stands out in the pictorial record is the dominant role that women played in rituals. The impression is reinforced by faience (fine glazed pottery) statuettes that have been found at several sites. These depict female figures – probably goddesses – holding snakes, or with snakes entwined about their bodies. Some researchers have argued from this evidence that women held a special position in Minoan society, even that a

matriarchal system may have applied. Another possibility is that the priestesses may have owed their conspicuous position to a fertility cult involving veneration of a Mother Goddess.

Bulls, which symbolised elemental power and strength, also played an important part in Minoan ritual. Stylised bull horns often appear as decorative elements on the roofs and balustrades of Cretan palaces, and memories of a bull cult seem to underlie Greek stories of the Minotaur. What the exact significance of the animals was for the Cretans remains unclear, although they also played a major role in Mesopotamian religion, where they were associated with gods of the sky and the weather. On Crete they seem to have been the preferred sacrificial animal in cult ceremonies.

Everyday life and death

The Cretan palaces were surrounded by urban settlements that clustered around their walls; archaeologists often find it hard to tell where the palace compound ends and the town begins. Within the towns, upper-class residents lived in elegant houses built of stone, while poorer citizens inhabited dwellings of mud-brick.

The rest of the island's population lived in villages scattered across the countryside. Two such sites have been excavated on the south coast, revealing communities of small, close-packed houses that between them were probably home to around 25 to 40 people. The villagers lived off the land, cultivating mainly barley, wheat, olives and grapes and keeping sheep, goats, cattle and pigs. They produced their own pottery, wool, oil and wine, but relied on the palace cities for other goods.

The Minoans buried their dead in communal graves that were round or rectangular in shape. In the north and east of the island, multi-chamber tombs predominated, while in the south the dead were laid to rest in domed vaults made of unworked stones rising in a beehive shape from a circular stone base. The corpses of the dead were laid in clay coffins or in *pithoi*. Analysis of the remains suggests that the islanders rarely lived beyond 30 years of age, and many suffered from bad teeth and from deficiency diseases such as osteoporosis and arthritis.

Disaster and renewal

A great catastrophe disrupted the Cretans' tranquil existence in about 1700 BC:

violent earthquakes shook the island and destroyed many of the palaces. The Minoans put all their vigour and drive, as well as their substantial resources of manpower and material, into the task of reconstruction. Knossos, Mallia and Phaistos were rapidly rebuilt, and new palaces were constructed at Kato Zakros and Galatas. Each of these complexes followed the Knossos model in general outline, although the new structures were smaller and less luxuriously equipped.

At Mallia, near the coast about 40km (25 miles) east of Knossos, the remains of many workshops and storerooms have been found, as might have been expected from the town's location; two ports lay nearby, making the area an important trading centre. Round buildings southwest of the palace are thought to have served as grain silos. Mallia also housed a large pottery factory and an important goldsmiths' workshop that was already producing genuine works of art in the 'Old Palace' period before the earthquake. Many beautiful pieces of jewellery, among them a dainty

A Mediterranean atmosphere
Minoan wall paintings are full of a Mediterranean freshness and vitality. These images of dolphins and of women carrying jars of wine and oil both come from Knossos.

Concentrated power
This bull's head, made of steatite, mother-of-pearl and crystal, was a libation vessel that may have held the blood of sacrificial animals during ceremonies.

the western part of the complex, has a monumental staircase which indicates that Phaistos may have staged spectacular religious ceremonies. Also, like Knossos, it has been suggested that Phaistos may have been the residence of a religious rather than a political leader.

The smaller palaces

Kato Zakros on the east coast of Crete was not as big as the other complexes, but objects found there include valuable works of ivory and stone and rock crystal vessels. Archaeologists investigating the palace also found the remains of a small laboratory evidently used to make perfumes, salves and scented oils. The palace of Galatas, discovered only recently in the centre of Crete, was smaller still.

After the earthquake the palace of Knossos remained, as before, at the heart of Minoan culture. If anything, its splendour increased in the wake of the disaster. In spite of their wealth, it appears the Minoans did not fear attack, as no signs of fortifications have been found.

The palace of Phaistos
Like all Minoan palaces, Phaistos (right) was aligned on a north–south axis. The round clay disc above was found in the palace ruins. It measures 16cm (6in) in diameter, and the symbols repeated in a rhythmic sequence around it were impressed into the damp clay with ready-made stamp seals.

Links with Egypt

Minoan culture was at its zenith from 1700 to 1520 BC. At this time the Cretans' supremacy in the eastern Mediterranean was unchallenged, and they maintained regular contact with all the neighbouring powers. Relations with Egypt were particularly close. The Egyptians had a penchant for the high-quality weaponry produced on the island, and also for Minoan jewellery. Saffron was much in demand, as were richly patterned textiles and a purple dye that the islanders produced from mollusc shells. Ceramics decorated with flower patterns or with designs featuring sea creatures also became fashionable at this time and found numerous buyers. The Cretan potters

bee pendant, have been discovered as grave goods in the local cemetery.

The palace of Phaistos was even more splendidly appointed. Set in a picturesque location in the centre of the island, it controlled the fertile Messara Plain. Living rooms ornamented with alabaster wall panels were grouped around pillared verandahs and courtyards. One of these, in allowed their imaginations to run riot: beaked flagons came alive with images of wind-blown grasses; octopus tentacles curled around vases and dishes; and crockery was adorned with starfish, schools of dolphins and spiny murex molluscs.

The Egyptians called Crete 'Ka-f-tu' – literally, 'island in the middle of the sea' – and showed their fascination with the Minoans in frescoes depicting Cretan bull-leapers and traders. Cretan artistic styles set fashions across the eastern Mediterranean. Remains of wall frescoes and floor decorations in the Minoan manner have been found in Syria and Israel. According to an old Syrian legend, the god of craftsmen and the arts originally came from Crete.

A violent end

The civilisation of Minoan Crete came to a sudden and violent end; all the larger Minoan palaces except for Knossos were destroyed and burned in about 1450 BC. The causes of its downfall are still shrouded in controversy. For a long time, the eruption of the volcanic island of Thera, about 120km (75 miles) north of Crete, some time in the 15th century BC was thought to be responsible. Recent research, however, has indicated that the volcano blew earlier than previously thought – well before the destruction of the Minoan palaces. The immediate effects of the disaster may also have been more limited than previously imagined, for there is no indication of a tsunami (tidal wave) hitting Crete at the time. It could be, however, that the Thera eruption was only the first of a series of seismic events that may have shaken the Minoan world over the ensuing decades.

Civil conflict and wars with foreign powers have been suggested as other possible reasons for the collapse of the Minoan civilisation. Archaeologists have found evidence of random destruction, as well as of personal possessions being buried – sure signs of troubled times.

There are also clear indications on the island of the growing influence of the Mycenaean culture of mainland Greece. Mycenaean ceramics put in an appearance on Crete as they did across the whole Aegean world. Burial customs changed, and large, Mycenaean-style domed tombs started to be constructed, equipped with grave goods that included weapons and sacrificed horses. Most significantly of all, the Cretan Linear A script was replaced by an early Greek one, known to scholars as Linear B.

All this evidence points to the inescapable conclusion that the Mycenaeans took control of Crete at this time. Evidence of the takeover has even been found in Egypt, where Rekhmara, vizier to Pharaoh Thutmose III, had the frescoes in his tomb chamber outside Thebes altered to replace Minoan tribute-bearers with Mycenaean Greeks, their Cretan-style loincloths retouched to turn them into the characteristic, pointed garments worn on mainland Greece.

Minoan culture survived for a time after the Mycenaean takeover, but its days were numbered. At first Knossos's new masters had the palace renovated and partially re-equipped in the traditional Cretan manner. After that, however, a clear break became apparent in the island's artistic heritage. The old playfulness disappeared, to be replaced by a much more austere and formal approach. The palace at Knossos itself was finally destroyed in about 1400 BC, possibly as a result of a local rebellion. With its fall the Minoan world lost its principal point of reference. Crete was absorbed into the Greek world and lost for ever its supremacy in the Aegean.

Marine motifs
The Minoans often decorated their ceramics with motifs in the so-called 'sea style'. Shells, squid, octopuses, seaweed and coral were all reproduced naturalistically and with great attention to detail.

Bronze – the metal that changed the world

In its splendour and savagery, the Bronze Age marked the culminating phase of prehistory. The art of manufacturing bronze not only encouraged an upsurge in economic activity across Europe but also fundamentally changed people's lives.

If a time machine had existed to shift a Neolithic farmer forward from, say, 5000 BC to 1500 BC, the smell of smoke in his village would probably have been the first difference he noticed. By the middle of the 2nd millennium, smoke fumes lay heavily over the settlements of Europe, as thick trails wafted up from the chimneys of foundries where copper and tin were being smelted into bronze. Spectators may well have clustered around to watch whenever a smith poured the molten ore, heated in small crucibles, into the moulds or hammered a piece of glowing metal into shape on his anvil. Perhaps they looked on in admiration as finished lance heads and daggers, dress pins and ornaments cooled and were taken from the moulds. For the smith himself, though, there was little time to rest. He would already be thinking of the next batch, spurring his assistant to stoke up the furnace with blowpipes or a primitive form of bellows.

Smiths needed specialised knowledge in order to mix and measure copper and tin in the right proportions to make bronze and to gauge the metals' smelting point – approximately 1000°C (1800°F). It is easy to imagine the aura of magic that must have surrounded the craft in those early days. The ability to make solid metals melt and then harden again into a different shape must have seemed little short of miraculous to the farmers who watched the new material being forged, by human hand, through heat, smoke and fire. It is not surprising that smiths were feared as much as they were admired and respected.

An alloy with many uses

Metal-working was not new to Europe when bronze first appeared. People had already been working small amounts of naturally occurring copper for several millennia. But bronze had advantages over copper: it was more malleable when molten, yet much tougher once cast. It was also suitable for a variety of uses: weapons, agricultural implements and personal ornaments could all be crafted from the honey-coloured metal.

Entirely new types of artefact were created by the smiths. The Nebra disc – found in 1999 on the Mittelberg, a hill in eastern Germany – is 3600 years old and

A swan chariot
Water birds symbolised healing and were frequently modelled in clay as religious offerings or grave goods, like this example found in Serbia.

The Nebra sky disc shows the crescent moon and the Pleiades alongside a golden circle that may represent either the full moon or the sun.

Ritual instruments
Among the most distinctive legacies of the Scandinavian Bronze Age are the extraordinary curving horns, known as *lurs*, usually about 1.2m (4ft) long. Rock engravings show them being used in religious rituals.

is the earliest known depiction of the night sky. It may have served as an agricultural calendar; metal arcs on either edge of the disc marked the range of sunrises and sunsets as seen from the hill between the summer and winter solstices. Equally striking were *lurs*, spectacular musical instruments made of sheet bronze that were used in religious ceremonies. Bronze was also used to make torques – necklaces of twisted metal – and ingots for use as currency.

Knowledge of bronze smelting probably reached central Europe in about 2300 BC from the Near East, where it had first surfaced a thousand years earlier. The process was complex, requiring access to copper and tin ores, which rarely occurred together in the same region. Metalworkers also had to be able to stoke furnaces to extremely high temperatures if they were to create the desired alloy and produce high quality finished goods.

Masters of fire

Metalsmiths were specialised professionals: casting bronze demanded experience and great care. Clay moulds had to be heated to about 400°C (750°F) if they were not to shatter, so the inventive smiths developed re-useable moulds made of metal and stone that allowed them to instigate a type

of serial production. Clay still had its uses, however, as smiths perfected the *cire perdue* or 'lost-wax' method to cast delicate objects; the clay moulds were shattered after cooling to reveal the finished bronze inside. Smiths also created thin bronze sheets by repeatedly hammering and reheating the metal. The sheets were then decorated using stamp-like tools called punches.

The first metal traders

Even the best smiths could produce nothing without raw materials. To fill the foundries and crucibles, ore-hunters sought metal deposits in mountainous regions and river valleys. The discovery of a viable lode usually triggered extraction on a large scale. As demand for bronze increased, mining spread across Europe, from the Hungarian lowlands through the Alps to southern Spain.

Wandering traders journeyed to and from the mines, using heavy wagons drawn by draught animals. Each trader would carefully check the purity of the ore on offer before accepting a wagonload. The traders needed courage and stamina to cope with the hazards of the road. With their heavily loaded carts they had to cross high mountain passes and dangerous marshes, only rarely enjoying the luxury of proper roads. One particularly well-served area was in northwestern Germany, where causeways made of wooden sleepers crossed the inhospitable moors and marshes. The paths, up to 2.5m (8ft) wide, were built of thick oak planks. From about 1800 BC, lighter spoked wheels introduced from the Aegean replaced solid wood, enabling the wagons to travel faster. To begin with, though, these were used only by the few wealthy traders who could afford them.

Europe's first Bronze Age culture takes its name from the village of Unetice in Bohemia where its artefacts were first identified. The Unetice people inhabited the Czech and Slovak regions, central Germany, southern Poland and parts of Austria between 2300 and 1600 BC. On the plains they lived in small villages of wooden longhouses; in hillier regions they built fortified settlements. Some lived in houses on stilts on the edges of lakes, the raised floors providing protection against both invaders and flooding.

Guarding the precious ores

The Uneticeans supported themselves by agriculture and stock-breeding, but it was bronze that made them wealthy. Some of their raw materials came from the distant Alps and Carpathian Mountains, but there were also more local supplies from the Harz Mountains and the Thuringian forests, as well as from the Erzgebirge – literally the 'ore mountains' – located on present-day Germany's border with the Czech Republic. Tin was the hardest to come by; it had either to be laboriously panned from river sands in the Erzgebirge, or imported from Ireland, Cornwall or Britanny. In exchange for the ores, traders bartered the 'white gold' of the Bronze Age – salt, mined in the Halle area.

The Unetice bronze traders went to great lengths to protect their stock-in-trade. Piles of bronze axes, daggers, torques and jewellery have been dug up in eastern Germany. Some of these would have been buried by traders in safe places until the stored objects could be recycled (melted down and used again), but the hoards were also hiding places for valuables and for artefacts

intended as offerings to the gods – the Uneticeans made a practice of burying bronze grave goods with their dead. These rich underground hauls give some idea of the region's great prosperity at the time.

Trade routes across Europe

The Bronze Age saw a vast expansion of long-distance trade as goods went all over Europe, often travelling great distances. Important routes led from the Carpathian Mountains westward along the River Danube, and from Italy over the Alpine passes to northern Europe. Metal was exchanged for amber in the Baltic region, and goods from Denmark and other Scandinavian countries travelled overland down the 'amber route' to Italy's Adriatic coast. From there, they were shipped by sea as far as Mycenean Greece.

Great rivers, notably the Rhône and Rhine, connected the Atlantic regions with the Mediterranean world. In the Mediterranean itself, experienced Minoan and Mycenean seamen handled the transportation of goods. In the coastal and inland waters of central and northern Europe, traders used rowing boats and dugout canoes, which were especially important in remote and thinly populated

Status symbol

The Bronze Age was a time of conspicuous display when chieftains visibly advertised their standing by wearing splendid ornaments like this metal necklet (below). Inequalities in wealth bred insecurity, however. Settlements were increasingly built with an eye to defence, either on hilltops or on wooden platforms extending over lakes, like the village of Unterruhldingen on the German shore of the Bodensee (Lake Constance, background picture).

Sea-going ships
Scandinavian rock drawings depict long ships propelled by oars. Their raised prows and sterns, decorated with spirals and animal heads, call to mind the dragon ships of the Viking era more than 2000 years later.

Scandinavia. Ideas and religious concepts travelled along the trade routes with the material goods, and it was probably this influence that caused a uniform type of burial to spread across central Europe in the mid 2nd millennium BC. In place of the shallow graves favoured in Uneticean times, the dead were now buried in wooden coffins under large mounds, usually 1–2m (3–6ft) high. Some burials were very grand indeed, illustrating a widening social divide in Bronze Age society. The powerful chieftains who controlled the trade routes and benefited from the traffic that passed along them were now able to amass great wealth.

A warrior aristocracy

Culturally, the Bronze Age warrior-aristocrats of Europe seem to have been cast in the same mould as the Homeric heroes of Mycenean Greece, whose influence penetrated to central Europe through the Carpathian region west of the Black Sea. Their lives revolved around glory in battle, conspicuous wealth and prodigious generosity to their followers. The ideals they lived by were mirrored in their burial practices.

As a sign of rank, leading chieftains were buried with valuable weapons, riding equipment and all the utensils needed for posthumous feasts; some of the richest graves in later Bronze Age times contained entire four-wheeled carriages. Other items that underlined a dead person's prestige included goods imported from the eastern Mediterranean, such as bronze beakers, razors, tweezers and jewellery.

Bavarian burials

The tumulus grave of a nobleman who was buried at Hagenau in Bavaria some time in the 14th century BC provides a fine example of the profligacy of the times. The chieftain was surrounded by an arsenal of bronze weaponry – bows, arrows, axes, daggers, and both short and long-bladed swords – along with gold rings and a bronze dress pin 50cm (20in) long. Another Bavarian burial, at Freising, featured a gold-trimmed ceremonial costume that harked back to Mycenean traditions, vividly illuminating the links between Bronze Age central Europe with earlier cultural centres.

Women aristocrats, too, were laid to rest in great pomp. A noblewoman from Lower Saxony, known as the 'Princess of Fallingbostel', was buried wearing eight bronze rings around her neck along with a necklace of amber beads and heart-shaped bronze pendants. Burnished bronze torques decorated her arms, and she had bronze rings on her fingers. Her clothing was made of wool, and her shawl was clasped with a wheel-shaped bronze pin. On her head she wore a cap covered in tiny, cone-shaped bronze caps and rods – a mark of her high status, for only one individual at any one time could wear such a crown.

A time of wealth and insecurity

The inhabitants of Bronze Age Europe enjoyed increasing wealth, which spurred population growth. Agriculture was making great strides: spelt (a species of wheat), millet and oats all came into cultivation, and green vegetables and pulses supplemented the diet. Pigs were reared in almost every yard.

There was, however, a downside to the new wealth. Not all regions profited equally from the bronze trade, and this inequality sparked jealousy among neighbours. Increasingly, people felt the need to protect their settlements. In southern Germany and the Alpine regions, lakeside villagers sheltered behind palisades that defended the landward approaches. Other communities built on high ground. The Heuneburg in the Swabian Alps became the seat of a hill fort that, in some ways, resembled a medieval castle. Although the site dropped away steeply on three sides to the River Danube, the inhabitants bolstered these natural defences by surrounding the complex with a wall, 2–3m (6–10ft) thick, that they secured at weak points with extra walls and ditches. Elsewhere, hillforts ringed by basalt walls and palisades of wood and earth protected important trade routes. Some show traces of fire, indicating that they may have been attacked. Other signs of conflict include broken weapons and evidence of hasty rebuilding.

Foreign competitors

The later centuries of the Bronze Age were a troubled period across much of the ancient world. The Hittite culture of Anatolia and Greece's Mycenaean civilisation both collapsed at this time, and even pharaonic Egypt was shaken to its core by the assault of the Sea Peoples.

In central Europe, a combination of population growth and a deteriorating climate of increasing drought saw people on the move. From about 1300 BC, tribes from the middle courses of the Danube began to migrate, and others followed their example. Wandering clans moved south across the Balkans towards the Mediterranean and west along the Danube to the Upper Rhine.

The atmosphere in Europe was unsettled and warlike. Hordes of armed men protected by metal helmets and armour, leather cuirasses and wooden shields scoured the countryside in search of fertile land on which they and their families could settle. These migrants were also traders, maintaining a far-flung network of mercantile contacts.

A further change in burial customs now spread across Europe. In place of the

Shield and helmet
Fighting equipment like this bronze shield and helmet from Denmark were popular grave goods for men, underlining their warrior status.

burial mounds that had marked the two centuries from 1450 to 1250, people now cremated their dead and put the remains in urns, which were buried in large burial grounds. The practices of what is now known as the 'Urnfield Culture' suggest a very different view of the afterlife from the one held previously. Whereas earlier generations had done their utmost to provide for the physical comfort of the dead in the otherworld, the Urnfield preference for cremation implicitly denied the importance of bodily survival after death. Instead, people now believed that the soul could reach the kingdom of the dead independently of the body that had once contained it. For the Urnfield warriors, the dead lived on in the memories of the living, finding their immortality in the lasting fame of their heroic deeds.

Rites and rituals

Apart from the mute testimony of burial sites, there is scant information on the religious beliefs of the times. There are, however, indications that a sun cult was widespread in Europe in the late Bronze Age, as attested by rock drawings, engraved sun symbols and cult objects such as the cone-shaped 'golden hats'. Made of thin sheet gold, these narrow, pointed conical objects can be up to 30cm (1ft) tall and are sometimes decorated with solar images. Scholars are uncertain of their exact function; some think that they were worn by shamans as part of their ceremonial regalia, while others consider it more likely that they were placed on wooden posts during religious rites. Whichever use they were put to, the cones must have created a remarkable spectacle whether glittering in the light of torches at night or else brilliantly lit up by the sun's rays. Rock engravings of

Mysterious 'golden hats'
Cone-shaped objects like this have been found at several sites across Europe. Some are covered with banded decorations and sun symbols that would have tested the goldsmith's skills.

concentric circles and multi-spoked wheels are usually interpreted as solar images, as are numerous metal discs. The best-known of all the Bronze Age cult objects is the famous sun chariot found at Trundholm in Denmark in 1902. Set on wheels, that perhaps allowed it to be pulled along in religious processions, it takes the form of a bronze horse pulling a gold-plated disc about 25cm (10in) in diameter. The chariot seems to embody a view similar to the ancient Greek belief that the god Apollo pulled the sun across the sky each day in a horse-drawn cart.

Religious rites were celebrated in the open air or in caves. Ceremonies featured music played on instruments that ranged from horns and clappers to sheet-metal gongs and drums. Animal sacrifices were offered on hilltops. Worshippers believed that springs, rivers, lakes and marshes represented gateways to the Underworld, so they buried valuable bronze gifts in their vicinity as offerings to the gods. Bronze chariots seem to have had a special ritual significance; they were paraded across the fields whenever there was a drought, apparently to bring on rain and stimulate crop growth.

The advent of iron

Whatever rites people performed to win the favour of the gods, they could do little to counter the growing insecurity of the times. The rising tide of violence was reflected in the ever-increasing importance of fortifications as the Bronze Age came to an end; settlements were equipped with higher and higher defensive walls, banks and palisades.

The situation only started to change with the spread of iron across the continent from about 1000 BC. This democratised metal technology and greatly reduced the importance of the old trade routes. The Bronze Age chieftains, whose wealth had been based on copper and tin, had to make way for a new elite. It was the end of their era of heroic display.

Homer's Greece

In the *Iliad* and *Odyssey*, the poet Homer left an incomparable portrait of ancient Greece in its Age of Heroes. In doing so, he drew on the legends of a culture that had disappeared many centuries before his own time – the world of the Mycenaeans.

The Trojans were amazed to find a gigantic wooden horse outside their city gates. For almost ten years they had been under siege by their enemies, the Mycenaean Greeks, but at last it seemed that the Greeks had withdrawn – their mighty fleet had disappeared over the horizon. Full of joy at their assumed deliverance, the Trojans dragged the horse into the city, taking it to the temple of

Symbol of power
A relief of lions caps the Lion Gate that led into the citadel of Mycenae. A fine example of Mycenaean architecture, the gateway was built in about 1250 BC.

The citadel of Mycenae
The site of Mycenae had been settled since Neolithic times, but the remains of buildings still there today date from the mid 2nd millennium BC. The circular tomb site in the foreground is among the oldest structures.

Servants had to ensure that the symbolic fire burning in the throne room never went out.

Early Mycenaean shaft graves were dug inside the citadel walls.

Behind the cemetery lay a number of small temple areas for religious ceremonies.

Athena as a victory offering to the goddess. But all was not as it seemed. Hidden within the hollow beast were a handful of Greek warriors: the devious Odysseus, who had hatched the scheme; brave Menelaus from Sparta, whose kidnapped wife, the beautiful Helen, had triggered the Trojan War; mighty Diomedes of Argos; Idomeneus of Crete, and others. When night fell and the unsuspecting Trojans were asleep, the warriors let themselves out through a hidden panel and rushed to the city gates to let their comrades into the undefended city. Then a

terrible massacre began. Troy, the great city guarding the mouth of the Black Sea, was reduced to rubble and ashes. The Mycenaeans had scored another victory.

Legend and fact

If the siege of Troy really happened – and academics still debate the point to this day – it must have occurred sometime during the 13th century BC, a troubled time across the ancient world. The stories that revolved around Troy were passed on by word of mouth for many generations before they were ever written down. It was only around the mid 8th century BC, when literacy returned to Greece after a Dark Age without written records, that the stories were collected. Homer's *Iliad* describes events at a crucial point of the siege, while the *Odyssey* recounts the adventures of Odysseus on the long journey home from Troy.

Some modern-day researchers have questioned whether an individual named Homer ever existed, suggesting instead that the epics were the work of a number of anonymous poets. At most, they suggest, Homer was the editor who assembled the tales into a cohesive whole. Whatever the facts of authorship, there is no doubt that many facets of Mycenaean history were accurately mirrored in the works attributed to Homer.

Anyone travelling on the Peloponnesian peninsula in Greece today will come across traces of Homer's heroes – perhaps in Mycenae itself where Agamemnon, the leader of the Greek army, reigned; or in Pylos where the ruins of a comfortable palace are said to be the remains of the home of old King Nestor, who according to the *Iliad* counselled moderation to his volatile warriors. The vast domed tombs of Mycenae are reminders of Clytemnestra and Aegisthus, Agamemnon's traitorous wife and her lover, who killed the trusting king on his return.

Mighty bulwarks

Even if the myths were only faint echoes of reality, later generations remained awestruck by the mighty citadel of Mycenae, which became the political and cultural centre of the Greek mainland in the years after 1500 BC. The stronghold was surrounded by fortifications nearly a kilometre (3000ft) long, and the average thickness of the walls was 6-8m (19-26ft).

The huge stones that made up the walls were dressed by Mycenae's masons and fitted together without the need for mortar; the gaps between blocks were filled with smaller stones. The oldest parts of the defences were in place by 1350 BC.

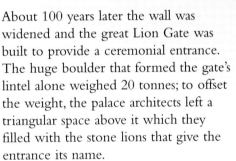

About 100 years later the wall was widened and the great Lion Gate was built to provide a ceremonial entrance. The huge boulder that formed the gate's lintel alone weighed 20 tonnes; to offset the weight, the palace architects left a triangular space above it which they filled with the stone lions that give the entrance its name.

The Mycenaeans cleverly secured the approaches to the Lion Gate with a defensive tower and a protruding fortified wall, which meant that attackers could be beaten back from above. The palace's North Gate was just as ingenious; it was concealed between two sections of wall in such a way as to make it practically invisible from outside. Astutely, the

▮ **Mycenaean influence**
● **Mycenaean citadels**
✳ **Mycenaean settlements in Asia Minor**

Monumental tomb
This domed burial chamber, or tholos, dating from the 14th century BC, is known as the 'Treasury of Atreus'.

builders also provided subterranean access to an underground spring located outside the walls that would provide a water reservoir in the event of a siege.

A fortified path led from the Lion Gate to the royal palace, which housed the private apartments of the ruler together with a central throne room, or megaron. This was equipped with a hearth 3.7m (12ft) across where a perpetual fire burned as a symbol of royal continuity. The throne stood on the room's south wall. Most of the other buildings within the palace complex were workshops, warehouses, or places of worship.

Warlike origins

But where had they come from, this people who were capable of such great military and architectural achievements? Little is known about the earliest phases of Greece's history. The Greek mainland had been inhabited since the Stone Age, but the people who scraped a living in its mountains and rugged valleys belonged to a simple peasant culture, quite unused to fortified settlements.

The largely peaceful existence of these farmers changed when foreign tribes migrated into the area from the north in the 2nd millennium BC. The newcomers, who spoke an Indo-European tongue, either integrated with the local inhabitants or else drove them out in the course of countless small wars. By the 16th century BC, an hierarchically structured warrior elite had established itself in central Greece and the Peloponnese, dividing the country into principalities under their rule. Important centres grew up at Mycenae in the Argolis region near the neck of the Peloponnese, and at Pylos on its western coast. Elsewhere on the mainland, the newcomers established strongholds at Athens, in Boeotian Thebes and Orchomenos, and at Iolkos in the northern region of Thessaly.

A strategic advantage

The rulers of Mycenae seem to have exerted a dominant influence over the other small kingdoms: they owned the largest fortresses, and by commanding the isthmus connecting the Peloponnese to the rest of mainland Greece they also controlled the road network, which radiated out in all directions past their city. Set high on a headland above the Bay of Nauplia, the citadel of Mycenae guarded the approaches to the Gulf of Corinth as well as the broad plain stretching to the Aegean coast. The site had been carefully chosen to take advantage of strong natural defences; it was protected by two deep ravines, which allowed access to the hilltop fortress only from the northwest.

Over the centuries Mycenae's wealth and power grew to legendary proportions: according to Homer, the city sent 100 ships against Troy – the largest contingent in the entire Greek fleet. In comparison, Agamemnon's brother Menelaus, the king of Sparta, supplied 60 ships, Crete sent 80, and even the mighty Nestor of Pylos could only manage 90.

In recognition of Mycenae's dominant position, scholars in modern times have given its name to the entire culture that blossomed in Greece between 1600 and 1200 BC. At the time, however, the Hittites who ruled in Anatolia referred to the people we call Mycenaeans as Achaeans – a term also applied to them in Homer's epics. No-one knows what the Achaeans called themselves.

An island inspiration

In its early years, Mycenaean culture developed under the influence of Crete. Greek sailors brought back fantastic tales of the palaces of the Minoans, with whom they traded. The Mycenaean ruling class copied the Cretan system of palace administration, and there was also close

A cumbersome load
Encased on all sides in heavy bronze armour, Mycenaean warriors usually proved more than a match for their opponents.

collaboration in the arts, with Mycenaean works often imitating Minoan models right down to fine details. Women in Minoan-style dress appear on wall paintings in Mycenaean palaces, and vases and amphorae are decorated with Cretan style sea motifs. Artists from Crete probably worked for Mycenaean employers and passed on their techniques to their mainland colleagues.

There were, however, clear cultural differences between the Aegean island kingdom and the mainland. In contrast to the peace-loving Cretan people, the Mycenaeans were manifestly warlike. They loved richly adorned weapons and fast horses, which they bred on the wide Argolis plains south of Mycenae. They had also adopted the war chariot, already familiar in the Near East. To judge from the rich hoards of gold found in Mycenaean tombs, war must have been an everyday business for the Mycenaean warrior nobility, who could never have earned such wealth from the natural resources of their relatively barren land. The gold is generally thought to have been plundered, although some may have reached Greece in the form of payment for the mercenary services of Mycenaean warriors abroad.

Equipped for battle

Mycenaean warriors were armed with long lances, swords of various lengths, and bows and arrows. For protection they wore bronze armour, including arm and leg greaves, and carried shields that were either small and round or else shaped like a figure of eight to cover the entire body. The head was protected by a leather helmet, sometimes plated with bronze or decorated with boars' tusks.

Mycenaean culture set great store by weapons and armour. The hero Achilles owned a suit of armour that, according to Homer, had been specially made for him by the divine smith Hephaistos. The showpiece was a great circular shield made of gold, silver and bronze and inlaid with

pictures of fields, herds, vineyards, cities, armies in battle, the sky, the sea, the Earth, Sun and Moon. After Achilles' death, Odysseus and Ajax vied for possession of this wonderful treasure, and Ajax committed suicide in a fit of madness when a counsel of Greek chiefs awarded Odysseus the prize. Receiving a suit of armour as a gift, or taking it from an enemy warrior defeated in battle, was a great distinction for a Mycenaean.

Luxury behind protective walls

Those who lived by war also risked dying by war, so Mycenaean warriors took care to protect their citadels with massive defensive walls. Later generations of Greeks found it hard to believe that the gigantic stone blocks of which the walls were built had been put there by human hands. Instead they ascribed the work to the Cyclops, one-eyed giants of Greek legend, and the massive masonry structures have been known as 'Cyclopean' ever since. To the south of Mycenae, the defences that surround Tiryns are as thick as 17.5m (57ft) in places – wide enough

Heroes' farewell
This detail from a fresco in the citadel of Mycenae shows a woman waving goodbye to two soldiers setting out for battle.

An unhappy marriage
This relief from a stele carved in 6th-century BC Greece depicts King Agamemnon and his wife Clytemnestra. After the war with Troy, the murder of Agamemnon by Clytemnestra and her lover Aegisthus threw Mycenae into bloody chaos.

Artistry in arms
Roughly 24cm (9in) long, this dagger from a Mycenaean tomb is inlaid with silver and gold illustrations of men hunting lions with spears and bows.

to conceal passageways for soldiers inside them. The most formidable fortifications of all were constructed at the citadel of Gla in Boeotia, where it seems likely they were intended to provide a refuge for the entire local population when under attack. The walls stretched for 3km (2 miles), punctuated by four gateways.

Inside their walled palace compounds, the ruling elite lived a life of sheer luxury. At the head of the social pyramid in every Mycenaean town was the *wanax*, or king. Above these local monarchs was the more powerful ruler of Mycenae – although the rulers of strongholds like Argos, Pylos, Thebes and Athens only reluctantly conceded his superiority. Quarrels and conflict were the order of the day; Homer describes in detail the petty jealousies that beset the Greek commanders, who squabbled incessantly over loot and women. In extreme cases their altercations stopped them from presenting a united front against the common enemy: the *Iliad*'s central theme turns on the unwillingness of the Greek hero Achilles to carry on fighting after Agamemnon, the commander of the host, robs him of his favourite mistress, Briseis.

Although the Mycenaean rulers often fell out, they also joined forces in certain military actions – as the war against Troy demonstrates. The pillaging and robbery that accompanied such ventures enabled them to amass ever more treasures.

Administration and society

Second only to the king in the hierarchy of most Mycenaean states was the commander in chief of the army, who was usually the ruler's son. The day-to-day administration of the community was left to a host of civil servants. Local governors answered to the *wanax* for the regions under their supervision; in the kingdom of Pylos, for example, there were 16 such districts grouped into two provinces. The population of the provinces included landowners with varying rights and prerogatives, as well as a number of free, mostly fortified villages whose inhabitants were known as demos, 'the people'; in later times these communities would become the nucleii of Greek city-states. Regional boundaries defined the areas controlled by the masters of the citadels.

Despite limitations on the power held by individual Mycenaean rulers, they were not prevented from boosting their self-esteem by building impressive palaces. A megaron, or rectangular throne-room, lay at the heart of each complex. Here, the ruler carried out his official duties and threw magnificent banquets, for which the Mycenaeans were renowned.

Centres of power

A visitor to one of the palaces would first have been ushered into a splendid pillared entrance hall, then from there into a vestibule before finally reaching the megaron. The central throne-room has been especially well-preserved in the palace of Pylos. Its floor, measuring some 28.8 x 11.3m (94 x 37ft), was made of stamped clay covered with decorated slabs of gypsum. The block immediately in front of the throne bore a stylised image of an octopus, perhaps a heraldic emblem. The room's walls were decorated with colourful frescoes of lions, griffins, birds and human figures.

The palaces at Tiryns and Pylos both had a second, smaller megaron, which might have been reserved for the women of the house. Women did not play as dominant a role in Mycenaean culture as in Minoan Crete, but it is likely that they were responsible for the observation of religious ceremonies. They also enjoyed sports and hunting and, like the men, rode out in chariots.

A successful economy

The numerous warehouses and storage rooms found in the remains of the Mycenaean palace complexes suggest that the economy of the kingdoms was organized centrally and regulated down to the last detail – a view confirmed by a multitude of small clay tablets inscribed in a script known as Linear-B, an early form of Greek. These describe the distribution of land to tenants, the supply of raw materials to local artisans, the employment of craftsmen – many of the best worked within the palace walls – and offer a detailed record of trade. Administrators monitored how much bronze was used for making weapons – the smiths had to account for every bit of ore they received. Grain surpluses were stored within the fortifications surrounding the palaces, along with finished goods ready for sale.

The Mycenaeans traded not only with the Aegean world but also with Asia Minor, Syria, Palestine, Egypt, Sicily and southern Italy. They exported olive oil, perfumes and ointments, and shipped wool, ceramics and weaponry across the entire eastern Mediterranean.

A change of guard

In the 15th century BC the Mycenaeans of mainland Greece took control of Crete, usurping the power of the Minoans who had long been their cultural mentors. They even took Knossos, the Cretan capital. By imposing their rule on the island they became masters of the Aegean shipping routes and a major naval power in the eastern Mediterranean. Miletus in Asia Minor became an important Mycenaean outpost, and there were other trading bases in Cyprus and Syria. Mycenaean dominance is illustrated by the widespread distribution of their pottery across the Mediterranean region in the latter half of the 2nd millennium BC.

Rich trappings for the afterlife

As the Mycenaeans grew in confidence – due in part to their successes in war and in part to their healthy economy – they demonstrated their success not just in

TIME WITNESS

Agamemnon and Nestor – Homeric heroes

In his epics Homer depicts Agamemnon, King of Mycenae, as a brave military commander, but also as a jealous and greedy general. His leadership of the forces assembled against Troy does not go unchallenged. At one point in the *Iliad*, Idomeneus of Crete threatens to withdraw from the siege taking his 80 ships with him unless Agamemnon agrees to share supreme command.

Odysseus and Diomedes, too, criticise Agamemnon for his impulsive behaviour. When the Greeks eventually emerge victorious, thanks to the intervention of the gods, new dangers await Agamemnon back home in Mycenae. During his ten-year absence his wife Clytemnestra has found a new lover, Aegisthus, and the adulterous couple conspire to murder the king in his bath.

Nestor of Pylos, in contrast, epitomises wisdom and goodness. Despite his advanced age, he speeds to Troy with his fleet and once there he consistently supports the Greek cause both in word and deed. He is always ready to mediate in the quarrels that divide the rival generals, and shows great compassion in personally treating the wounded.

The face of a hero
This gold plaque, which measures 25cm (10in) across, was uncovered by Mycenae's first excavator, Heinrich Schliemann, who named it 'the mask of Agamemnon'. Scenes from Homer's epics were often depicted in decorative classical friezes (background, above).

their splendid palace-fortresses but also in the way they buried their dead. The modern world had its first glimpse of the splendours of Mycenaean civilisation in the late 19th century when German archaeologist Heinrich Schliemann uncovered some stunningly well-equipped shaft graves located within the fortifications of Mycenae itself. The dead warrior-kings buried there entered the afterlife with valuable weapons, including lances, daggers, arrows and elegant bronze knives with curved blades. Many of the items were engraved with hunting or battle scenes. Some wore priceless gold masks. Women were buried in fabulous jewellery: princesses were found with massive gold earrings and arm bands and necklaces of golden beads or pearls, as well as crowns made from beaten sheet gold. Amethysts, carnelians and amber from the Baltic seem to have been especially prized as gems, and the tombs also housed splendid gold sacrificial vessels.

Divine opulence
This sacrificial vessel in the form of a lion's head was found in one of the shaft tombs inside the citadel of Mycenae. Measuring about 20cm (8in), it was fashioned by a Mycenaean smith out of pure gold.

Shaft graves and beehive tombs

Early Mycenaean tomb construction was fairly simple: shafts were sunk into the earth to a depth of about 4m (13ft) and the graves were set within circular cemeteries demarcated by upright stone slabs. Individual tombs were marked with slabs or stelae on which hunting or battle scenes were depicted.

By the mid 1st millennium BC, however, shaft graves no longer sufficed.

Mycenaean rulers now built huge domed tombs known as tholoi (singular, tholos) whose construction represented an outstanding architectural achievement. A particularly beautiful tholos stands outside the walls of Mycenae. Schliemann named it and its contents the 'Treasury of Atreus' after Agamemnon's father, a legendary king who, in about 1250 BC, seized power from the ruling Perseid house to create his own dynasty. Like many other Mycenaean rulers, he eventually died at the hands of one of his own relatives.

The path to the tomb was flanked with colossal stone walls, 36m (117ft) long, that followed the slope of the hill. A gigantic doorway over 5m (16ft) high with a lintel weighing 120 tonnes provided access to the burial chamber. Inside, a 3m (10ft) long passageway led to the beehive-shaped tholos, which was hollowed out of the hillside. Built of large stone blocks, this rose up to a dome standing a full 13m (42ft) above the tomb's floor. To create the dome, the architects designed a corbelled roof, with the stone blocks staggered so that each layer extended slightly above the one below.

The protruding edges of the blocks were later chiselled away to provide a smoothly curving surface. Nail holes in the ceiling suggest that it was once covered with decorative bronze or gold rosettes. Funeral rites took place in the domed chamber and the body was then laid to rest in a smaller side-chamber. Nine of these impressive round structures were found at Mycenae alone, their construction coinciding with the peak of Mycenaean culture. Lesser mortals were buried in somewhat smaller chamber tombs, though these, too, were domed. Long passages dug into the sides of hills led to round or oblong tomb chambers that were often used for generations.

The Mycenaean pantheon

Little is known about the religion of the Mycenaeans, but it is likely that they worshipped a Mother Goddess and conducted fertility rites in much the same way as the Minoans. Ceremonies probably took place mainly in the open air, at sacred sites and in groves as well as in the palace compound. However, small cult buildings – in particular a shrine at Eleusis near Athens – are clearly antecedents of the classical Greek temple.

Although the Mycenaean pantheon was not as fixed as that of classical times, the gods of Olympus can already be identified. At this time, Poseidon was venerated as the principal deity; later he would be relegated to god of the sea. The Earth Mother Demeter along with Zeus and Hera, and possibly Apollo and Dionysos, were also revered.

Between Mycenae and Argos stood the Heraion, an important sanctuary dedicated to Zeus's wife Hera. In later times this building became the focus for famous celebrations and competitive games in the goddess's honour. The practice of ritual ablutions in sacred waters was familiar to Mycenaean priestesses, and each spring the faithful made a pilgrimage to a local river to celebrate the marriage of Hera and Zeus. The cult sites of Delphi and Olympia, which became so important in classical times, also had Mycenaean roots.

The collapse of Mycenae

For all their martial skills and mighty fortifications, the Mycenaeans could not prevent their ultimate decline. The seeds were sown in the second half of the 13th century BC, when great migrations shook the eastern Mediterranean world. Previously unrecorded 'Sea Peoples' invaded Egypt, and unknown assailants sacked the Hittite kingdom in Anatolia. The Mycenaeans, too, had to contend with foreign invaders. In about 1240 BC, the royal residence at Pylos was reduced to ashes. There was destruction too at

Elegance in the afterlife
This gold Mycenaean cup came from one of their beehive-shaped tombs.

Mycenae and Tiryns, followed by hasty rebuilding of the defensive fortifications. The two citadels were finally destroyed about a hundred years later.

The heavily armoured Mycenaean warriors were no match for the invaders – lightly-armed foot soldiers who fought with throwing spears and long swords. Mycenaean military tactics that relied heavily on the deployment of war chariots proved to be a liability in battles against highly mobile enemy forces.

Internal factors also underlay the Mycenaean collapse. There are some indications that the hold of the ruling elites in their powerfully defended citadels had already been loosened from within. Natural catastrophes including earthquakes and bad harvests may have weakened their grip. Tensions and rivalries within the warrior caste itself may also have played a part, preventing the rulers from organising effective defences against the hostile tribes.

The stuff of legend

Whatever the causes of the Mycenaean downfall, the results were grim. The splendid fortress-palaces were burned down, settlements were abandoned, the population was drastically reduced, and the Linear-B script was lost along with knowledge of writing itself.

Greek-speaking tribes, specifically Doric peoples from the Balkans, moved into the ensuing power vacuum. Cultural life died almost completely and the heroes of Mycenae lived on only in memory, as wandering bards commemorated their deeds in their songs. Courage, intelligence, strength, nobility, an obsession with honour and fame – all these warrior virtues would in time find their apotheosis in the *Iliad* and the *Odyssey*, which would eventually carry the ideals of these Bronze Age warriors into the modern world.

Delicate decoration
Jewellery featuring motifs from the natural world, like the laurel leaves on this coronet of gold, were popular with wealthy Mycenaean women.

AMERICA

The first Americans

America was the last of the Earth's major landmasses to be settled. The first North Americans adopted flexible strategies to enable them to cope with the enormous environmental changes that followed the end of the last Ice Age.

Estimates of when early American settlement began vary enormously, from the traditionally accepted theory of around 15,000 years ago to as much as 40,000 years ago based on very recent discoveries. The scenario postulated in the traditional theory is that a group of Ice Age hunters probably set out from the north-eastern tip of Asia and simply went farther east than any had gone before. At the time the Bering Strait – the strip of water that separates Asia from America – did not exist. A land bridge connected the continents and the early settlers took this path to reach new hunting grounds, not realising that by so doing they were opening up the Earth's last virgin landmass to human settlement. Other groups may have followed later.

The landscape they found can hardly have been very inviting. Two huge ice sheets covered much of present-day Canada, but a narrow corridor ran between them, forming a path to the south. Even the regions that were not icebound at the time were largely treeless: the vegetation consisted of dwarf birch trees, heather and grass, much like today's Siberian tundra. Nevertheless, some large animals were able to support themselves in sizeable numbers on such terrain, notably mammoths, steppe bison, wild horses and caribou.

In the ensuing centuries more groups of nomadic hunters followed the first arrivals, pursuing the herds ever southward. Over the course of several thousands of years they spread out across all of North America.

Cunning and courage

The tundra landscape stretched right down to the plains of America's present-day Midwest, while the lands to the east and west were covered with forests. The climate was harsh: short warm summers, followed by long hard winters. The early settlers had to adapt to these difficult conditions. Small bands, only a few people strong, roamed the land, supporting themselves by hunting and harvesting wild plants. They lived in caves, under overhanging rocks,

Living with nature
Fishing was the mainstay of the hunter lifestyle in the Arctic and coastal regions of North America. This pictograph of a whale was found in Ozette in Washington State. Like today's Inuit, their present-day successors, these early peoples dressed in warm furs to protect themselves against the cold (background illustration).

or in camps sited on the banks of rivers or lakes. They built shelters of simple, hut-shaped frames covered with mammoth or bison hides. Their preferred prey probably included mastodons – a large mammal that resembled an elephant – and mammoths, both now extinct, as well as caribou and bison. Wild horses, which roamed North America at the time, were another source of meat.

A group of hunters could live for weeks off the meat of the largest mammals; whatever they did not eat immediately, they dried or smoked to keep in storage. The animal hides and bones were used to make warm clothing, weapons and wind-breaks, and the fat was burned in stone lamps – an important source of light in the long, cold winter months.

It took experience and courage to kill a mammoth. The hunters needed intimate knowledge of the migration cycle of the herds in order to ambush them, most probably at watering-holes. The aim would be to separate one or more of the animals from the rest of the herd, then if possible drive the chosen victim over a cliff or into a marsh. A handful of the hunters might try to create a distraction from the front so that others could creep up unseen from behind. The coup de grâce was delivered with a spearthrust into the vulnerable underbelly.

Quality tools from simple materials

These early Americans have left ample evidence of their tool-making abilities. The materials that they used, both for hunting weapons and for the tools they used in daily life, were stone, bone and wood. From about 9500 BC they are known to have been making delicate but deadly stone tips for their spears. These have become known as the Clovis points after the site in New Mexico where they were first found, but spearheads like these have since been unearthed all over North America. The points would probably have been fixed to spear shafts with twine and resin. Bone or wood were used to make

spear-throwers that dramatically increased the range and penetration power of the weapons. The Clovis people also used razor-sharp scrapers and knives for skinning and butchering animals. Modern experiments with these Ice Age tools have shown that their cutting power almost matches that of modern steel knives.

A time of drastic change

However harsh the climatic conditions faced by the first Americans, they would rarely have been forced to go short of

Scenes from North America
Some of the early settlers from Asia probably used what is now Oregon as their access road to the south. Their traces can be seen in rock pictures, like this one, along the path of the Columbia River.

An ancient weapon
An early American tool-maker created this fine stone spear point about 12,000 years ago. Known as the Sandia point, it is about 7cm (3in) long and is now displayed in the Maxwell Museum of Anthropology in Albuquerque, USA.

food. The huge continent was sparsely inhabited, and if game became scarce in one area, a tribe had only to move on to fresh hunting grounds. Around 10,000 BC, however, the climate began to warm up.

The Ice Age came to an end and within just a few thousand years environmental conditions changed drastically across North America.

As the northern ice shields withdrew, the land bridge between Asia and America was flooded, creating the Bering Strait. The landscape of North America gradually took on its present-day appearance: coniferous forests spread over areas of Canada previously covered by glaciers, and dense deciduous forests blanketed much of the eastern part of the present United States. Vast expanses of prairie stretched across the Midwest, while much of the Southwest became desert. These huge environmental upheavals had an enormous effect on the animal world. Many of the larger Ice Age mammals – including mammoths, mastodons, wild horses and sabre-tooth tigers – rapidly became extinct. No-one knows for sure how far humans may have contributed to their extinction through overhunting.

Survival strategies

The disappearance of many of the large herding animals had acute consequences for the early Americans. As their principal food sources melted away they had to come to terms with hunger, hitherto an unknown problem. As a result, in the years after 8000 BC the unified culture of the early hunters gave way to a range of different life styles that were adapted to the changing environmental conditions. Small bands of hunter-gatherers no longer wandered freely across the continent; instead they settled down in fixed areas and adopted ways of life specifically adapted to the resources that their new surroundings provided.

The one large game species to escape the post-Ice Age extinctions was bison. They continued to graze the vast prairies as they had before, and they became the main quarry of the Midwestern hunting tribes. The hunters came to rely on tried-and-tested methods to kill large numbers of animals. First, they carefully observed the movements of a herd. When the animals approached the top of a cliff, hunters camouflaged with bison skins would close in, suddenly shouting or otherwise creating a commotion to startle the beasts and drive them towards the drop. Panic-stricken, the animals would take flight, galloping over the edge of the chasm to their deaths. Where no cliffs were available, the hunters constructed wooden pens concealed by the brows of low slopes. They would then chase the bison into the trap where they could be easily slaughtered.

New weapons for new situations

External conditions encouraged the early Americans to develop a versatile arsenal of weapons. They started arming their spears with shorter tips – the so-called Folsom points – or with points made out of deer antlers in which they embedded small, sharp stone blades. These spears were more suitable for hunting smaller animals. Other tribes used spears with detachable heads that remained fixed within the prey after it had been hit. One advantage of such weapons was that the shafts could be reused simply by attaching new heads, saving hunters the chore of having to carry several different spears.

Using what nature provided

In the other regions, too, the post-Ice Age people developed new survival strategies. For the inhabitants of the Pacific Northwest and the ancestors of today's Inuit in the Arctic region, the sea provided the means of survival. The main occupations in these regions were fishing and hunting whales and seals. The hunters developed special harpoons with bone points, and also boats like the kayak that were adapted to local conditions. Kayak remains found in western Greenland have been dated back to around 2000 BC.

On the coasts of California the local tribes found themselves in rich fishing grounds. They supplemented their diet of fish and seafood with wild plants, seeds and nuts, among them starch-rich acorns, which were laboriously ground up in stone mortars. The resulting flour was then soaked in water to leach out the bitterness before being made into an edible dough.

In the arid Southwest, the indigenous peoples lived in caves or established simple hunting camps near the region's few lakes and marshes, where they fished and also hunted water birds. Archaeologists have discovered striking evidence of some sophisticated hunting techniques. In Lovelock Cave, Nevada, naturalistic raffia decoys have been found that were evidently used as lures. Hunters concealed in the reeds attracted the birds' attention by making splashing sounds; when the waterfowl approached the decoys, they became easy prey.

For the inhabitants of the Eastern Woodlands, the forests with their abundant fauna and edible plants provided a varied range of nourishment and a rich

source of raw materials. Here, people lived in camps of wood-framed huts covered with deer skins, bark or woven mats. They still used tools and blades of flint, but these now came in a variety of different shapes and sizes. Every activity undertaken by the villagers now had its appropriate tool, whether it was a scraper for removing fur from skins, a drill for boring, or selected knives for hunting, carving or whittling.

The start of metalworking and agriculture

In the centuries that followed the arrival of the first settlers in North America, tribes and tribal groups of varying sizes gradually developed, each of which evolved its own language, art, culture and lifestyle. Over the course of time these groups moved restlessly around the continent, just as people did in other regions of the Earth, adapting to the surroundings that they found in their new homes.

The migrations led to the development and exchange of new technologies. By about 3000 BC, tribes in the Great Lakes region had discovered the art of copper-working by cold-hammering techniques, and from about 2500 BC the first simple ceramic vessels came into use in the coastal areas of what is now Georgia.

In the Southwest, villagers began cultivating domesticated plant species such as maize, gourds and beans, and were thus able to compensate for the unpredictable food supply of the hunter-gatherer lifestyle in semi-desert. These people were an exception, however; in most of the rest of North America hunter-gathering rather than farming remained the usual way of life for as long as conditions allowed.

The one other region in which agriculture caught on was the Eastern Woodlands, where a settled lifestyle gradually evolved. From about 1000 BC, large settlements resembling towns developed there, opening up a whole new stage of cultural development.

The Olmecs – makers of mighty monuments

The Olmecs made their first appearance in southeastern Mexico in about 1500 BC. They carved extraordinary sculptures from huge blocks of stone and their religion and art influenced all later Central American civilisations.

Stone tomb
Constructed from carefully worked slabs of solid basalt, this tomb belonged to a member of La Venta's ruling elite.

The eyes are almond-shaped and the gaze unfocused. The rounded face, with its flattened nose and full lips, seems profoundly sad, although the turned-down corners of the mouth suggest anger, or perhaps grim determination. The head bears a tight-fitting covering resembling a helmet. The majesty and sheer size – almost 3m (10ft) tall and weighing over 20 tonnes – of this freestanding sculpture still impress, more than 3000 years after its creation.

Mystery surrounds the people who created these colossal stone heads, of which 17 have survived. No-one knows where they originally came from or even what they called themselves. Centuries later, the Aztecs referred to them as *olmeca uixtotin*, 'the people from the land of rubber'. The Olmecs certainly used latex taken from the abundant rubber trees of their homeland, working it into balls used to play the ritual ball game that they first introduced and which became a feature of all subsequent Mesoamerican cultures.

A thousand years before the Maya civilisation, the Olmecs founded the first urban settlements on Mexico's Gulf Coast. They also built the earliest ceremonial centres north of the Isthmus of Panama, complete with courts for the ball game, and created a multitude of magnificent works of art from basalt, clay, wood, iron and, above all, jade. The little-understood symbolism of their art and architecture suggests they already had a complex world view, expressed in religious rituals to honour their gods. In addition, they devised a calendar, a system of numbers and a hieroglyphic script, although as yet this has been only partially deciphered. Theirs was the founding civilisation of the Central American area, and it eventually extended from central Mexico to the Pacific coast of El Salvador.

An inhospitable region

Set in dense primeval jungle, with extensive swamps and a labyrinth of rivers, streams and lagoons, the Olmec heartland between the Gulf of Mexico and the volcanic Tuxtla mountains might not have seemed the most propitious choice for settlement in the early 2nd millennium BC. A lengthy rainy season brought prolonged downpours that regularly caused severe flooding, threatening the survival of human settlements and making it difficult to find clean drinking water. To counter the flooding problem, the Olmecs built their villages on high ground

The colossal Olmec stone heads stare unflinchingly into eternity. Some, like this one, sport headgear thought to be connected with the Olmecs' ritual ball game.

GULF OF

CAMPECHE

YUCATAN

PENINSULA

Tres
Zapotes

La Venta

MEXICO

San Lorenzo

PACIFIC OCEAN

- Olmec heartland
- Olmec centres
- Olmec expansion
  and influence

complexes were surrounded by ramparts and adorned with monumental stone sculptures. By then, the farming communities must have been producing surplus food, which enabled some among them to turn their attention away from subsistence agriculture and look towards ambitious, large-scale public works. At the same time, their egalitarian society underwent a transformation as a ruling elite arose, possibly through ownership of the best agricultural land, or perhaps because they possessed specialist knowledge or leadership qualities. This minority promptly set about demonstrating their claim to power in a display of organisational and logistical skill that was without parallel, at least in the Mesoamerica of that time.

Ingenious engineers

The greatest of the early Olmec centres, San Lorenzo, flourished between about 1250 and 950 BC. Its builders chose an area of ground rising 70m (230ft) above the River Coatzacoalco. They secured it against erosion by building terraces and drainage ditches, then levelled its top to form an artificial plateau, which involved thousands of workers shifting at least the top 10m (30ft) of earth by hand.

On the western, northwestern and southern sides of this huge plateau, the builders erected six monumental earthworks, along with 12 reservoirs and an underground system of water pipes. These were constructed by digging a ditch and lining it with basalt stones, which had been carved into a U-shape and were butted up end to end. This guttering was then covered with flat basalt lids and the ditch backfilled.

and raised their huts on artificial hillocks of mud and sand. For the floods also brought benefits – they made the land fertile. By repeatedly depositing rich alluvial soil on the riverbanks, they enabled Olmec farmers to harvest two crops each year. The grew maize and beans, as well as manioc, squashes and chilli peppers, and watered and drained their terraced fields through an ingenious system of irrigation ditches. For eggs and meat they kept chickens and small, edible dogs, and hunted deer and peccaries, a species of wild pig. Fish, mussels, turtles and alligators provided extra protein.

Around the middle of the millennium, Olmec culture took a great leap forward when the first ceremonial centres and earth pyramids were constructed. The

A monolithic throne
The lifesize central figure in this throne from La Venta wears a conspicuous pectoral ornament and a decorative headdress made of eagle's feathers. In his right hand he grips a cord that is knotted around the wrist of another figure carved on the back of the block. A stylised jaguar bares its fangs above the man's head.

A structure known to archaeologists as the *palacio rojo* (red palace) was constructed on a purpose-built earth mound in the centre of the complex. All that remains is some 60m² (650sq ft) of reddish flooring material, along with some of the stones that made up the steps and the stumps of huge basalt pillars that probably once supported a wooden roof.

Houses for about 1000 people stood on 200 other, smaller mounds dotted around the complex. They had floors of compacted clay and gravel, walls of wattle and roofs of palm thatch. Like other Olmec centres, San Lorenzo apparently sheltered a small elite in large, centrally located dwellings. Craft-workers and merchants were housed in designated quarters on the outskirts of the complex. The bulk of the workers, along with the farmers and fishermen who helped to support it, lived in small villages nearby.

Monolithic monuments

Archaeologists have recovered about 70 carved stone monuments from San Lorenzo, including ten colossal heads – some seem to have been ritually buried. The heads, with clearly differentiated features, probably represented leading dignitaries, perhaps rulers or high priests. Most are shown wearing the same distinctive headgear pulled tightly down over the forehead – a feature that resembles the helmets worn in later Mesoamerican cultures for the ritual ball game, traditionally the preserve of the ruling elite. Ball courts, along with the rubber balls used to play the game, have been found in other Olmec settlements, but not at San Lorenzo itself.

Three basalt thrones found at San Lorenzo have an equally monumental feel. It was once thought that these monoliths – which

weigh up to 30 tonnes each – were altars, particularly since the Olmecs ritually buried artefacts under and around them. More recent opinion is that the figures depicted on the front of each block, shown crouching or sitting in a carved niche, represented Olmec rulers. This is inferred from a number of symbols that the ancient stonemasons used to suggest majesty and power – a headdress made from the feathers of the harpy eagle, for example. In later Mesoamerican cultures such headgear formed part of the garb shamans wore when making journeys to the spirit world. Its image at San Lorenzo suggests that the city's rulers also performed sacred duties, perhaps even serving as high priests.

Waterways for transport

Whatever their exact status, San Lorenzo's ruling elite evidently provided efficient leadership. They not only succeeded in

Ritual gathering
These 16 small jade figures have been reassembled in front of standing stones in the positions in which archaeologists found them, buried in sand under a courtyard at La Venta.

providing for the several thousand workers employed on the site but also arranged the transport of the massive basalt blocks used in its construction from the Tuxtla mountains 70km (45 miles) away. The city's location on the Coatzacoalco River, one of the region's most important trade arteries, was no doubt a considerable help. The huge stone blocks were dragged on sleds or rollers to the riverbank, then floated on rafts to stonemasons' workshops where they would be worked on.

Superior skills with stone tools

Masons used stone chisels and hand drills to smooth the blocks, which would have been only crudely shaped at the quarry; large amounts of sand were used as an abrasive. In addition to the colossal heads and stones for building purposes, sculptors fashioned statuettes of gods, sarcophagi and steles decorated with reliefs and inscriptions

recounting Olmec myth and history. Other skilled craftsmen shaped arrow tips, blades and scrapers out of a hard, glasslike substance known as obsidian. Jewellery, ceremonial knives and other status symbols for the ruling elite were at first made mostly from serpentine; jade was introduced in a later period.

Olmec blacksmiths made beads and concave mirrors from a variety of metals including haematite, ilmenite and magnetite. On ceremonial occasions the ruler wore a concave mirror on a leather thong around his neck. Whoever stood before him would have seen his own reflected image in the mirror, upside-down and with the features distorted.

Trade networks in the rainforest

Raw materials came to San Lorenzo by the river route, often arriving from distant locations. Haematite, for instance, originated in Oaxaca 200km (125 miles) away, while volcanic obsidian came all the way from what is now Guatemala. To ensure a constant supply of the goods they needed, whether precious minerals or cocoa beans, the Olmecs established a far-flung chain of trading bases – two were at Tlatico and Chalcatzingo in the vicinity of modern Mexico City, for example, and even on the Pacific coast of present-day El Salvador. They traded their own products for the materials they needed, with the result that Olmec pottery and statuettes have been found at Copán in Honduras 1100km (680 miles) away, and even at Cuello in Belize. But then something

Child statuettes
This lifelike ceramic figurine of a small child is one of many found in the Olmec lands. Some researchers believe that they may have represented infant 'were-jaguars', half human and half beast; others argue that they embodied household gods. Their true significance remains a mystery.

dramatic happened. Sometime between 950 and 900 BC, San Lorenzo was abruptly abandoned. Some of the colossal heads and other monuments were ritually defaced before being buried. No-one knows why this happened; perhaps there was a workers' revolt, or a civil war between different sections of the ruling class.

La Venta

At about the same time that San Lorenzo fell into disuse, another complex was coming into its heyday at La Venta, near the Gulf Coast 100km (60 miles) to the east. Some 18,000 people lived in its environs, among them fishermen, farmers, artisans and merchants. Here, too, the reins of power were held either by a priest-king or by a secular ruler reigning in conjunction with an elite caste of priests. There was never a unified Olmec state; rather, there were more than 50 ceremonial centres serving regions of different sizes and competing with one another for influence.

La Venta was situated on an island about 4.5km (2.8 miles) long. The vast complex that rose there from around 1000 BC onwards was built in four main phases and was oriented on a precise north–south axis that could only have been achieved through careful astronomical observation. To the south the Great Pyramid, one of the largest earthworks in Mesoamerica, rose 30m (100ft) high. To build it, the Olmecs piled up around 100,000m³ (3.5 million cu ft) of clay and multicoloured sand. To judge from its irregular, non-rectangular base, and the way in which it is oriented toward the Tuxtla mountains to the north, they designed it not so much as a pyramid as something resembling the

cone of a volcano. Some scholars believe that the grave of an Olmec ruler lies beneath the mound, but this theory is unproven.

Immediately to the north of the mound was an open area 80m (250ft) long, enclosed by earth ramparts, which may have been a ball court. Beyond lay another plaza, which was walled with upright basalt slabs.

Buried artworks

Beneath this open space one of the great mysteries of the Olmec world lay hidden. Over the course of about four centuries, hundreds of serpentine blocks were buried there, at five separate points along the north–south axis. In one, the diggers excavated a pit 20m (65ft) square by 4m (13ft) deep, then filled it with the green stone slabs. At the four other sites, they spread yellow-orange sand on the bottom of each pit, then arranged the blocks in a mosaic which they then covered over with earth. One of the mosaics is thought to be a jaguar mask or the face of a supernatural being, but the purpose of these so-called 'stone sacrifices' is still unknown.

So far, experts have also only been able to guess at the purpose of a shaft, spread with red sand and paved with serpentine slabs, that was dug into the earth mound at one end of La Venta's ceremonial centre. A number of jade axe

Stone figure
The Olmecs buried this carved stone stele, seen here from the back, near the great earthen pyramid at La Venta. The loin cloth the figure is wearing was standard dress for Olmec men, but the feather headdress suggests this individual was a noble – perhaps an envoy or a priest. The object in his hand is probably a ceremonial hatchet.

heads were placed inside it in a cruciform pattern, along with a large, empty, stone sarcophagus decorated with a relief of a grotesque figure with gaping, crocodilian mouth. Like the pits, the shaft was sealed off until reopened by archaeologists in recent times.

One theory is that the serpentine blocks may have represented the waters of the underworld. Deceased souls could enter through the alligator's mouth – the creature's amphibious nature suggests a link between the worlds of the living and the dead. The cross made by the axe heads may have stood for the World Tree, which is the order of the Mesoamerican cosmos.

Elsewhere, too, the Olmecs buried precious artefacts at ritually significant sites. Jade and serpentine statuettes, carved stones and ceremonial knives and hatchets were all placed at specific points along the main axes of the ceremonial centres or under flights of steps, presumably to ensure the gods' protection. In addition, the Olmecs singled out natural sites that they held sacred, including mountain peaks, which they regarded as the seat of the gods, caves, which were entrances to the supernatural world, and springs, which required divine attention because they supplied vital drinking water.

Sacrificial springs

In about 1600 BC, Olmec builders enclosed a spring at El Manatí, southeast of San Lorenzo, within a sandstone wall. Over the ensuing centuries they made regular votive offerings there, throwing polished obsidian cleavers and blades, serpentine beads and rubber balls into the waters. Later, in about 1100 BC, the spring was the scene of a strange ceremony. Celebrants carried 40 lifesize busts – painted red and black and with the prominent eyes, flat noses and full lips of the colossal heads from San Lorenzo – to the edge of the pool. They wrapped them in rush and leaf matting and dropped them in, weighted down with an assortment of serpentine knifeblades, carved wooden sticks, balls of haematite, chains and ear pegs. Finally, they covered the offering over with a thick layer of plant matter.

The bones of young people have also been found at the spring, as at other sacrificial sites connected with water, leading scholars to speculate that the Olmecs sacrificed children in ceremonies considered vital for the fertility of the land. Olmec reliefs, however, show only the sacrifice of adults, so perhaps there is some other explanation.

Infants in clay

Strange, hollow-clay, infant sculptures have been found buried as grave goods with Olmec dead. The figures, which can be almost lifesize, look like babies of a few months old. The chubby tots are naked, and many appear to be holding their arms out to an observer. On most, the mouth is wide open, as if screaming or snarling. The Olmecs often left jade or stone statuettes in the laps of these clay infants. Both male and female figures have been found, along with androgynous ones whose gender is impossible to discern; some have half-human, half-animal features.

Like so much Olmec iconography, the clay infants raise more questions than they answer. What did these child figures mean to the Olmecs? Who were they meant to represent? Why did they have such a significant role in Olmec art, and why did childhood hold such fascination for these people? Did the figures hold some religious significance – and if so, what might it have been? The lack of written sources makes it impossible for researchers to do any more than guess. The figures may be linked to fertility rituals, but their purpose remains a mystery.

Exported craftware
The abstract pattern on this elegant bowl was made by scratching through the black glaze. It was found at Las Boca, in the Mexican highlands, where it must have been taken via the trade routes.

Animal gods

The Olmecs clearly held the jaguar in great reverence (see Backround panel, page 167), and were probably the first Mesoamerican civilisation to do so. They immortalised the big cat in countless sculptures, and stylised jaguar masks adorned steles and thrones. In a cave in the Mexican state of Guerrero, west of San Lorenzo, a fresco depicts a ritual of an almost erotic nature involving a human and a jaguar. Some sculptures show a human figure clinging onto the back of a big cat, perhaps on a journey to the otherworld – jaguars apparently provided a link. Similar mystery surrounds the hybrid figures, displaying half-human and half-animal (usually catlike) features, that frequently crop up in Olmec art.

About ten Olmec gods besides the jaguar deity have now been identified. They include divinities associated with harpy eagles, pumas, alligators or caimans, and snakes, as well as a corn god. A relief at San Lorenzo shows a man holding the head of an enormous feathered boa constrictor, with the snake's body wrapped around his torso; on a stele from La Venta, a huge rattlesnake looms over the figure of a ruler. Perhaps such images were intended to suggest that the beasts' innate powers could be transferred to certain humans, or perhaps that the ruler was protected by the animal depicted.

Unanswered questions

Many questions about Olmec society remain unanswered. Their pictographic system of writing remains only partially deciphered, and the artworks they left behind are still little understood. We do not know, for example, whether Olmec culture was spread by war or by peaceful trade networks. What is certain is that they influenced an ever larger area of Mesoamerica. Olmec civilisation was the most advanced in the region up to the 6th century BC; and their hierarchically ordered population lived in an economy based on the division of labour.

Olmec potters created high-quality ceramics with unique stylised patterns. The same can also be said of their jade and serpentine artefacts, all made without the aid of metal tools. These ceramics and carvings were sought-after export commodities, and their makers' skills were much in demand.

Yet there is still no generally accepted explanation as to why first San Lorenzo and then La Venta were abandoned, in each case after large numbers of artworks had been defaced and buried. Similar mystery surrounds the abandonment of the other Olmec settlements, up to and including Tres Zapotes, the last major centre, which was located 120km (80 miles) northwest of La Venta near the Gulf Coast. It is also not clear what happened to the Olmecs' descendants after the last remnants of their civilisation disappeared, sometime in the final half of the 1st millennium BC.

A long-lasting legacy

Even though they themselves vanished, the Olmecs left an enduring cultural legacy. Later Mesoamerican civilisations inherited from them a tradition of monumental architecture and ceremonial sites oriented with the heavens. In addition they left behind the ritual ball game and a pantheon of gods with their associated iconography.

The Olmec numerical system consisted of a combination of dots to denote the numbers 1 to 4 and a stroke to represent 5. This is seen again in the system used by the Maya, and the Mayan hieroglyphic script is based on Olmec pictograms. For the Olmecs themselves, no antecedents have been found whose work they could have built on. They stand right at the start of the Mesoamerican tradition, making their own achievement unique.

Artistry in jade
Jade artefacts, whether in the form of necklaces, earrings and nose ornaments (background) or worked into ritual objects like this ceremonial hand-axe (above), were highly prized status symbols among the Olmec ruling class.

Jaguar people – the Chavín of Peru

The first of the great South American civilisations, the Chavín worshipped a jaguar-god as their principal deity. The technological and artistic achievements of this people would influence all later indigenous cultures of the Andes.

Stirrup handle
The hollow stirrup handle of this red-glaze pottery vessel is typical of Chavín ware. It is embellished with a striped snake design and dates from the Late Period of Chavín culture, around 200 BC.

Gateway to a pyramid
The old temple at Chavín de Huantar is thought to date from the 9th century BC. This monumental portal or gateway opens onto stairs leading up the step pyramid, which rises to a height of 15m (50ft).

Some 3200m (10,500ft) up in the Andes mountains of Peru lies an ancient shrine that has lent its name to the first great culture of Peru. Today, the only way to reach it is by truck, and the bumpy ride on winding tracks, over vertiginous mountain passes, calls for strong nerves. At one point, the road leads through a tunnel that opens like a gaping black mouth 4700m (15,400ft) above sea level, then descends steeply via a series of sharp hairpin bends. Visitors arrive with a sense of relief at the modern village of Chavín with its two-storey adobe houses. The trip is worth the effort, however, not least because nearby, ringed by snowfields that never melt, lie the remains of the most important site of Latin America's Early Horizon cultural epoch, which has lent its name to the extraordinary culture of the Chavín peoples.

The ruins of Chavín de Huantar cover an area of about 250m² (2700sq ft), and display a striking interplay of raised terraces and sunken plazas. Constructed to a complex plan, the site demonstrates a degree of architectural sophistication that can only have been built up through a wealth of past experience. Historians think that the various phases of construction took place over several centuries, with earliest buildings probably dating from about 1300 BC.

By the time of the Spanish conquest of Peru, the shrine had been deserted for many centuries. Even so, the chronicler Cieza de Léon, who undertook the hazardous journey to Chavín in 1533, was sufficiently impressed by the massive walls

of the temple pyramid, with their perfectly fitting stone blocks, to suggest that the complex must have been created before the dawn of time by a race of giants. Even now, visitors must find themselves wondering who these master builders might have been, and how, with only the most basic tools at their disposal, they managed to create such imposing monuments in this remote mountain spot.

The big cat and its priests

To judge from the effort that went into building the huge, stepped pyramid with its labyrinthine internal passageways, religion played a central role in the lives of the Chavín peoples. The artworks found in the vicinity of the shrine indicate that the cult that brought them together had a highly developed mythology. Stylised images of a big cat reappear time and again on earthenware pots and stone reliefs, suggesting that a god in animal form was the main focus of devotion. Although both jaguars and pumas are native to South America, it seems most likely that the creature is a jaguar, judging by the markings that potters and masons depicted on its flanks. (Jaguars have vividly blotched coats, but pumas are only spotted for the first four months of their lives.)

In time the influence of the Chavín culture spread westward from the high Andes all along the coast of northern Peru. From early on, the Chavín world seems to have been structured in a way that freed up large numbers of people from the demands of subsistence agriculture so they could work as stonemasons and sculptors, or serve as priests.

The Chavín had no writing to record how their civilisation began, but given the importance of the weather for

Stone warrior
Wearing a loincloth and protective headgear, the warrior depicted on this stone carving from Cerro Sechín on the Peruvian coast is brandishing a weapon that may be either a club or a battleaxe.

Death mask
This gold mask from a Chavín grave displays the fang-like teeth that are regularly seen in depictions of the anthropomorphic jaguar-god.

a relief carving of a hybrid creature, part human and part big cat; serpents decorate its body, and the locks around its face end, Gorgon-like, in snakes' heads. We can only speculate about the sacrificial rituals that must once have been practised where it stands.

Equally hard to decipher is the so-called Raimondi Stone, a relief carving named after the Italian traveller who came across it in 1855. The carving on the stone depicts a figure known as the Staff-bearing God, so called because it is invariably depicted between two upright batons, one clenched in each claw-like hand. The Raimondi figure displays multiple feline masks, worn one above the other – so many, in fact, that they take up three-quarters of the entire stele. The masks have the fanglike teeth and staring eyes typical of Chavín art.

The Tello Obelisk, a third monument discovered near the temple, takes its name from the Peruvian archaeologist who unearthed it. It features another hybrid creature, sometimes referred to as the Caiman God, whose body is garlanded with big-cat paw prints and designs representing food crops. The figure probably represents a fertility deity.

Sanctuary among the summits

Chavín de Huantar lies in a narrow, steep-sided valley whose main crops today are potatoes, corn and agaves. The location can never have supported a large population, yet for centuries people travelled to the site to extend and beautify the shrine, some of them bringing construction materials with them. Religion was evidently the motivating force; adherents of the jaguar cult were apparently happy to make long journeys on foot over the mountains to participate in the rituals practiced in the temple.

farming communities, it is possible that people started studying the heavens to help forecast the weather, attributing sun or storms to the will of the gods. From here it would have been a natural step to the worship of deities controlling the forces of nature, with a ruling hierarchy of priests venerated for their ability to intercede with the gods. If this was the case, the sanctuary at Chavín de Huantar may have served not just as a ceremonial centre but also as an observatory.

The most impressive of Chavín de Huantar's surviving monuments was probably erected on the orders of priests seeking the favour of the jaguar-god. Known today as El Lanzon ('the Dagger'), this huge, pointed monolith stands 4.5m (15ft) high in an underground chamber at the heart of the old temple, surrounded now by fluttering bats. It is adorned with

In Chavín times the inhabitants of the coastal settlements lived in houses built of adobe bricks on stone foundations; their gabled roofs were covered with rush thatching. They fed themselves mainly through fishing, which they supplemented with some agriculture. The fields on which they grew their crops often lay some way from the villages, in woodland clearings where the soil was more fertile.

Chavín villages have also been found inland, in the river valleys that serve as oases of fertility cutting through the dry lands of the Peruvian coastal desert. Life can never have been easy in the valleys, which were isolated from one another by large stretches of arid land.

The people who lived in these villages would probably not have looked very different from the indigenous population of modern Peru, with dark brown skin and a stocky build. The mountain-dwellers would have had little difficulty in walking long distances to Chavín de Huantar and other shrines as their bodies and lungs would have been adapted to the rarefied atmosphere of the high Andes.

also other sea creatures, which were then burned on sacrificial altars during communal devotions.

One intriguing theory holds that the roots of the jaguar cult lie farther north, possibly even as far as the Gulf of Panama or beyond. Its proponents argue that immigrants from what is now Mexico introduced revolutionary innovations – such as the cultivation of corn, the use of earthenware ritual vessels and the worship of animal gods – to Central America, from where they may in turn have penetrated to Peru's north coast, affecting the behaviour and beliefs of the local people.

There are indeed striking similarities between Chavín artefacts and those of the Olmecs, a culture that radiated out from Mexico's Gulf Coast. Pottery found at Tlatilco, an Olmec site near modern-day Mexico City, bears a striking resemblance to Chavín ware, displaying the peculiar stirrup-spouts and impressed zigzag patterns beloved of Andean potters. Both civilisations may also have practised skull deformation and worshipped a jaguar-god.

Recurring motif
The stone faces in this relief combine human features with a jaguar's fangs. They adorned the side walls of the temple complex at Chavín de Huantar.

The roots of Chavín culture

There is little doubt that there was active communication between the coastal dwellers and their fellow jaguar worshippers in the mountains. Large quantities of bright red Spondylus shells from the sea have been found at Chavín de Huantar and other highland sites. Travellers would have taken several days to journey from the coast and through the passes of the Cordillera Blanca to enter the high valley where the shrine lay. They brought with them not only the mussels, which apparently played an important part in Chavín rites, but

Half man, half beast
One of the best-known Chavín artworks, the Raimondi Stone depicts the deity known to scholars as the 'Staff-bearing God'. The face combines human and animal features, and snakes writhe around the head.

The mysteries of Cerro Sechín

In recent years, excavations on Peru's north coast have significantly enhanced our knowledge of daily life in the Chavín period. Sites in the Chicama, Nepena and Casma valleys have all yielded impressive examples of skilled artistry. The brick temples and step pyramids found there have clay-plastered walls decorated with multicoloured paintings in Chavín style.

One site in particular – Cerro Sechín in the Casma Valley – has aroused widespread interest and stirred controversy. The temple complex there consists of several platforms built one on top of another and linked by a staircase. The perimeter wall surrounding the shrine is decorated with an extraordinary stone relief depicting human figures. Some are evidently warriors: dressed in loincloths and wearing helmets decorated with feathers, they grasp axes or clubs in their hands. Others, however, have neither headgear nor weapons and exude a despondent air. Smaller, roughly hewn blocks of stone have been unearthed bearing images of truncated heads; others show skeletal remains and dismembered torsos, arms and legs. No one has yet been able to determine conclusively whether this frightful parade represents a battle scene, complete with victors and victims, or a processional scene of ritual sacrifice.

In style and technique the Cerro Sechín relief differs markedly from the intricate, sophisticated works of art from Chavín de Huantar. In stark contrast to the ornate, highly stylised carvings found at the Andean site, the coastal carvings are relatively crude and fleshed out with few details. Current dating methods indicate that the Cerro Sechín works are several centuries older than the ceremonial centre of Chavín de Huantar and may possibly belong to the very earliest period of the Chavín culture. Intriguingly, even in this early site, the link with Mexican art is plain to see: the warriors on the frieze at Cerro Sechín are strongly reminiscent of the so-called *danzantes* – the Olmec-influenced dancers found at Monte Albán in southern Mexico. The outlines of the figures were chiselled with an amazing sureness of touch straight into the smooth surface of the stone.

Elaborate irrigation systems

The coastal deserts of Peru are among the driest lands on Earth, and cultivation can never have been easy. Water drained from the Andes mountains was available in the river valleys, however, and in seasons when there was heavy rainfall in the highlands, it was even plentiful. But supplies had to be carefully guarded if they were to last through the long dry months. The Chavín

farmers used the building skills shown in their temples and carvings to create impressive irrigation systems which improved the yield of their harvests. They grew several varieties of corn, as well as squashes, beans and cotton.

In the Nepena Valley, for example, Chavín engineers constructed a dam between two mountains to prevent their crops from being washed away by the torrential spring floods. The impounded water was channelled through two conduits into a reservoir, where it was stored until it was needed. Extended and improved over the intervening centuries, this complex system is still in use today.

For the afterlife

At an altitude of some 2100m (6900ft), on a mountain called La Copa, the Chavín built another place of pilgrimage, known today as Kuntur Wasi or 'the House of the Condor'. Here, archaeologists have found not just a buried temple complex but also a cemetery containing rich grave goods, gold and precious stones among them, alongside pottery and textiles. All these goods were intended to smooth the passage of the deceased into the afterlife and make life there more pleasant.

Yet the richest evidence of living conditions in the Early Horizon period has come from necropolises closer to the coast. In graves at Cupinisque, the dead were interred in their finest clothes and with their favourite jewellery – but only after their flesh had rotted away, for the bones had been covered in a cinnabar-red powder before burial. Most of the grave goods were decorated with religious symbols, often featuring the ubiquitous big-cat so familiar from Chavín art.

To prevent the dead from suffering hunger or thirst on their journey to the afterlife, they were provided with pottery vessels containing food and drink to sustain them. The rotund, handcrafted containers are extremely thick and robust; coloured black or brown, they are often equipped with the familiar stirrup handles.

Almost all are decorated with abstract patterns featuring stylised plant or animal motifs that were no doubt intended to have a magical effect.

Unresolved questions

Although researchers investigating Chavín culture have made many exciting discoveries in recent decades, many questions remain unanswered. For example, scholars still have much work to do to decipher the complex iconography of Chavín art.

The greatest mystery, however, is how the jaguar priests spread their cult across all of northern Peru – and whether they used military force to do so. Was there perhaps some sort of proto-Peruvian state, led by the high priests of the jaguar cult?

If they are ever to unravel the mystery, archaeologists know there is a need not only to find new sites but to preserve those that are already known. Chavín de Huantar is under constant threat from flooding; in 1945 a mudslide buried both ceremonial centre and village, forcing the excavators to start work all over again.

Double jug
This curious vessel from the late Chavín period, around 500 BC, consists of two separate bowls linked through hollow handles to a single spout. Both containers have a dark-brown glaze and are decorated with stylised images probably representing big cats.

The mystery of the temple guardians

In the Chavín cult's heyday, the outer walls of the temple at Chavín de Huantar were lined with three-dimensional stone heads, sited below a ledge decorated with a relief of striding jaguars and condors. Now, only one remains in place, fixed to the wall with pegs.

The gargoyle-like head seems to combine human and animal elements in its staring eyes, wide mouth and flared nostrils. The expression on the lone face seems almost friendly, but once the walls held more than 40 heads of various sizes, and like the El Lanzon sculpture inside the temple, they were most likely designed to inspire awe and fear. It is easy to imagine devotees entering the temple and feeling a spine-tingling shiver as they glanced up at these guardian visages staring down on them.

Sole guardian
The flaring nostrils and wide mouth on the one surviving sculpted head call to mind some aspects of the Chavín jaguar-god.

OCEANIA

On the track of the Aborigines

Australia's first settlers successfully adapted to the harsh living conditions of the arid Outback, developing a lifestyle that endured for many thousands of years.

Nobody knows how the first humans came to Australia. What is known is that about 40,000 years ago, or possibly even earlier, seafaring people from southeast Asia reached its shores. During the Ice Age sea levels were as much as 90m (300ft) lower than they are today, and land bridges existed that have long since been flooded. Sumatra and Borneo were still connected to the Asian mainland, and Australia was linked to Tasmania and New Guinea forming a huge single landmass. The seas around Australia were also considerably shallower than they are now.

Even so, the proto-Australian continent was out of sight of other land, and people would have had to sail 70km (45 miles) to reach it. So what made them set out on a journey into the unknown? Perhaps fishermen from the Asian mainland were blown off course, landing in Australia by accident. Perhaps adventurers saw smoke drifting from bushfires set off by lightning strikes, indicating the presence of land just over the horizon. Whatever the motive, the continent these settlers discovered forced them to adapt to an environment very different from any they had previously known.

A unique weapon
The Aborigines used boomerangs for cult purposes as well as for hunting. Smaller versions of the curved throwing-stick were used to bring down water birds.

A hunter-gatherer civilisation
Like all Earth's peoples at the time, these early Australian settlers lived by hunting and collecting wild food. Unlike their counterparts on the Eurasian landmass,

however, they continued doing so into modern times, long after the agricultural revolution had transformed the lands to the north. This may have been because there were no native animals or plants suitable for domestication, or perhaps the Aborigines simply saw no need to change their lifestyle. Instead, they evolved a hunter-gatherer civilisation based on a pattern of seasonal migrations.

The Aborigines soon learned that their best chances of survival given the Outback's scarce resources was to live in nomadic groups of about 20 to 50 people. Several related groups formed a tribe. In time, some 500 to 600 separate tribes grew up, usually numbering between 100 and 1000 individuals.

With spear and boomerang
As in virtually all early cultures, hunting was a job for men, and they developed extraordinary tracking skills. They were able to mimic bird and animal calls almost to perfection, and could make out the faintest of animal tracks. Sometimes they sniffed out game – literally – using only their acute sense of smell to follow a spoor. Mostly, though, they would stand motionless for minutes at a time until an animal approached; then they would strike it down with a spear.

Spears, cut from acacia or eucalyptus, were the most important hunting weapons, used even to catch fish. Some

Aboriginal rock art is widespread in Australia and styles varied from tribe to tribe. This figurative example depicting childbirth is in the Kakadu National Park in northern Australia.

The Aborigines hunted herbivorous (plant-eating) marsupials such as kangaroos and wombats. In the early days, giant species provided large quantities of meat when killed; there were kangaroos up to 3m (10ft) tall and wombats the size of donkeys. There were also relatives of the emu – flightless birds much bigger than today's species.

The last giant animals disappeared about 15,000 years ago, when the end of the Ice Age triggered radical climate changes that turned Australia into the driest and hottest land on Earth. Smaller species, such as the red kangaroo, evolved in response to the new environmental conditions.

Putting fire to use

The Aborigines often used fire to trap animals during a hunt. To start a fire they used a fire-drill – a hard wooden stick; one end was inserted into a hole in a softer piece of wood, then the stick was rotated back and forth very fast. The friction generated heat, causing the wood dust to smoulder. With care and the addition of fine tinder, the hot embers could be coaxed into a flame.

Fire was also used to clear land. Early on, the Aborigines noticed that grassland recovered surprisingly quickly after bushfires, so it was a logical step to start conflagrations deliberately in order to renew the land. In time, they staged regular burn-offs, and by doing so they became active protectors of the environment, stopping the grass savannah from turning into desert. Controlled fires still play a part in the management of Australian ecosystems to this day.

While the men hunted, the women and children gathered fruit, roots, herbs and seeds, along with insects, insect larvae and small lizards. They could usually collect enough to support themselves in just two or three hours a day. The pickings were stored in baskets woven from plant fibres – the women used the same technique to make fishing nets.

Colours of earth
Red and yellow ochres dominated the palette of colours used by rock painters, as in this powerful image of faces. Black was obtained from wood charcoal and white from naturally occurring gypsum.

had stone tips, fixed to the wooden shaft with resin. The most famous Aboriginal weapon is, of course, the boomerang, which was already being made along its aerodynamic lines more than 10,000 years ago. These curved wooden throwing sticks could be used effectively up to a distance of about 50m (160ft), and were generally used to drive animals into traps.

Boundaries in the desert

The Aborigines lived their nomadic existence within strict boundaries. Each tribe had its own area or territory, which was precisely defined by natural features, and the tribespeople would only cross these invisible boundaries if the neighbouring tribe gave permission – perhaps during a food shortage or famine.

Under normal circumstances each wandering clan remained in its own terrain, moving from one waterhole to another. To protect themselves against cold or rainy weather, the Aborigines built simple, cone-shaped huts out of branches, which they covered with tree bark or grass. The shelters were easy to construct and did not require the use of special tools, whose extra weight would have been a hindrance on long treks.

A religion grounded in Nature

Each tribe was intimately bound to the land it occupied, and the legends that each one passed down stressed the relationship with their surroundings. Natural landmarks featured in stories of the mythical past, along with the animals that were hunted. Aborigines referred to this epoch as the Dreamtime – a term that has nothing to do with dreams in the usual sense, but refers to the mythological era when life began, as well as to its continuation.

A common belief among all of the tribes was that the landscape, all natural phenomena and the whole gamut of living things were created by mythical ancestors in the distant past. Once the process of creation was completed, these ancestors then became part of the landscape they had formed, living on in sacred sites imbued with spiritual power, as they still are for Aboriginal peoples today. Probably the most famous of these spiritual sites is the world's largest sandstone monolith, called Ayer's Rock in colonial days, but now known by its Aboriginal name – Uluru. Located in the dry centre of the continent, Uluru was venerated by several tribes and remains a sacred place to this day.

Totemic ancestor figures, including animals and plants, created continuity between the Dreamtime and the present. Successive generations of tribespeople were duty-bound to care for the places designated by their mythic ancestors, and would carry out ceremonies to renew the spiritual energy originally generated in the Dreamtime. Men might mimic totemic animals in ritualised dance ceremonies, re-enacting the life and activities of the creator beings and seeking their protection and help. Special paths known as songlines connected the sacred sites; the ancestors had trodden them in the Dreamtime, and their progeny followed in their tracks.

Sacred symbols
Rock painting was the preserve of privileged male tribesmen. The act of drawing or restoring an image, which regularly took place in a ceremonial context, played an important part in the Aborigines' ritual life.

Ochre – the colour of earth

Ochre is a very dense type of clay with a high iron content that comes in shades of red, yellow and brown. It was an indispensable raw material for Aboriginal sacred art – it was used not just in rock painting but also in ceremonies and for body decoration.

Red ochre was particularly sought after for ritual use, and large-scale expeditions were organised to obtain it. Sometimes traders embarked on journeys that lasted many months and stretched right across the continent. The main ochre deposits had great religious significance, and the creation of the coloured earth had its own part to play in aboriginal mythology.

An extinct giant
The diprotodon was a giant wombat-like marsupial that could weigh up to 1.5 tonnes, making it easy prey for men with spears. In their search for food, the Aborigines hunted some species to extinction.

Bound to the earth

The first Australians believed that after death, the person's spirit was born again in the body of another living being, or else in inanimate matter such as a rock or a river. Everything was connected, and everything returned in designated cycles. The Aboriginal peoples felt inextricably rooted to the land, deriving their very identity from it, and so always treated it with respect. They never made violent incursions into other people's territories, and the theft of land was unknown – one could even say unimaginable.

Aboriginal art can only be understood against this spiritual background. The Aborigines never developed a written language; instead, they passed on the Dreamtime myths from one generation to another orally or through dance or drawings. Markings left on trees and rocks were actually coded messages that had meaning only for people who had learned to decipher them. On one level the marks acted as signposts; on another, they passed mythological information along the length of the songlines.

Rock engravings and drawings are the most widespread Aboriginal art form. These are found all over the Australian continent. The pictures reflect the cultural diversity of the Aborigines, who believed that their Dreamtime ancestors had

created distinctive motifs for each separate region, which have been copied and recopied ever since. In the south, abstract images including symbolic spirals, lines, lozenges, stripes and snake patterns prevailed; in the north, figurative representations were more common. The oldest images of all were simple finger signs, which were scratched or chiselled into the soft walls of limestone caves; these date back 20,000, maybe even 40,000 years.

The power of art

The Rainbow Snake – a multicoloured mythical serpent – played a part in the creation stories of many tribes. In northern Australia, for example, the serpent was thought to have emerged from the Earth and, through its zigzag motion, to have created channels for the continent's great rivers.

One of the most distinctive of the Aboriginal rock art styles, the so-called 'X-ray style', appeared in the last 3000 years. In this style a drawing of a kangaroo might display, as if in an X-ray photograph, the animal's spine, the two lobes of the lungs, the heart, the oesophagus, the liver, the bowels and the kidneys, which were prized for their fat content.

Aboriginal artists varnished their works with bees' wax, plant juices or animal protein to protect the surface and ensure long life, not just for the drawing itself but for the spiritual power it contained. They believed that as long as the pictures survived and were renewed, the plants, waterholes and animal species depicted in them would continue to flourish and their own way of life would be preserved.

That the Aborigines kept their unique culture alive in isolation from the rest of the world for so long is thanks largely to the rise in sea levels after the Ice Age. The land bridges linking the Indonesian islands to continental Asia were flooded, and New Guinea and Tasmania were separated from the Australian landmass. This allowed generations of native Australians to follow the dreamline paths undisturbed.

At home on the ocean – the seafarers of Polynesia

Starting more than 5000 years ago, seafarers from eastern Asia headed across the ocean in outrigger canoes. Their dangerous voyages to the lonely, uninhabited South Pacific islands rank among the great feats of marine exploration.

Imagine the scene before the start of an early voyage into the massive expanse of the Pacific. Two large outrigger canoes lie ready on the beach, stocked with food and drinking water for a journey of several weeks. Perhaps the sailors were waiting for the wind to change. Many prayers would be offered up to the stone statue of the local god, begging for a lull in the south-easterly trade winds. When at last the wind was favourable, the journey could begin. The all-male crews made a final check of their provisions and scanned the skyline, then pushed the great wooden boats – each one made from a single hollowed-out tree trunk – into the water. To the sound of anxious farewells from wives and children, a journey into the unknown had begun.

Many such scenes must have been played out over the thousands of years that it took to colonise the islands of the South Pacific. From the Asian coast and the island of New Guinea, mariners travelled eastward, exploring chains of islands stretching over 12,000km (7500 miles) in search of new lands to settle.

The easterly direction forced them to sail against the prevailing winds for much of the time, yet this seeming handicap actually served as a safety precaution; if they wished to return, the trade winds could be relied on to carry them back to

Totemic figurine
Seafarers setting out to seek new island worlds may well have taken with them animal-like figures such as this one. Standing 20cm (8in) tall, it was made from greywacke in prehistoric New Guinea, where it was found in the Yombu Valley.

Sailing by the stars

At the end of the 19th century, a German sea captain discovered a mysterious object on the Marshall Islands, part of Micronesia. It was made of the spines of palm fronds connected at various points by cowrie shells, and at first sight it seemed to form a random pattern; local people referred to it by the native name of *mattang*. In fact, it turned out to be a sea map or chart. The palm spines represented the major ocean currents in the vicinity of the Marshall Islands, while the shells marked the positions of the individual islands. The map only made sense when viewed upside down, with the south uppermost – the natural perspective for travellers in the southern hemisphere. It is possible that the ocean voyagers did not actually take the chart with them on their long journeys but carefully memorised the information it contained before setting out.

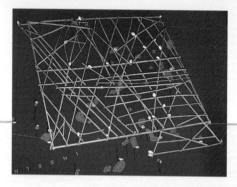

Navigational memory aid
Three-dimensional sea charts like this one were in use in Micronesia into the 19th century.

their point of departure. Even so, it is hard now to imagine how people from as early as 3500 BC could roam the ocean without the aid of compass or sextant. The settlers of Polynesia, however, were not rash adventurers but experienced sailors. They had well-equipped boats and had mastered all the sailing and navigational techniques they needed for their ventures.

Knowledgeable boatbuilders

Contemporary rock drawings give us some idea of the appearance of the ships used, which were constructed by methods that have barely changed up to modern times. The Oceanian peoples used dugout canoes provided with one or more outriggers to increase the craft's stability. To make a canoe, they used fire or simple tools to hollow out a tree trunk, then laid wooden planks within it that they bound into place with ropes twisted from plant fibres. Finally, they sealed the inside of the boat's hull with the resin of an indigenous species of nut tree.

Over time the boats got bigger until canoes as much as 15m (50ft) long

became quite common. The vessels were propelled by one or more triangular sails made of raffia fabricated from the inner bark of mulberry trees. Using wooden mallets, the islanders laboriously pounded the bark strips into paper-like leaves, broad but thin. They then laid several layers on top of one another, weaving them into substantial mats that were resistant to salt water. With such sails and a favourable wind, the boats could travel up to 240km (150 miles) in a day.

Sailing by the stars

Over the centuries the peoples of Oceania accumulated a huge store of nautical knowledge. On sea voyages they orientated themselves by careful observation of the heavens, as well as by noting weather conditions, ocean currents and the behaviour of birds and sea creatures.

They followed the daily motion of the sun, even in cloudy conditions, and were familiar with its movements through the seasons. They read the winds and cloud formations as navigation aids, and they kept a close watch for seabirds or any sign of plantlife drifting in the water – a sure sign that land was nearby. They were also on the lookout for an unusual natural phenomenon of the region: in the daytime, and at dawn or dusk, the green water of lagoons can be seen reflected in the sky, another indication of the presence of land long before the land itself comes into sight.

It was the position of the stars, however, that was the single most important factor in early Oceanian navigation. The mariners knew the difference between fixed stars and planets, and had special names for such bright, clearly visible bodies as the Pole Star (north of the Equator) and the Southern

Cross. They would usually set sail in the late afternoon to make maximum use of the night sky, and then only if they knew they could count on good weather and clear visibility. Once it was dark, they sought out a familiar star to serve as a compass, then picked one or two other stars that lay close to the horizon in the general direction in which they were headed to serve as guides. Using such methods, they generally managed to reach their intended destination.

The sea's victims

As an additional safety precaution, boats travelled in convoy, keeping each other in sight. Yet however carefully the seafarers prepared for their journeys, some must never have reached journey's end.

It is impossible to know how many were lost at sea over the course of thousands of years of ocean travel, but estimates ranging between a quarter and half a million may not be far from the mark.

The reasons that drove the islanders to search out new shores are also unknown. Overpopulation and local rivalries may have played a part. The real trigger, however, may have been the islanders' own close relationship with the sea – coupled with an inbred thirst for discovery.

Long ocean journeys came to form part of the cultural traditions of these seafaring peoples. By about 1000 BC they had reached the Fiji Islands, Tonga and Samoa, hitherto uninhabited archipelagoes far out in the Pacific.

Natural materials
To catch swordfish and other large sea creatures, Oceanian fishermen used solid fish-hooks made of tortoiseshell firmly anchored in a piece of bone.

Boats for master mariners
Outrigger canoes equipped with sails were the vessels of choice for the Polynesian mariners who explored large areas of the South Pacific.

Finding new homes

Not every lonely island made a suitable new home, however. Explorers had to check that there was a sufficient supply of drinking water, and that the soil was fertile and the land not too rocky. If the verdict was positive, they would make the journey to and from their home island several times to familiarise themselves with the sea route before finally setting out with their wives and children to take possession of the new land.

Journey to a new life

Once the decision to move had been taken, the home village became a hive of activity. Pots, utensils and other equipment had to be carefully selected and packed in the boats. Even more important was choosing the best seedlings to take along to cultivate in their new home. One favourite crop was the yam, a vegetable common throughout the Pacific region that grows particularly well in dry soils. Its tubers, weighing 2–5kg (4–11lb) and with a starch content to rival that of the potato, could be stored for months, providing a valuable food reserve.

When the day of departure dawned, the pace must have quickened even more. Some of the men would have checked the boats and sails, while others stored fresh water and provisions in the hulls. Perhaps the children, meanwhile, were busy rounding up pigs, dogs and chickens, for the animals too had to make the long journey to their new home. Throughout the day, the villagers probably kept casting anxious glances at the sea and sky: was the wind picking up? Were clouds blowing in? Finally, in the late afternoon, the time came to set out. Men, women and children took their seats in the narrow boats, while the animals struggled against the unfamiliar plant-fibre ropes that tethered them in place. Finally, the long-awaited moment came. At a given signal the boats set sail, and the journey into an unknown future began.

Elegant and practical
Spacious Lapita-ware pots, with a typical decoration of geometric lines, were used as storage containers by the people of Polynesia.

The Lapita culture

The people who made these great journeys belonged to what is known as the Lapita culture, so called from a site in New Caledonia where their pottery was first found. Lapita ware spread eastwards from Melanesia, eventually finding its way across much of Polynesia and the South Pacific. Its makers mixed clay with sand or crushed seashells to form coils or blocks that they then shaped into cooking pots, bowls and plates.

They decorated their pottery with complicated geometrical patterns or stylised faces that they pressed into the moist clay by means of small, toothed stamps. To complete the process, the finished items were fired at low temperatures over open flames.

Adzes were an indispensable and characteristic product of these active seafaring peoples. Experienced craftsmen fashioned broad, heavy blades out of giant sea shells, which they fixed at right angles to wooden handles. The resulting tools were well-designed for whittling tree trunks and hollowing dugout canoes.

Living around water

Lapita settlements were usually situated on the coast. Dwelling were straw-walled and built on posts, in some cases set out over the water. On many of the islands fishing supplied a large part of the diet. The islanders lived on a mixed catch that ranged from shellfish, sea snails and crabs through to mackerel, manta rays, shark, swordfish and sea turtles, which were usually caught in shallow reef waters at the edge of the open sea. Ocean-going fishermen used fish-hooks made from sea-shells along with nets and funnel-shaped basketware traps fashioned from creeper stems or coconut fibres.

The Polynesians also practised some farming, leaving the land to lie fallow at regular intervals so as to avoid exhausting the soil. Ploughs were unknown; tubers and cuttings were planted in individual holes sunk with a digging stick. When rain was scarce, the islanders sometimes turned to artificial irrigation.

In addition to yams, they also cultivated taro, another starch-rich tuber. The coconut palm was one of Oceania's most useful trees; its flesh and milk provided food, while the wood, fibres and coconut shells were put to many different uses around the house and the village.

The only domestic animals known to the Oceanian islanders were descendants of those they had originally brought with them from the mainland. Meat was only eaten on special occasions. Pigs were considered to be a particular delicacy and the possession of a large herd was the mark of a wealthy family or clan.

On some of the islands, a local species of rat was considered a tasty morsel; it too may have arrived with the settlers, in this case travelling as a stowaway. Hunting on land was not especially important on the islands, although pigeons and seabirds were killed for their feathers, which were needed for ceremonial purposes.

Bonds across the sea

The Oceanians never lost touch with their original homes or with other islanders. Such contacts were necessary because the islands were subject to natural catastrophes such as floods and tsunamis (tidal waves), which could make them uninhabitable within minutes. In such an eventuality, the inhabitants would either return to their old home or else seek sanctuary on a neighbouring island.

Trade relations kept the islanders in touch, even over long distances. They exchanged pottery, pearls, necklaces and bracelets, and above all, obsidian. This black volcanic glass was a favourite raw material for the manufacture of sharp cutting tools.

Tattooing of both men and women was part of Lapita culture from an early time and, like all Oceanian art, was motivated by religious belief. Polynesian myths tell how its secrets were originally passed on to humankind by spirits from the otherworld. Tattooists used delicate bone chisels that were dipped in dyes and tapped into the skin with a stone hammer. Men often had every part of their bodies tattooed, a process that would have required them to endure this treatment through numerous sittings spread out over months or even years.

Placating the ancestors

Other works of art were drawn on rock walls. Images of birds appeared frequently, for birds across the entire Pacific world were symbols of the souls of the dead. As the spirits of dead ancestors had to be constantly placated to avert bad luck, it was hardly surprising that many Polynesian cult images bore birdlike features. Boats were another common motif – naturally enough for a people so at home on the seas. In all, the Oceanians sailed to and settled as many as 800 separate Pacific islands in the years up to 900 BC.

Conspicuous adornment
Necklaces were normally made out of dog, pig or fish teeth although, unusually, the teeth of a sperm whale were threaded together to produce the example shown at top. Oceanian craftsmen skilfully worked and polished stone to make tools such as axes or clubs (background illustration), as well as bracelets and other jewellery (above).

Abbeviations: t = top, c = centre, b = below, l = left, r = right, T = Timeline, B = background.

akg = akg-images
BPK = Bildarchiv Preußischer Kulturbesitz
BAL = Bridgeman Art Library
TAA = The Art Archive

Front cover: TopFoto
Back cover: (from top to bottom) Erich Lessing/akg; Erich Lessing/akg; National Museum La Valetta, Malta/TAA; Dagli Orti/TAA; Eye Ubiquitos

4/5: Werner Forman/akg; 6 and T: akg/Hessisches Landesmuseum; 6/7 B: Shaen Adey/Gallo Images/Corbis; 7: A. Sperber, Hamburg; 8/9: J. Reader/Agentur Focus/Science Photo Library; 10: Bildarchiv Preußischer Kulturbesitz; 11 G. Steinmetz/Agentur Focus; 12 T and b: G. Baldizzone/Corbis; 13 Andras Zboray (www.fjexpeditions.com); 14 t: E. Lessing/akg; c and T: W. Grunwald/akg; 15 W. Forman/akg; 16 t: Dagli Orti/Museo d'Egizio Turin/TAA; b: Dagli Orti/Museo d'Egizio Turin/TAA; 16/17 B: Martens/Mauritius; 17: E. Lessing/akg; 18 and T: W. Forman/ akg; 19: R. Wood/Corbis; 20/21: Trip/D. Harding; 21 t: W. Forman/akg; c: Corbis/S. Vannini; 22 t: J. Liepe, Berlin; b: BPK; 23: J. Liepe/PBK; 24: Corbis; 24/25 B: Workbookstock.com/Mauritius; 25 t and T: Vidler/Mauritius; b: W. Forman/akg; 26: R. Wood/Corbis; 27 and T: BPK; 28: F. Guenet/akg; 29: Die Illustratoren/J. Willbarth; 30: R. Wood/Corbis; 31: J. Liepe, Berlin; 32: W. Forman/akg; 33: E. Lessing/akg; 34: Dagli Orti/Corbis; 35: R. Wood/Corbis; 36: J. Fuste Raga/ Corbis; 37 and T: T. Bognar/Corbis; 38: BPK; 39: M. Büsing/PBK; 40 t: L. Lecat/akg; b: E. Lessing/akg; 41: W. Forman/akg; 42: Dagli Orti/TAA; 43: M. Büsing/BPK; 44/45: Erich Lessing/akg; 46: Asian Art & Archaeology, Inc./Corbis; 47 and T: The Institute of Archaeology, Peking; 48: L. Georgia/Corbis; 49: Asian Art & Archaeology, Inc./Corbis; 50: Asian Art & Archaeology, Inc./Corbis; 51: Dagli Orti/Museum of Anatolian Civilisations Ankara/TAA; 52: Dagli Orti/Archaeological Museum Amman Jordan/TAA; 52/53 B: Weltbild/Interfoto; 53 t: BAL/Bildarchiv Steffens; b: Y. Arthus-Bertrand/Corbis; 54: Dagli Orti/Museum of Anatolian Civilisations Ankara/TAA; 55 and T: E. Thiem/Lotos Film; 56: Dagli Orti/Corbis; 57: BPK; 58: Dagli Orti/Corbis; 60 t: E. Lessing/akg; 60/61: BAL/Bildarchiv Steffens; 62: BPK; 63: E. Lessing/akg; 64: J.-L. Nou/akg; 65 t and T: Dagli Orti/National Museum Karachi/TAA; b: G. Degeorge/akg; 66: J.-L. Nou/akg; 67: BAL/Bildarchiv Steffens; 68: Jean-Louis Nou/akg; 69 l: BAL/Bildarchiv Steffens; r: Robert Harding Picture Library; 70: Dagli Orti/National Museum Karachi/TAA; 71 and T: akg; 72 t: Dagli Orti/National Museum Damaskus, Syrien/TAA; 72 b: E. Lessing/akg; 73: Dagli Orti/Corbis; 74: E. Lessing/akg; 75: Corbis/Archivo Iconografico, S. A.; 76: O.M. Teßmer/Vorderasiatisches Museum Berlin/BPK; 76/77 B: Nik Wheeler/Corbis; 77: Prof. Dr. M. Krebernik/Friedrich-Schiller-Universität Jena; 78: W. Forman/akg; 79: C. Hellier/Corbis; 80 and T: Dagli Orti/Museum of Anatolian Civilisations Ankara/TAA; 81: D. Forman/Corbis; 82: BAL/Bildarchiv Steffens; 83: Vorderasiatisches Museum/BPK; 84: Amaudet/RMN; 85: Dagli Orti/Musée Cernuschi Paris/TAA; 86: E. Lessing/akg; 87 t: Bildarchiv Steffens/Orient Impressions Photo Stock; b: T. Ollivier/RMN; 88 b, T and 88/89 B: Asian Art & Archaeology, Inc./Corbis; 89: The Institute of Archaeology, Peking; 90: RMN; 91 T: Ollivier/RMN; 92, 93 and T, 94, 95: E. Lessing/akg; 96: RMN; 97: Dagli Orti/TAA; 98, 99: Zev Radovan, Jerusalem; 100: E. Lessing/akg; 101: akg; 102, 103: E. Lessing/akg; 104 and T: W. Morgan/Corbis; 105 t l: E. Lessing/akg; t r: akg; 105 b l: J. Reader/Science Photo Library/Agentur Focus; b M: Dagli Orti/TAA; b r: S. Pitamitz/Corbis; 106 t: W. Ruppert/BPK; b: D. Gifford/Science Photo Library/Agentur Focus; 107 l: J. Reader/Science Photo Library/Agentur Focus; t r: T. Stephan, Munderkingen; b r: Corbis; 108 t: BPK; b: K. Göken/BPK; 109 t l: akg; t r: BPK; b: akg; 110/111: R. Martin/Agentur Focus; 111 b l: akg; t r: Dagli Orti/TAA; 112/113: National Museum La Valletta, Malta/TAA; 114: J.G. Berizzi/RMN; 115: W. Ruppert/BPK; 116 and T: akg; 117: E. Lessing/akg; B: Jens Firsching; 118 and T: BPK; 119: Fotoarchiv Südtiroler Archäol-ogiemuseum; 120 and T: T. Schulze, K. Schauer/dpa; 121: E. Lessing/akg; 122 t: Fotoarchiv Südtiroler Archäologiemuseum; b: C. Hellier/Corbis; 122/123 B: Landesgendarmeriekommando für Tirol; 123: BPK; 124: National Museum La Valletta Malta/TAA; 125 and T: J. Hawkes/Corbis; 126 t: AGE/Mauritius; b: E. Lessing/akg; 127: Dagli Orti/TAA; 128: A. Woolfitt/Corbis; 128/129 B: Jens Firsching; 129: Dagli Orti/National Museum La Valletta Malta/TAA; 130: BPK; 131: akg; 132 and T: P. Connolly/akg; 133: akg; 134: U. Hoffmann/BPK; 135: J. Hios/akg; 136: BPK; 137 t l: P. Frilet/Agentur Focus; t r: A. Garozzo/Agentur Focus; b: akg; 138 t: Dagli Orti/Heraklion Museum/TAA; c: Dagli Orti/TAA; 139: BAL/Bildarchiv Steffens; 140 and T: Dagli Orti/BPK; 141: B. Wüstenp/ dpa; 142 and T: W. Forman/akg; 142/143 B: W. Reuter/ Bildarchiv Steffens; 143: Dagli Orti/Historiska Museet Stockholm/TAA; 144: akg; 145 l and T: BAL/Bildarchiv Steffens; r and T: E. Lessing/akg; 146: G. Blot/RMN; 147: L. Janicek/Bildarchiv Steffens; 148: P. Connolly/ akg; 149: Dagli Orti/'TAA; 150: Dagli Orti/ Archäol-ogisches Museum Nauplia/ TAA; 151: Dagli Orti/ National Archeological Museum Athens/TAA; 152 t: Dagli Orti/Archäologisches Museum Sparta/TAA; b: Nimatallah/akg; 153 B: akg; b: H. Kraft/BK; 154: BPK; 154/155 B: Bildarchiv Steffens; 155 r and b: Bildarchiv Steffens; 156/157: Dagli Orti/TAA; 158 B: Ohio Historical Society; b: Michael Fogden/Bruce Coleman Inc.; 159: Dr. Harold Bergen/Burke Museum Seattle; 160/161 B: L.L. Rue Jr./Bruce Coleman Inc.; 160: W. Forman/akg; 162 and T: Charles Lenars/Corbis; 163: Dagli Orti/TAA; 164: H. Stierlin/Bildarchiv Steffens; 165: Dagli Orti/National Antropological Museum Mexico/TAA; 166: Bildarchiv Steffens; 166/167 B: Anton Schnell; 167: Dagli Orti/TAA; 168 b: H. Stierlin/Bildarchiv Steffens; 168/169 B: Dagli Orti/Museo de Jiquilpan, Mexico/TAA; 169 r: Eileen/Museum of Mankind London/TAA; 170 t: H. Stierlin/Bildarchiv Steffens; 170/171: Dagli Orti/TAA; 171 r and T: Dagli Orti/ TAA; 172/173 B: Charles Lenars/Corbis; 172 t: Mauritius/SST; 173 b: Charles Lenars/Corbis; 174: Dagli Orti/Corbis; 175 t: Dagli Orti/E. Poli Collection Lima/TAA; b: R. Ergenbright/Corbis; 176/177: Eye Ubiquitos; 178 and T: South Australian Museum; 179: H. Bock/akg; 180/181 B: J. Beck/ Mauritius; 180: Kleist/Frobenius Institut; 181: P. Mayall/Bildarchiv Steffens; 182: akg; 183: National Gallery of Australia; 184/185 B: Mauritius/Age; 184 l: Museum für Völkerkunde Hamburg; 185 t: J.G. Berizzi/RMN; b: D. Graf/Ethnologisches Museum Berlin/BPK; 186 and T: Australian Museum/Nature Focus; 187 t: Dagli Orti/TAA; b: J.G. Berizzi/RMN; B: J.G. Berizzi/RMN.

Maps originated by Müller & Richert GbR, Gotha, Germany; translated into English by Alison Ewington

The Illustrated History of the World:
THE DAWN OF CIVILISATION was published by The Reader's Digest Association Ltd, London.

First English edition copyright © 2004
The Reader's Digest Association Ltd
11 Westferry Circus, Canary Wharf, London E14 4HE
www.readersdigest.co.uk

Reprinted with amendments 2005

Reader's Digest English Edition
Series editor: Christine Noble
Writer: Tony Allan
Translated from German by: JMS Books, Peter Lewis
Design: Jane McKenna
Copy editor: Helen Spence
Proofreader: Ron Pankhurst
Index: Hilary Bird, Marie Lorimer
Colour proofing: Colour Systems Ltd, London
Printed and bound by: Arvato Iberia, Europe

Reader's Digest, General Books
Editorial director: Julian Browne
Art director: Nick Clark
Prepress account manager: Penelope Grose

We are committed to both the quality of our products and the service we provide to our customers. We value your comments, so please free to contact us on 08705 113366, or via our website at: www.readersdigest.co.uk

If you have any comments or suggestions about the content of our books, you can email us at: gbeditorial@readersdigest.co.uk

First published as ***Reader's Digest Illustrierte Weltgeschichte: DIE ENTSTEHUNG UNSERER ZIVILISATION*** © 2004 Reader's Digest – Deutschland, Schweiz, Österreich Verlag Das Beste GmbH – Stuttgart, Zürich, Vienna

Reader's Digest, German Edition
Writers: Karin Feuerstein-Praßer, Andrea Groß-Schulte, Marion Jung, Heike Kolb, Karin Prager, Otto Schertler, Karin Schneider-Ferber, Dr. Holger Sonnabend
Editing and design: Media Compact Service
Colour separations: Meyle + Müller GmbH + Co., Pforzheim.

ISBN: 0 276 42986 9
CONCEPT CODE: GR 0081/G/S
BOOK CODE: 632-001-2
ORACLE CODE: 351600008H.00.24